Artifact: A Memoir

Michael Rutledge Riley

Purple Breeze Press, LLC

purplebreezepress.com

Artifact: A Memoir

© 2026 Michel Rutledge Riley

Artifact: A Memoir reflects the author's recollections of experiences over time. Some names and descriptions have been changed. Events have been drawn from memory. Some dialogue has been recreated or reimagined.

Library of Congress Cataloguing in Publication Data

Names: Rutledge Riley, Michael, author

Title: *Artifact: A Memoir* / Michel Rutledge Riley

Description: First edition. | Purple Breeze Press, 2026

Library of Congress Control Number: 2026910736

ISBN Paperback: 979-8-9954928-1-8

All personal photos are from the author.

Book designed and copy edited by Meg Vezzu / megvezzu.com

Cover design by Mary Welcome

Artifact: An object made or modified by human workmanship, as opposed to one formed by natural processes.
(*Oxford English Dictionary*, def. 1.a)

Artifact (Science): A spurious result, effect, or finding in a scientific experiment or investigation, esp. one created by the experimental technique or procedure itself. Also as a mass noun: such effects collectively.
(*Oxford English Dictionary*, def. 2)

[Referencing a line-drawing on the label of a wine called Silence]: A fib, artifact, flat line. An EKG with artifact means there's outside interference giving you a false read. Might be movement, a hairy chest.
(Julie Gardner, RN)

Dedication

For my parents:

To all the mother and father figures, and they are legion, who welcomed me into their homes and lives and allowed me glimpses of the kind of family I wanted for myself someday.

To Mama and Darius, who showed me through their devotion to each other and to the craft of their professions the transformative power of love and doing good work.

To Papa, for giving me a few great stories and life lessons and a million things to care about. This memoir exists less because of Mama's numerous books published and more because, unlike Darius, you never saw yours all the way through. This is a book I always had to write for you.

Contents

Part I: Founding   1

Vienna, Gun Club, 1934   3

Vienna, Bedtime Stories, 1945   10

Vienna, Passport Stamps, 1957   13

Vienna, In the Garden, 1972   17

Where I'm From   28

Little Rock, Arkansas, Hard Times, 1928–1964   30

Little Rock, Heels by the Poolside, 1958   34

Denton, Texas, Kick the Can, 1970–72   42

Acapulco, Mexico, Family Vacations,1970   50

The Grand Canyon, 1971   53

Garden Lore   56

Part II: Foundering   59

Houston, TX, Taking our Pops, 1972–1975   60

Little Rock, Arkansas, Summers, 1975–1980   79

Little Rock, Hospital Slippers, 1970s   99

Hamden, Connecticut, First Snow, 1974–1981   110

Albert   136

Part III: Seeking   139

   Lake Folk, Nisswa, Minnesota   139

   Wye Mountain, Arkansas,
   Parking Lot Stripes, 1979   140

   Pullman, Washington,
   High School Dances, 1981   145

   New Haven, Connecticut,
   A Pennsylvania Quaker, 1982   165

   Pullman, Washington, Sagebrush Navy, 1984   173

Part IV: Finding   199

   The Palouse is a Big Lovely Lady   199

   Sunshine Slough, Alaska, Slime Line, 1989   201

   Somerville, Next to the Star Market off
   Porter Square, Boston, Massachusetts,
   Wingtips, 1989   214

   Hawthorne Valley Farm, Ghent,
   Harlemville, New York, Root Crops, 1990   228

   Seattle, Washington, The Hobart, 1992   253

   O'Dell Farm, Omak, Okanogan Valley,
   Washington, Apples and Pears, 1993   262

   In the Pears   262

   Little Rock, Arkansas, Church Ladies, 1994   273

The Palouse Region, Washington,
Kamiak Butte, 1995   277

Part V: Arrival   287

Palouse, Washington, The Bungalow, 1996   289

Little Rock, Arkansas, The Favorite, 1997   306

Portrait of a Cousin (or the First Law of
Thermodynamics)   310

Little Rock, Arkansas, Death of the
Patriarch, 2016   311

Coda: Greenville, South Carolina,
A Body of Work, 2025   318

When Mama Actually Passed   323

Acknowledgements   325

About the Author   326

Part I: Founding

I'm always surprised at how little effort was made to stamp me in an image of effort and ambition. As the youngest son of an immigrant mother who came to America looking for a better life for herself, and a highly educated, ambitious father who planned for his first child to be President of the United States, I wasn't encouraged to be anything in particular. I wasn't shamed or excoriated for my inexplicably bad academic record. I never felt the need myself or the push from outside to participate in sports, church, extracurriculars, dating rituals, or any of the roles children are routinely given to prove themselves worthy of being produced in the first place. I meandered, sauntered, ambled, and moseyed through my childhood and all through my teen years. Beyond that, if I'm being honest, into my thirties.

This slow trajectory into being fully me seems to me now, having just turned sixty years old, to have been the blessing of my life. Things that might have seemed a waste of time when I was doing them for the first time became lessons in how to do something in the right-for-me way. Picking paper grocery bags full of pecans for a nickel apiece, washing nursing home windows, milking cows, and teaching twenty-six years in the same middle school building, all of that work, and the lessons that taught me how to do them well, remain to me as a body of modest achievement. It might not be wisdom, but these lessons and experiences leave me a not-so-old man with very few dreams unrealized. In the immortal words of the Price's Pimento Spread jingle I learned as a young kid in Texas and always kept close to my heart, "Staying the same, that's progress."

Vienna, Gun Club, 1934

Helene and Josef Kastinger, my Austrian grandparents, had two kids: Helene, or Helli, and Josef, known as Seppi. Josef Senior was a man I never met. When he was a young man with a young wife, he was a straight up socialist firebrand. In the early 1930s, he joined a group called the Vienna Gun Club to practice shooting fascists in preparation for the political changes sweeping Austria and Germany and Italy. When the far right Austrian government finally flexed their muscle to root out dissidents, there was a pitched battle between the Austrian police force loyal to them and my grandfather and his gun club associates. There was house to house fighting for a matter of hours before the resisters were killed or first captured and then killed. In my mom's stories that she heard as a little girl, troops lined up the anarchists against the wall and shot every fifth one. Since the man next to my grandfather could count, and wanted to save the young family man, he switched places and was shot dead. Another story, maybe more credible, was simply that all of the older men responsible for the fight were killed and my grandfather was spared initially because of his young age. In any case, court records reveal that my grandfather was sentenced to *Tod durch Erhängen*, or death by hanging.

-2-

wegen Verbrechens des Aufruhrs nahh §§ 73, 74 StG. ver-
handelt worden.

Über den vom Ankläger gestellten Antrag hat das
Gericht am 16. Februar 1934 zu Recht erkannt :

Die Beschuldigten Emmerich S a i l e r, Josef K a s
t i n g e r und Johann N o s k o sind schuldig:

A.) Sie haben am 12. Februar 1934 in Wien 5., Margarethen
gürtel Nr. 104 - 110 (Reumannhof) an einer Rottie-
rung teilgenommen, wobei es bei der Zusammenrottung
durch die Widerspenstigkeit geg n die von der Behörde
vorausgegangene Abmahnung und durch die Vereinigung
wirklich gewaltsamer Mittel soweit kam, dass zur Her-
stellung der Ruhe und Ordnung eine ausserordentliche
Gewalt angewendet werden musste; dem Aufruhr musste
durch Standrecht Einhalt geschehen.

Sie haben hiedurch das Verbrechen des Aufruhrs nach
§ 73, 74 StG. begangen.

Es werden dafür v e r u r t e i l t .

Emmerich S a i l e r und Josef K a s t i n g e r
gemäss § 74 StG., 442/1 StPO. und § 13 StG.

zum Tode durch den Strang.

Johann N o s k o gemäss § 442/1StPO. zur Strafe
des s c h w e r e n K e r k e r s in der Dauer von

7 (s i e b e n) J a h t e n , verschärft durch
1 (einen) Fasttag vierteljährlich.

Zuerst ist Emmerich S a i l e r und dann Josef
K a s t i n g e r hinzurichten.

Gemäss § 55 a StG. wird dem Johann N o s k o auf

The court document that sentences my grandfather, Josef Kastinger, to death by hanging.

ARTIFACT: A MEMOIR

Translation:

> *Tried for the crime of sedition under Sections 73 and 74 of the Penal Code.*
>
> *On the motion filed by the prosecutor, the court rightly ruled on February 16, 1934:*
>
> *The accused Emmerich Sailer, Josef Kastinger, and Johann Nosko are guilty of:*
>
> *A.) On February 12, 1934, in Vienna 5, Margarethengürtel No. 104-110 (Roumannhof), they participated in a riot, during which the gathering escalated due to their defiance of the prior warning issued by the authorities and the use of genuinely violent means, necessitating the use of extraordinary force to restore peace and order; the riot had to be suppressed by martial law.*
>
> *They thereby committed the crime of sedition under Sections 73 and 74 of the Penal Code*
>
> *The following are sentenced:*
>
> *Emmerich Sailer and Josef Kastinger according to § 74 of the Penal Code, 442/1 of the Code of Criminal Procedure and § 13 of the Penal Code. to death by hanging,_*
>
> *Johann Nosko according to § 442/1 of the Code of Criminal Procedure, to the punishment of severe imprisonment for a period of 7 years, aggravated by one fast day quarterly.*
>
> *First, Emmerich Sailer and Josef Kastinger are to be executed.*

It was a fate he managed to avoid, thankfully for me, and maybe for him. He was instead imprisoned first and then sentenced to work in factories for the German war effort. Again, later in the war, he was sentenced to confinement in a concentration camp for sharing food with a Jewish fellow factory worker. When he came back from the war, he didn't go back to Helene and his children. Instead, he got a divorce and started a new family and never spent time with them again. The war broke a lot of stuff, both human and material, but the Kastingers managed to survive. Perhaps my mom was the only one of them who thrived, but she might have been the only one who was creative enough to want to thrive, and ambitious enough to make it happen. I didn't inherit her ambition, but I did learn to muddle through, to move forward, to do enough to give myself a chance at a better life. I created less than her but enjoyed it more.

When my mother was still quite young, maybe five years old, in the mid-1940s, she and her mom were moved to a farm in the Austrian countryside, where they stayed for some months until the end of the Second World War. At that time, Vienna was facing a concerted and continuous bombing campaign and was deemed too dangerous for small children and the elderly. Evacuations were ordered. Her apartment was on *Reinprechtsdorferstrasse*, a major road leading to the *Westbahnhof*, the main train station and a prime target of Allied bombers. Little Helene walked to school along that route every day. One day she stayed home, troubled by a sense of deep anxiety and gloom, or perhaps a bad stomach, and that morning her school was bombed and everyone in it died. Some Allied pilots, weary or scared or just clearly aware of their odds after too many missions, found it easier to drop their bombs before reaching the stiff defenses around the train station, and as long as they came back empty, no one asked too many questions. And so, the evacuation and my mom's short-lived rural farm life experience.

A young Helene Maria Kastinger,
(1949)

I would listen to her stories from that time, entrenched in our artificial suburban neighborhood, and they developed into a quiet yearning in me. After all my years of schooling, when I could finally make choices of my own, I generally chose the countryside. When I was twenty-something and working on a dairy farm in upstate New York, she visited for Thanksgiving, and I cooked the big meal. Taking a break from the holiday to do the morning barn chores, she reveled in a chance to shovel the sawdust and manure into the barn gutters and enthused about the fresh smell of cow shit. I wondered how she could feel that way after a lifetime in academia as a professor in German, when we'd never gotten our hands dirty in the years under her care, but then I remembered the romance of the farm she'd passed to me. Not romance, per se, as much as the mystery of experiences beyond our ordinary lives. And I understood her. Something that happened seldomly enough that it gave me great joy. Mama, the farm girl. When our adult lives had even small areas of overlap, it seemed strange to me. In all other ways we were so different.

When my mom returned as a teenager to the wartime farm refuge from the bombs, the farm wife, standing in the yard, failed to recognize her. My grandmother explained how they'd stayed there, with the old Nazi, and they were coming back to say their thanks. A light went off in the old woman's eyes and she declared, "Ah, *das Schreiendes Kind*! The screaming child! I wouldn't recognize you, standing there so pretty and quiet and smiling. Those dimples! I never saw those when you were here last." They walked around and refamiliarized themselves with some of the most-remembered spots. Here was the pig pen, currently occupied by an enormous sow and nine little piglets, and here the side courtyard where they slaughtered the pigs. Mama never forgot waking in the early mornings to the high-pitched screaming they made as their throats were cut, the sound slowly dimming as the pails filled with blood for sausage-making. And over the wall there was the potato field where she, in lieu of schooling, did the important work of walking down the rows, burlap bag in tow, collecting potato beetles for hours on end for one *Reichspfennig* per bag.

When they met in the kitchen for coffee and *küchen* after the tour around the farm, they all remembered at about the same time that they hadn't really liked each other all that much: the farm wife had been paid to board them, and wasn't overly generous or kind; Helene the mother had been exceedingly talkative, bothersome and flirtatious with the men; the child Helene, the *Schreiendes Kind*, was all that her nickname entailed, a fragile and high-spirited and emotional little girl who didn't know how to work. Always, it seemed in hindsight, screaming.

They had survived the last months of the war together, but that was their only bond. And it wasn't enough to keep them there until lunch. So, rather quickly, they finished the coffee, said their goodbyes, and the Helene Kastingers headed back to the city.

Vienna, Bedtime Stories, 1945

After the war ended, there was a national health initiative in Austria to feed the children who'd been force-fed a diet of violence and privation. My mom was skinny. She was in school by then, but her mother, known to her as Mutti, was working full time in that other major initiative: rebuilding some kind of normalcy after the war had bombed whole neighborhoods in the capital of Vienna into rubble. Everyone was busy, and just the opposite from before the war when no one had work, now there was zero unemployment, and the city was one big hustle and bustle. There was work to be done and Helli was old enough to fend for herself and her little brother, Seppi.

Into this gap of neglect stepped the federal government and took the two kids away from home again, this time to be fed and fattened into children who would show the Austrians and the world that they were capable of taking care of their own. Once again Helli was in the countryside, this time with a regimented exercise and feeding program to get her into the Austrian idea of the "healthy" weight category. Healthy for Austrians was apple cheeks, dimpled knees, plump. Helli was not plump. Nor would she allow herself to be made that way. First fiercely authoritarian, the workers gave her huge platefuls of *kartoffeln*, kraut, and wurst, with glasses of milk to wash it down. They threatened with the direst consequences any failure to clean her plate. Austrian kids are raised on the stories of *Struwelpeter*, a boy who fails to make culturally acceptable decisions based on what his parents dictate and ends up getting his fingers chopped off for not cutting his fingernails and becoming thinner and thinner before disappearing altogether for failing to eat his meals.

My mom had heard all the stories already and, a realist as only wars can make of children, she called their bluff. She refused anything but sweets. As time went on, bullying from her minders became frantic pleas to follow the program. The poor women in charge of her were required to take daily weight measurements, and Helli was still in the category of Undernourished. "You'll get us fired! You must eat!" Always her response was, "I'll eat pastries and pancakes and ice cream and chocolate, and nothing else. Feed me those and I promise I'll gain weight." "But these are not healthy! They are not allowed!" Of course she won the battle. It was not a fair fight. It was the first of many times the established order of things would run into the brick wall that was my slight, stubborn, and fiercely motivated mom. In her wake, she would leave shattered careers that had thrived on the careful following and breaking of rules. She was seven years old and she was just getting started.

At various other times, Helli and Seppi were sent away, as kind of work war orphans. Once to Denmark and another time to Switzerland, where my mom was taken in by the minor nobility in the town. They were so charmed by her they sent for Seppi as well, to have the matched pair. For the two children, it was a kind of wonderland. Switzerland had managed to avoid being bombed and occupied and spent the war in relative peace, while Europe and the world burned around them. Living in a quiet mountain hamlet in relative opulence, they thrived.

The home was tidy and clean. There were fresh linens and pretty curtains. The interior was well-lighted by windows with expansive views, and warm lamps shone on broad bookshelves and thickly padded comfortable furniture. All of this luxury was used, so there was no fear of touching this or even breaking that: it was a home, not a showplace. And it was comfort that was shocking to the two kids who'd experienced hardship and poverty. Most shocking of all, they were cared for. Helli and Seppi were good-looking children, smart and curious. For the first time in their lives, someone noticed. And appreciated them. But as always, whether in a good placement or bad, after a matter of some months, my grandmother's crisis passed, and the kids were recalled home to Vienna. To a place that was too small, too empty of love or supervision to be much of a home at all.

Vienna, Passport Stamps, 1957

My father, Edward Rutledge Riley, and my mom met at a dance in Copenhagen, a place neither of them had any good reason to be except that they were young and ambitious and knew how to make a lot happen with just a little bit of fluff and a spark. He was twenty-nine and working as a correspondent for the Army, and she was seventeen and looking for a fun night. They spontaneously combusted. I'm always reminded of that Johnny and June Carter Cash song "Jackson" when I think of them meeting. Ed was the youngest son of a successful Little Rock, Arkansas, merchant, Harvard-educated and athletic, an AAU boxer who could take a hell of a beating but hadn't let it damage his good looks. He had eyes that could draw you in and mesmerize, a charming smile. He was a gadabout and always the smartest man in the room. My mom was a slight, young, beautiful chameleon, able to make herself into whatever she needed to be. That night, apparently, they both liked what they saw. He followed her when she left for home to Vienna and within a short time they were married.

In the wedding photograph from after the civil ceremony, Ed and Helli stand together, smiling, surrounded by her few family members. In the top left-hand corner stands my grandfather, looking out of place. As of course, he was. My grandmother is smiling, smitten with Ed as well. I'm pretty sure that she immediately loved him more than she loved her daughter, because Ed was easy and charming and confident and American, and my mom was a whirlwind of passions and plans, anything but easy. It was enough that he had arrived to take her daughter off her hands, finally, and she was well and good with that. And so, take her away he did.

The wedding party of Edward Riley and Helene Kastinger in Vienna, Austria in 1957. Josef, back left, is now an outcast. My grandmother stands in the front left. Leopold, my Nazi uncle, positioned in the middle, between the young couple.

ARTIFACT: A MEMOIR

My mom's passport from this period is filled with overlapping entrance and exit stamps from every country in Europe, the Middle East, Oceania; they traveled the world at a dizzying pace. They went everywhere, in a time when you could do that. They saw richly vibrant cities of Dacca and Tehran, Amman and Cairo, no great city or country was outside of their avaricious reach to experience. And when Mama got pregnant, they traveled until late in the pregnancy, when Ed rushed them home so that his child could become President one day by virtue of their birth in the United States of America. When the child was born, Papa, the great liberal and well-educated intellectual, laughed that they needn't have hurried, since it was a girl. Soon again, they were off traveling, first to Vienna to drop off the baby, Schatzi they called her, with Mutti so the young vivants could continue making waves in some of the most interesting places in the world. When Mama became pregnant a second time, two years later, Mutti refused any more childcare duties and the couple moved back to Little Rock for good. For a good little while. Long enough to have two more kids and keep trying to figure out whether to take them traveling or leave them. Or both.

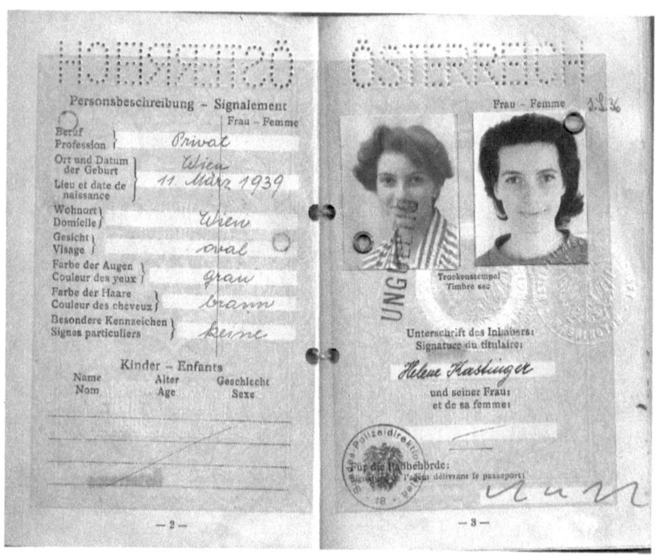

Helene Kastinger Riley's passport (1955)

Vienna, In the Garden, 1972

That summer, newly divorced and desperately needing research materials only available in Vienna to finish her PhD, Mama brought all four of us kids back to her home and dumped us. Mutti got Mama and Schatzi in the new apartment in *Reinprechtsdorferstrasse* which, after it was rebuilt, my grandmother was allowed to buy. That was a special and unthought of luxury in the postwar period. It was around the corner from Great-grandmother's old flat on *Margaretenstrasse* with the kitchen and one big bedroom full of beds and the shared toilet in the main hallway. When we all slept there, I got the bed closest to the door because of my status as the youngest and was told by my brothers that if a robber broke in, he'd kill me first. They had already prepped me for terror by telling me that the German Shepherds in Austria would bite my ears off, so the robber-murderer was just an extra layer of fear for me.

At that time the new place was less than thirty years old, built on the rubble of the former apartment where little Helli learned about schools being bombed, neighbor's dogs being shot in the street, and other hard lessons. My two brothers and I were to spend two months at the country garden plot with our Uncle Rudi, my grandmother's companion. I really don't remember my mother being with us at all, and she must not have been, really. She was off doing her research, and therefore we were pretty much left alone. Whenever we were in the city with Mutti, she would tire of all of us kids in the tiny apartment and give us money to go get *eis* from the ice cream vendor. Schatzi shepherded us, I think, and we all understood that we were to disappear for an hour or two. So we went out to kick the soccer ball around in the city parks. We'd stand for what seemed like hours outside the Spiel und Sport looking at the action figures and board games and sports gear, all way outside our spending range, which was really almost nothing. And after we'd squandered our required time and Mutti had gotten her small bout of silence, we returned to the six-hundred square feet space of our temporary home.

ARTIFACT: A MEMOIR

In the Vienna allotment garden with an aunt, Uncle
Rudi, Helene, Jesse, John, and Michael (1971).

I was always particularly aware of how things could change monumentally, very quickly, but I was never privy to know when it was going to happen. We always just moved with startling finality. The trip in '72 and us staying in the *garten* was like that. We arrived at the little square of green grass with a few wormy cherry and apple trees, a small seasonal two-room cabin rustic enough to almost be mean, and it was an oasis from everything I'd ever experienced before. There was a quiet, village-like aspect to the garden neighborhood, with mostly modest cabins or cottages and lots of trees and hedges and grass. It felt quiet in a way I'd never experienced life being.

Across the street and a bit down, there was a house where it was anything but quiet. For all hours of the day and night, anonymous workers we never actually saw filled the big garage with sparks from grinders and arc-welders and cutting torches lighting up the area. Cars showed up and cars left. Uncle Seppi was by now the cool, motorcycle-riding uncle who would take us on short rides and drag race other bikes from the city stop lights. The uncle who would buy you your first underage beer. He had a job working for the government traveling all over Europe to return cars that had been stolen in Austria. They would fly him to Italy, and he would drive home in a stolen Alfa Romeo and return it to its owners. He told us this house was a chop shop, where stolen vehicles were reduced down to their component parts. We didn't question how he could know this, how this was literally his job, and he could just let it happen and go unreported. That was just the way Seppi lived his life, by letting things happen. On a lower level of criminal behavior, but always so much closer and personal that it felt more dangerous somehow, was our Mutti's habit of going to the corner newspaper machine every morning and fake putting in her coins, pulling out her free paper and walking nonchalantly back to our place. It was such a bold and obvious misdeed. She was so unrepentant and comfortable, the opposite of her American grandkids who were awed and amazed and, maybe, proud of her. She always had her shopping bags visible on her arm from the chicest department stores in Vienna. She would buy a small trifle at these stores and then ask for a big bag to carry them, as an advertisement of her high status and good taste. Appearances mattered to her. Every time she went to the Sparkasse bank, she would return with branded bank trinkets to hand out to us, like a queen bestowing a boon. She was the antithesis of our Grandmother Riley, an old Southern belle, and we loved her, but with a kind of wariness.

Mutti was rarely there with us in the garden, and we were almost completely under the care of Uncle Rudi. Such as that was. As a young teen, Rudolf Hostek was taken to the Dachau Concentration Camp for being Jewish. He survived through the entire war, somehow, and when he was released from the camp and given traveling papers by the Americans, he found himself in the Russian part of Vienna, the city divided like spoils to the victorious Americans, British, and Russians. The soldiers quickly found that Rudi was quite the entertainer when drunk and plied him with drink to enjoy his antics. One time his behavior was found lacking and he was bashed in the temple with a rifle. No one wanted to be in the Russian subdivision, because fresh off twenty-four million casualties, they lacked the friendliness of the late-comer Americans or the efficient rule-following of the British. At some point, he came into my grandmother's life and helped to fill the void left with my grandfather's leaving. He became her lifetime companion, and he never left, except for their daily leave-taking, usually accompanied with threats and yells and screams as he left for his own apartment somewhere nearby, stumbling crookedly with his afternoon drinking and mumbling under his breath. She reiterated her refrain of "He's awful, that guy," and shouted all the swear words that I would learn and take home to share with my friends.

*Rudi on the far left in his concentration camp uniform
(1945).*

I didn't know what being Jewish meant and I certainly didn't know what Concentration Camps were at that time, but I knew Uncle Rudi was a little different. The war had damaged all of my Austrian family members in one way or another, but Rudi, in his quick, fiery rages and endless muttering was fascinating. Not normal. Every day he marched right off the rails that others were bound by, and to me that made him wonderful. He was tiny, around five feet tall, but powerful in his presence, like a storm squall. There was a whiff of danger; anything might happen around him. I was later told that Rudi was a cook in the camps, and it's true, he was a terrible cook. I think there was an old stove in the corner of the cottage with a few burners, but I also remember him cooking outside over a fire. Everything he made was burned, and the only two things he made were *grieskoch*, basically Cream of Wheat, and bachelor spaghetti of simply noodles and tomato sauce. Not only were they always burned at the bottom and permeated with an undesirable smokiness, but they also shared a similarity in taste and color because he never washed the pans very diligently. Me and my two brothers were no help at all and so the meals were awful. Rudi's only rule was that we had to finish our plates. That was non-negotiable. Arguing this point would bring him from absentmindedly pleasant to an instantaneous rage.

We three boys, at eight, ten, and twelve years old, were always hungry. But Uncle Rudi's cooking put that hunger to a real test, and we had various ways of dealing. Trying to wait him out was not a good tack. Once I sat at the table, obstinate, and Rudi roared, "Mikey, you must eat!" and shoved my face into my plate of spaghetti. It was hot. I remember the burn, but more so I remember the black centipede, which my face-imprint had exposed among the separated noodles. After that I'm unclear. Did I barf? Cry? Did a big centipede move even Uncle Rudi to compassion so that he tossed it? All I know is that our asking price among brothers for treats wagered to finishing another's food went up. What had previously been a "I'll finish your Crisco for a candy" became "I'll finish your spaghetti for a chocolate bar or ice cream." The black market was alive and well in the garden. And even if eating in the garden wasn't ideal, there were a couple of days a week when we lived off the fat of the land and could stockpile food for the leaner times.

Rudi never lost the alcohol habit he picked up just after the war ended, so every few days we boys would put ourselves into his care and walk a circuit of every *gasthaus* bar in the area, a matter of a few miles. We would leave in the midmorning, Rudi locking the fence gate behind us, and we'd walk to the first pub. Rudi was a tiny man in stature, although we didn't think so then because his gruffness and style made him seem large. He was thick, he moved with sounds of grunts and veiled conversations to himself, and he was big with all of his combined mannerisms. And though small, he could consume an enormous amount of beer. While he drank, we boys would sit and eat chocolates or *Manner Schnitten* until lunch, when we'd have a big plate of sausage and potatoes, bread and sauerkraut, coca-colas, and whatever else. After a few hours or so, we'd move on to the next place and repeat the process, with another big meal down the road at dinner. By nightfall we were headed home, guiding Rudi through various spots of rugged terrain, shepherding him to somewhat appropriate peeing spots beside hedges or off the road to stream sides, he, struggling with his zipper, belt, and shirttails. When we got back to the garden, we steered his fat little sausage fingers and the key into the lock, he beside himself with laughter, short snippets of song, and good spirits. We would get him situated into his cot and then we'd do the same. Lights out. And, inevitably, a short while later, the great crash resounded as he rolled off the bed and onto the floorboards. More mutters and curses and laughter and then a snoring silence. I would look back at those days of us boys all together under the loose supervision of Uncle Rudi and remember that routine with a sheepish fondness. Plenty of good food and a happy drunk. It wouldn't always be so in the coming years.

Another of the mainstays of our weekly round in the country was going down to the end of the street and crossing the bigger connecting road and heading overland to the river. The river was really more of a causeway or canal, but it was big enough across and fast-flowing that we weren't tempted to try and cross it. It provided a boundary that no adult put on us, hemming us in from wandering too far. In between the road and the canal was a small forest and stream that we would follow until it cleared into a field bisected by a long, sloping, stone-paved waterfall to the river. I only have a few pictures from this time, but in every one of them we are tow-headed, shirtless, and wearing shapeless black swim trunks and brown plastic jelly sandals that were cheap enough to break and buy again, no questions asked. Not shown were the rips and tears, mended or not, that got such wear on the backsides from us sliding down that water and moss-covered stone falls. We spent hours there. I remember it hurting, that slide where some rocks jutted a bit more than others, but we must have gotten calluses and inured to the pain, because part of the fun was standing up at the end of the ride and rubbing your injured butt with a squinched-up face and the laughter of the other brothers. The human and nature interface became a big part of our childhood, because unlike the adults in our family, the outside was always present and accounted for. Always there. The natural world, such as it was in our suburban world growing up, was our teacher and parent and entertainment all in one. With the outside, we were never in want. Inside, with our people, that was not a sure thing.

Uncle Rudi in his prime (nd).

One memorable night we were hunkered around the small black-and-white TV in the cabin. I think it was John who was manning the antenna, moving the metal assembly this way and that trying to get the best coverage for the Summer Olympics. We'd been on the *gasthaus* round with Rudi already and had pestered him enough that we had made it home in time to catch the men's basketball gold medal game between the US and the Soviet Union. Through the snowstorm of bad reception, we coddled and cadged the set to the end of the game. And then to the second end of the game. We must have cried and shouted our anger at the referees, who refused to end the game with the US in the lead, again and again adding time to the clock, loud enough for the guys in the chop shop across the street to hear us. Midway through the last extended period of play, Rudi rolled off his bed with a crash and the set went dead. A mighty wail went up, followed by a resounding cheer as the TV came back on, doggedly determined to show us the snowstorm golden game. We lifted and shoved Rudi back into bed and watched as time ran out and the Soviets celebrated their unfair victory. It was the first time the Americans had lost the basketball Olympic gold. We howled our anger into the night as Rudi snored, the chop shop chopped, and Mama researched in the city somewhere near us and altogether too far away.

MICHAEL RILEY

Where I'm From

I'm from poor proud folks
from an old, white-bearded
Patriarch with seven brawny boys
ranged beside him
with bacon and butter and
cold milk and cornbread on their breath

I'm from streets that smell of rain on hot concrete and
asphalt
whose gutters run with water and
Crawdads and gangs of boys
chasing in flat summer sun
where locusts swing from the ends of strings
and Junebugs swarm the streetlights
in the sweaty sleeve-stained night
Thunder and kicked cans booming

I'm from fields full of cold morning and warm
burnt-orange sunrises
from burrs in dun cotton canvas
and cold-stung fingers harvesting Kale

I'm from sandpaper and sweat
from vinegar and honeysuckle
Juniper and mint
and stubborn, tight-fisted ground
where those born from the dust return home to it
with the green smell of tomato vines still on our hands.

My great-grandfather, John Rutledge Riley, the patriarch, and his seven sons. My grandfather, John Rutledge Riley II, is fourth from the right (1918/19).

Little Rock, Arkansas, Hard Times, 1928–1964

My father, who I'm more curious about than my mom since I know him less well, was raised in a staid and nurturing environment quite different from my mom's. Born in 1928, youngest son of a Little Rock, Arkansas, dry-goods businessman, Bauxite mine investor, timber entrepreneur, do-everything-to-get-by father and a tough, sweet, beautiful mother, Ed Riley was a fortunate child. I have a picture of him riding a goat, but it was a middle class and ironic picture of a boy on a goat. Even in the picture of him from the mid-1930s fishing with a rowdy group of older boys, his clothes fit better and were in better repair and were worn with more confidence than mine ever were at the same age.

My dad, Edward Rutledge Riley, on the left, as a child(nd).

My dad's oldest brother, John Rutledge Riley III, died in childhood from complications after a fall from a tree in the front yard of their prosperous home on 24th Street. This family tragedy was soon to be followed by the national tragedy of the Great Depression. The Riley fortunes were soon to take a hit, but my grandfather was a hopeful and tenacious man, and he wasn't about to give up. This is the environment my father was born into: one of loss and striving, and a belief in the ability to better yourself. I think it was a cardinal responsibility to improve yourself in the Riley worldview. They were forced to move from their 24th Street home in the economic downturn and into a house on 34th Street, an address farther from "town" and an indicator of their declining financial situation. My Uncle

Pat, always business savvy, sold apples and newspapers on street corners to add to the family income. As the youngest, I think my dad was probably shielded from some of those hardest times and had a good childhood in which he was never homeless or hungry, something a lot of Depression-era folks could not claim.

As the Great Depression ended and the WWII economic boom began to be felt, the Riley financial outlook improved. Bauxite is a key element in the aluminum needed for airplanes, and my grandfather had an interest in some mines as part of his diverse portfolio of business affairs. Their address changed again, and they left hard times behind for 1921 W. 22nd Street and the home we always knew as "The White House." It was a house to send a signal: tall, straight, and prosperous. It would be the height of grandfather's achievement in social standing.

The Rileys were big believers in the upward movement potential of education, and all the boys and girls went to the best colleges. My dad earned a Pepsi-Cola scholarship to attend Harvard University, after graduating from Central High School as a sixteen-year-old. Once there, he immersed himself in college culture, and he became a boxer, Young Democrat, and a member of the cross-country team. His older brother, my Uncle Pat, a Harvard Business guy, always said of his boxing days, "Your dad could take a hell of a beating." I always found that to be true in my experiences with my dad, too, but it wasn't a skill he would need to lean into during the late fifties, as he married, began a family, and faced forward into a bright-seeming future.

An eighteen-year-old Ed Riley heading out to play tennis (1950).

Little Rock, Heels by the Poolside, 1958

After the whirlwind tour of the world, after their whirlwind romance and marriage, my parents must have experienced a realization that money was short, babies were on the way, and someone better get a job and a place to live. They ended their epic walkabout, packed up my baby sister and a few other small things, and left Vienna for Little Rock. The destination would have been a natural choice for Papa: head to the only home he'd ever known and the source of his parental benefactors. Go where the money and cheap living were to be found. The contrast couldn't have been more extreme for Mama, though. Switching from the life in a great city of Europe to a mid-sized parochial city of the American South was bound to be jarring. Little Rock couldn't match the buzz, the culture, the style or flair of Vienna, but Mama was young and daring, and she brought that with her.

She knew very little English, so she got a German-English dictionary and started in on reading *Gone with the Wind*, translating word by word. She would have known the movie, the White House gave a fair imitation of an antebellum mansion, and she was married to a charismatic and handsome dark-haired Southerner. It fit her view of the story she was telling herself. Mama wasn't an academic by training, which was one of the reasons she left Vienna, where the most she could hope to achieve in the workplace was to be a secretary. She did know how to bear down and work. She learned English and the dialect, started homekeeping and delved into at least the surface domestic arts, and jumped into the society she found herself in. Everyone loved her. Helene was a perfect complement to Ed: beautiful, vivacious, wonderfully different in her accent and clothing. Her mother-in-law, India, was a gracious Southern woman, and invited Helene into the family and into her home on West 22nd Street. The White House, with its Doric columns and stately lines, was a commanding presence on the street and an impressive step up for Mama. Here was something my mom couldn't have in her home city, where small apartments and shared bathrooms were the norm. She moved in and took over.

*Little Rock School Board Campaign Picture for Edward Riley
including Ed Riley (standing), John, Helene, holding Michael, Jesse,
and Schatzi (around 1965).*

Mama was a cultural avatar for Vienna. She had an insatiable love of learning and practicing arts of all kinds, and she immediately began painting wall-sized murals in the big white hallways of her new home. She practiced the piano and joined the Second Baptist Church choir so she could add her strong soprano to the mix. And stand out from the midst of it. I have a picture of her dressed in men's work attire, worn blue jeans, striped shirt open at the chest, straw hat, and a painted mustache. She would wear tiger-stripe bathing suits and high heels to the poolside. She was audacious, and a match in every way to her handsome, stunningly intelligent husband. I can't help but think Little Rock must have felt a little taken aback by the infusion of sultry instead of staid, liberalism in a conservative town. Wherever they went, they left a mark.

Helene being creative (about 1959).

The Riley Clan was growing up and moving up, as all of Ed's siblings married and moved up various rungs of Little Rock society. Literally up, into the Pulaski Heights, where the cream of the financial elite rose to the hills looking down over the rest of the city. Gone were the rebuilding years and homes on 34th Street and 24th Street. Gone, too, was the patriarch, John, who died in 1957 and never got to meet his charming young daughter-in-law. But Ed, the youngest, and Helene were living on 22nd Street, in the White House. The family was growing. Confidence was high.

On May 26, 1960, my dad found himself in front of Little Rock's Central High School just as Daisy Bates was being accosted by a police officer. Papa had attended Central High before leaving for Harvard, and he knew very well who she was. Everyone in Little Rock knew Daisy Bates. Three years earlier, she and her husband, L.C., were instrumental in implementing the Supreme Court's Brown v. Board of Education decision in the high school. As the NAACP liaison for the nine African American students integrating the school, she would shepherd them through the difficult and dangerous year, holding press conferences at her home, seeing that the kids all got to Central High, and problem solving with the local school board in finding solutions to the myriad problems that were tossed at the students from a rebellious and unkind student body and citizenry.

News story of Ed's arrest in front of Central High School for speaking up in support of Daisy Bates, the Little Rock 9 mentor and President of the Arkansas Chapter of the NAACP (1960).

As the police officer yelled at Mrs. Bates and proceeded to give her a ticket for double-parking in front of the school, my father said, "Officer, it's your car that is blocking traffic." The officer turned and said, "Do you want to make something out of it? Come on, what are you going to do about it?" My dad responded calmly, "There's nothing I can do but protest. And report you." And then he added, as an aside to Mrs. Bates, "We know why he's bothering you." The officer threw the ticket at Bates and turned, furious, to my dad. A few words ensued, out came the "slapper," a leather billy club. Down went Riley. Later that night my mom got a call from Mrs. Bates informing her that Ed Riley had spoken up for her and was downtown in the Little Rock Police city lock-up. The officer later stated in court that my dad was drunk and had taken off his glasses "in an intimidating manner," and that he resisted arrest. My dad was fined a small sum and wore the arrest and time in jail as a badge of honor. It was a small knockdown, but one that would resonate in our family stories for years to come.

Papa worked in journalism at the *Arkansas Gazette* newspaper, in philanthropic organizations like the Red Cross, and as a speechwriter for a US Senator for a while. As he amassed a collection of worthy but short-term jobs, he and my mom also continued to add to their family, with a new child coming every two years. When I was born in 1964, my mom asked the doctor plaintively, "How did this happen?!" She had been trying to use contraception, and after three children and a miscarriage, she wasn't relishing another newborn and all the work it would entail. The doctor replied, "Well, Mrs. Riley, this is your fourth child, so I do hope you know how this happened." Ed had dreams of a big, bustling family of six or eight kids, but after my birth my mom drew the line: four was enough. My cousin would later tell me that I had the worst case of diaper rash she'd ever seen. Four might have been a little bit more than enough.

As the youngest, I've always felt a bit left out of our family history. And I've always recognized that as a kind of positive, missing out on a lot of the drama and stress of a new and dynamic young family of two charismatic, brilliant, and ambitious parents. By the time I came into consciousness, much of that had already passed. Facing a harried home full of babies and an overwhelmed wife wondering where her dreams of career glory had suddenly disappeared to, my dad decided to disappear as well. Education had always been a strength of his, and he decided that now might be a good time to pursue a master's degree and a PhD. The terminal degree always had a cachet for me, and it must have for him as well. He left my mom with his mom in the big house and left for the Bay Area to pursue an MA in journalism from Stanford. How that worked for Mama is a dead question, but it was a creative time in her life, and perhaps she got by with painting and music and biding her time. When Ed came back and was eager to pursue a PhD from Indiana University, Mama insisted that the family follow him. She found time in Bloomington to take classes in the arts while keeping the kids clothed and fed and cared for, mostly, and when Papa finally finished with his terminal degree, they picked up once again and moved to Texas and a waiting teaching position in political science at Texas Women's University.

Denton, Texas, Kick the Can, 1970–72

When my dad started at Texas Women's University (TWU) in Denton, Texas, it was a small school in a small town. Our home was in a raw new subdivision, with empty lots still on either side of us soon to sprout houses, and a big section of horse pasture that extended far and wide beyond the back of our property. In the front yard was a small willow tree and a bed of marigolds. There was a small strawberry patch out back, a woodpile that sometimes harbored rattlesnakes, and after some green grass and a barbed-wire fence, pastureland stretching for what seemed forever. This was the first place I would know from my memory, instead of hearing about it from others. It was in many ways a perfect place for a kid to grow up. We roamed the neighborhood with so many kids our own ages, there was room to run and play in the street with only slim chances of being run over by cars, and the subdivision was still newly carved from the landscape, so there were a host of wild little verges to play and explore and to learn about the natural world. I loved it with the total abandonment of judgment and caution of a clueless youngest child. Even the willow tree was magical to me.

Michael and Jesse in front of the Denton, Texas, house on Greenbrier (1970).

We Rileys were all towheads at that time from being in the Texas sun all summer long, and I can't remember wearing shoes. Stubbed toes and sunburns were the bane of our existence, and we tanned brown as pecan shells after layer upon layer of skin peeled and healed. We stayed out at night playing Kick the Can under the lights clouded by June bugs; we stayed out in the warm summer rain and caught the crawdads in the fast-running gutters and then put them together to watch them fight. There was always one of them with one big, oversized claw like the arms of a cartoon character superhero. We caught lightning bugs in jars and let them light our rooms until their batteries died. We caught fish from a deep hole we knew about and sold them from house to house, even if we rarely found buyers. This rural kidhood, kind of a *Lord of the Flies* abandonment with breakfast and dinner, always felt like enough for me. There were tensions and disagreements between my parents, but it was what I knew and so it kind of washed over my head, water from a duck's back. Papa was teaching; Mama was taking classes in music and fine arts because that's what she knew, loved, and wanted to get better at. She played to her strengths. I occasionally got left at university daycare, and the staff had to drive me home. I noticed, but maybe more because of the distress and anxiety of my care providers than any of my own. I didn't think much of it. As the last of four, my mom would go down the list of Jess-John-Je-Michael if she had to call out for me. I was the quiet one who didn't gather much notice. I think that makes me the lucky one.

Our neighborhood on Greenbrier was a self-contained community for a kid like me. We had our extended range on Halloween night, and forays to the Piggly Wiggly grocery and five-and-dime store to buy pastel-dyed chicks at Easter, and everything else all the time, but I don't remember much more of the town of Denton. Our street had plenty of opportunities to amaze and delight, so we didn't stray much. We had a gay couple as neighbors to one side of us, and those guys made amazing ethnic food that I couldn't pronounce or recognize that they would always share with us for dinner. Mama collected their recipes and learned from them. My siblings knew their names, Carlos and somebody or other, but I always remember them as the Galloping Gourmets after the TV show. On the other side was a family of radical hippies, the Francises, who ate whole-grain foods and were nudists behind their big, boarded backyard fence. I didn't know what that meant until one day I put my eye to the missing knothole of one plank in the fence and forever burned my little eye with their old-person nakedness. We had a dog named Nakita, after Khrushchev, and had a turquoise Ford Falcon. Each of our families were our own kind of fabulous.

Collectively, we thrived as a neighborhood as well. We kids all ran in packs, the next-door neighbor Francis kids and the down-from-them Clampitts and us Rileys: from dawn to well after dusk on any non-school day, we were playing ball in the street and chasing around going nowhere in particular. There were always enough kids to make teams. Being inside was not yet a thing that we did, except for Saturday morning cartoons. The Ramseys from across the street were big gardeners, and Mr. Ramsey grew marigolds and morning glories fit to take over any available space. He grew lots of watermelons, too, and the highlight of the summer social season was their harvest. He would invite the whole neighborhood, and there was a loaves and fishes element to the event: we would feast until our stomachs were round as the melons, but he never ran out of stock. Afterwards, the kids would collect all the uneaten rinds and have fights with them. I don't remember any of us getting hurt by a dead-on throw or having to pick up the mess afterwards. It was an idyllic life for us kids.

Every year, the Francises would have a big garden in their backyard, and in the spirit of Tom Sawyer, Mrs. Francis would get all of the neighborhood kids to help her collect her fertilizer by having a battle of the sexes, boys vs. girls, to see who could collect the most manure from the horse and cattle pasture out behind our houses. Whichever team collected the most would get first choice of pies and cookies and cakes. And Mrs. Francis was a killer baker. It was basically a cow-pies-for-apple-pies equation and so, for us kids, it was irresistible. She'd gather us all up, give us the "On your marks! Get set! Goooooo!" commands, and we were off. It was no delicate task. If the cow pies were good and dry, they were easy to pick up and put in our burlap bags. They also made great frisbees, which might have played heavily into the boys' annual loss, because hitting a girl mid-stride with a swiftly spinning disk of manure, which on contact exploded into poop- and hay-dust and an equally explosive bout of indignation, was a win in and of itself, and well worth the second choice at pies. There was plenty of manure to go around on acres of well-grazed pasture, so waste was not a thing. Getting your hands into a deceptively dry-looking manure patty was part of the game, too, and by the end, we were all fairly considered cowboys and cowgirls, if only by our smell. The pie and cakes at the end were gravy, and life was sweet indeed.

Next to the Ramseys were another older couple, and the old guy would take all of the neighborhood kids to the fair that visited every summer and pay for rides and food from the midway. He would also drive the bunch of us out to his farm and give us tractor rides and show us the real country life outside of our subdivision. None of us or our parents were aware of any risk involved in this kind of behavior, of allowing kids time away from adult supervision, but my sister Schatzi later told me the guy was a pedophile and was generous of his time and money with kids for a reason. My sister narrowly avoided being abused when the old lady found her alone with him in their living room and sent her home. After we'd moved away, I heard that he died by falling off his tractor seat and getting run over by his old red Farmall.

Every July we would set in a huge store of fireworks and fret with how to use them before the Fourth finally rolled around. Someone had the bright idea of filling up a Coke bottle with water, putting a bottle-rocket inside pointing down, and lighting the fuse. Everyone took off running, but I, the youngest, was asking a question about the mechanics of fuse and water, and looked around to see everyone in the distance, booking it. Just as I got ready to run, the rocket exploded and I got hit with multiple pieces of glass, the biggest one carving a four-inch furrow in the skin and meat of my shin. I woke up in someone's front yard, and I wasn't hurting, just confused. But one look down at my leg, and the green grass all around it red with blood, and I started hollering and blubbering. When Mama showed up with a screech of the tires, dragged away from classes by an emergency phone call, she was furious. "I can't leave you kids alone for a minute without something going wrong!" No one mentioned that we were alone most hours of the day. We were dumb, but not that dumb. I was the one furious, later, when I looked down at my leg in the hospital bed to see the results of the minor surgery: brown stitches. "Brown?! I asked for green! Or blue or red or anything but brown!" I cried some more.

Mama was pragmatic in all things. Perhaps she had to be, but it could be tough on a kid. I had a favorite toy, a big green turtle that you sat on and rode around on wheels. A precursor to the Big Wheels we'd later love and ride until the plastic tires wore out and our legs got too long to cram onto the pedals. The turtle steered with a varnished black wooden handle. I rode it everywhere. I came home one day to find it almost completely intact but broken beyond repair. Where the driving handle once shone proudly, there was nothing. Just a thin metal rod. Bare. I ran into the house and Mama was cooking dinner. I yelled and cried about my turtle and asked her what had happened. She looked down at the frying pan on the stove, and I followed her gaze to a new, shiny, black varnished handle. I always hear William Carlos Williams and his narrator talking about plums when I hear her tell me, "The frying pan handle broke, and I needed to cook dinner. I saw the handle, and it fit." So little love in a poem, in a frying pan, in an Austrian mom who needed to cook dinner.

But small crises endured and big ones avoided, Denton remains for me a bright spot in my childhood. The simplicity of having everyone in one place, a house and family just like the other kids, a belonging and acceptance, even if it was an acceptance of not knowing. I didn't know the danger our gay neighbors must have faced and the fear they knew if the wrong people knew about them. Or that the kindly old neighbor farmer was grooming my twelve-year-old sister for sex. The shouting and arguments and emptiness of our home, when we kids were the only ones around and Mama and Papa were separately elsewhere. That was all I knew and all I expected. But for my older siblings who'd known another time, known other parents, really, I think it must have been hard. For me, too, coming up on the horizon, not knowing and togetherness were coming to an end; storm clouds looming, and they were bringing more than cold rain on a summer day and crawdads running in the flooded gutters.

Acapulco, Mexico, Family Vacations, 1970

We went driving from Denton across the border to Mexico a few different times over the years. Mama would start making grilled ham-and-cheese sandwiches for the road, much different from the ordinary fare of peanut butter, which we would partially eat and then throw behind the freezer in the pantry off the garage. A special treat that signified change was in the air. We'd pile in the car and drive for what seemed to me forever, but which might have been a couple of days. I always knew when we'd crossed the border into Mexico because we were eating cantaloupes for breakfast. Another harbinger food. We would arrive in Acapulco and our new home in a palapa near the beach—for a longer stay of a month or until the money ran out—or a hotel, for shorter stays of a week or two. My parents traveled like migrating birds: they knew where they were going and good stops along the way, but there wasn't a lot of planning.

ARTIFACT: A MEMOIR

On one long stay, one of the local kids in a neighboring palapa, Pepe, would come over to play, and he had magical skills. He could catch birds in his hands. He knew names of the different lizards that inhabited our houses and ways to have fun with them. He knew which ones would change colors, knew to feed them flies and mosquitos and other bugs so that they would live longer in captivity, and knew which ones would lose their tails if you grabbed them wrong. He could sing and talk with us without either knowing the others' language.

Mama and Papa would switch out driving on some of the drives and once, in the mountains, they were arguing pretty vigorously about something and Mama stopped the car and said, "Get out!" Papa, always game and always on the losing side, got out. Mama sped off down the road to the uneasy silence of us four kids. I think of Mama as a person who would always win a game of chicken. She'd been in enough wrecks of all kinds of life that she was driven to succeed, even if that meant heading straight into the path of a vehicle accelerating directly towards you. She feared but was fearless. An unstoppable force. Papa was just naive and charming and too smart for his own good. Mama drove. She went far enough that we all started complaining and crying, and then she went some more, before stopping and turning around. When we got to Papa an hour or so later, still sitting by the roadside, he was hot and meek. He got in and we resumed our trip to wherever, and that present silence made our former kids' silence seem loud. We motored down the road to the sound of tires on pavement. Years later, when I was a married man myself and having a similar difficult road trip, I unknowingly turned down an olive branch, makeup offer from my wife when we finally stopped after an interminable driving session. "A Shamrock shake?! Green ice cream? Yuck!" She went white and ordered me out. When she didn't drive off without me, I was grateful.

On the road and along detours to and from Acapulco, we traveled to some famous pyramids of the ancients, and all of us would trudge up the steep steps, terrified of falling and becoming a stand-in tourist sacrifice to the old gods. The local kids made a living off tourists at the site and would trade clay figurines and handcrafted art for ballpoint pens. We were amazed by our good fortune. We would go to restaurants and try to eat American food and avoid the tap water to protect our pampered American digestive flora and fauna, but it was always the burgers and fries that ended up making us sick. Nowhere in the world is a burger a burger unless it's in America, something I have had to learn time and again from childhood and into my adult years. We swam in the turquoise waters, went to see the famous cliff divers, made sandcastles on the beach, and played with our friend Pepe. Then a day would come, and like the birds gathering in flocks, all knowing, obeying the same impulse, we gathered up and left. The money was gone, the university break was over, the living without confines and in close quarters grew too burdensome. A decision was made like a light switch being flipped, and we were gone.

The Grand Canyon, 1971

One year we piled into the car and took part in that great American institution, the family road trip. Mama made the grilled ham-and-cheese sandwiches, Papa told us stories about this mystical destination, and we kids buckled up (metaphorically, because I don't think all the seats had seatbelts yet) for a long and learning-filled experience. We drove for days, and at one point we left Jesse at one of the gas and food plazas. There were metrics to the driving that we kids were not privy to, and so when we stopped, we went about the important business of filling up and losing our loads. Pee breaks didn't happen after the tank was full and food was for beginnings and end and, sometimes, briefly, midway through the day. Jesse always needed to eat and that time it caught him out. We remembered him some ways down the road, and he was patiently making his way through a sit-down meal, none the worse.

Before there were screens in cars or listening devices, there was reading and road-trip games. There was no way to insulate yourself from everyone else in the car, no personal space at all, so we had to work together to pass the time. Uneasy alliances in the face of incalculable boredom. There was "99 Bottles of Beer on the Wall" singing, which really was more punishing than fun, kind of a way to put our non-consensual boredom to a tune and force it upon the others. If you were singing, your voice kind of shielded you from the experience. Then there was Slug-Bug, which was dangerous because it gave John a free chance to hurt you. Often. And I-Spy, working your way through the alphabet, A to Z, using only the signs that we passed at sixty miles per hour, and poring over the gas-station maps that showed us where we were going, and where we weren't. We spent the time honing our skills of observation and being present, while also practicing the coping skill of not noticing anything at all. Both were necessary family survival skills.

Papa would spend hours of factual lecture and storytelling prepping us for the Grand Canyon, but we'd also stop at random places of interest along the way. Once, as I lay sleeping, everyone packed out of the car and went out to the rim to look out over Meteor Crater in Arizona, and I woke up to car doors slamming and the excited hubbub of chatter about the sight. I was heartbroken and indignant that they would leave me out (as the youngest, I was used to that feeling) and aghast at their priorities. They were protecting my sleep? By abandoning me in a hot car and letting me miss the most exciting thing since we left Jesse? It was a wrong I carried with me forever.

I had been dreading our arrival at the destination, but it turned out my dread was for all the wrong reasons. I had the thought that we would be hiking down the canyon like Army soldiers, rappelling down the cliff sides. And on other parts of the journey down, riding donkeys just on the edge of tumbling down into the rocky ravines. It turned out that there was a nicely groomed dirt and rock path down into the canyon, no rappelling necessary, and the donkeys cost too much, so we just walked, hugging the rock-side inner path while the riders tiptoed on the edge of disaster. Midway down, we dunked our T-shirts into the communal water trough to cool down and made it down to the bottom triumphantly. I don't recall the trip up, or the car ride back home, for that matter. My childhood memory is a one-way trip only.

That evening or the next, we stopped by Carlsbad Caverns to see the bats and camp for the night. I know some people who love bats, but I'm not one of them. Seeing that black stream of blood-sucking *fledermaus*, literally "fluttering mice," was primally scary and emotionally overwhelming. I was awestruck. A wing of night left the darkened cave for the star-streaked and ambient light of the desert evening, fear and wonder and experience colliding into an unforgettable nature experience. And since that was part of the purpose of the trip, it was a success from my parent's perspective. When we settled into our covered concrete pad campsite for the night, no tents or sleeping bags for my family, the brutally hot day gave way to a hard frozen and interminable night. We piled beneath scratchy blankets for the shared body heat and squirmed for position nearest the center, our frozen noses poked into the night air. By morning, when we woke sore and muscle-strained from the tai chi of our sleep positioning, the cramped confines of

the car seemed like a kind of paradise, and we started the
unmemorable way home.

Garden Lore

Failure to thrive is nothing new
I teach my students the history of ours.
All of us from someone, elsewhere, even here, grown in
Arkansas was how I came labeled.

I pull for the weedy kids in my classes:
(really, that's all of them)
the ones in raised and razed/made and unmade beds
all forced in my garden classroom.

I'll bring in kitchen herbs to jog their memories,
say, "Smell this!" Be just a little sad
for the ones who name the Rosemary,
Mint and oregano.
Happy for the kids who say, Trees. Gum. Mary Jane.
We all have our blind spots.

The Bronze Fennel, Tomatillos in my plot that
tenaciously outlast
lack of water and hoe, all marginally out of line
volunteers
master and husband themselves to grow
where cossetted and factoried seeds fail.
I want my kids to make it through
just like that: struggle and despair and, finally,
fruit.

ARTIFACT: A MEMOIR

We're all taught what to love and hate.
My students that I'm warned about—the ones
that co-workers caught strangling or stealing or speaking
out of turn
end up graduating, bartending, giving me Shakespeare.
"Good" ones sometimes not so well,
find themselves useful, successful, full
of rubrics and not much else.
Picking winners and losers isn't what I do.

I mind the riotous growth, nurture
the one who says, "These buds remind me of a friend
who liked Chamomile tea, and the day we drew pictures
of flowers
all day in the basement."

Part II: Foundering

While I have subtle and shadowed memories of my parents' marriage falling apart, of arguments and silences and odd periods of neglect, I was too young to pick up on much of it more than an emotional sense that things weren't good at home. My father was having affairs at the university, perhaps my mom as well, and there was a lot of shouting. Papa was fired for erratic behavior and was showing the first signs of the bipolar disorder that would define the second half of his life the way his strong promise and fine academic achievements had defined the first. But a tipping point was reached, and we packed up, whether from Denton or Mexico I was too young to remember, and ended up at a duplex in Houston. Our new home.

Houston, TX, Taking our Pops, 1972–1975

Mama must have done the preparation for leaving while finishing her BA in fine arts and graduating magna cum laude in Denton and applying for her advanced degree at Rice University, but that was far from anything that was shared with me. This seemed like just another random road trip in the life of Michael, except that we were in a new place, and Papa had stayed home. The apartment had a large chain-link-enclosed backyard, where grass grew haltingly and fire ant colonies thrived, and the front was a big concrete parking pad that segued seamlessly into street. The front living room had avocado-colored long shag carpet, and the rest of the decor went downhill from there. I remember, if anything, a lot of white space. All three of us boys shared a room with bunk beds, and at our bathtime we were still small enough to share that space as well. We would have contests to see who could stay underwater longest, which John always won. Sometimes he'd jokingly hold me underwater, and that panicked inability to breathe kept me fearful of water and sporting events among brothers for years to come. Mama and Schatzi, the oldest and a girl, each got their own rooms.

Papa didn't move with us, which seemed strange to me, but he was always somewhere nearby. Sometimes he would appear at our apartment and stay the night. I had just learned the basics of the concept of divorce, and I was confused about why Mama and Papa would want to separate and still be together. He would occasionally round us up in his white Ford Econoline panel van that he used in his new business for airport transit and other people-shuttling events and take us down to Galveston for a day at the beach. I can remember most clearly the waiting in gridlock traffic, windows open to the ninety-degree heat, watching the engine temperature gauge rise deep into the red and smoke starting to rise from under the hood. For sure there was the tepid, tea-colored ocean water, massive sunburns and ice cream, but as with every one of our childhood vacations, the overpowering memory is of anxiety and foreboding. That and "99 Bottles of Beer on the Wall." It was a childhood of waiting for bad things to happen. Or maybe just waiting.

I started first grade at Gus Grissom Elementary, which was only two blocks from our duplex apartment. Jesse must have been there with me, but school was a lonely thing for me, and I don't ever recall having company to help me endure it, friends or family. John and Schatzi were across the street at the middle school. Mama was on campus working feverishly to get her PhD at Rice in record time. And Papa was . . . somewhere. In school I learned that kids generally didn't like to read. On my first trip to the school library, I got a big book and sat down in the bookshelves to read it, and a kid told me, "You don't have to get a big one with words. You can get away with just picture books." I told him I liked big books, and he shrugged and left me alone.

In PE class, we got lined up and the big man told us, "Ya'll want to quiet down now. Anyone wants to keep on talking, you can get five pops. Anyone want five pops? FIVE POPS!" Everyone quieted down and we got into the educational mode of silent activity. Papa never hit us, and Mama stopped the day in Denton when she grabbed one of her trusty weapons of child management, a rubber baseball bat toy with a big goofy smiley-face on the barrel and spanked one of the brothers with it. She used to say with a wicked grin and a thick German accent, Gestapo-like, "The rubber, it leaves no mark." On that day we'd had enough, and all in cahoots, we stole the bat, dug a hole out back in the horse pasture, and buried it without honor or fanfare. Mama figured that if we'd steal and destroy our own property, maybe it was time to stop hitting us. The schools in Texas didn't come to the same realization, unfortunately.

I don't know what you had to do other than talk in PE to get pops from the paddle each teacher had, but apparently it wasn't much. Pain and humiliation are great for setting memories, and I can remember getting called out into the hallway, told to bend over and take the swinging belts of pain, and then walking gingerly back inside, trying to sit down back in the hard wooden seat with my butt stinging like fire, all the kids snickering. On another occasion, I was called to sit at a desk on the big cafeteria stage during lunch, eating alone under the bright lights while every kid in the room stared at me. At least it felt that way. Not quite a dunce cap in the corner, but I'm sure that would have been preferable to the spotlight for a shy kid like me. I guess if Gus Grissom could serve his country by flaming out in a cosmic crash, I could take a little heat in his namesake institution. I doubt that's the way the teachers justified it because, really, it was Texas. A little pain was to be expected.

My favorite part of first grade, other than the library visits, was my end-of-the-day speech pathology class. I didn't know that's what it was, but I knew it had something to do with me being special and wrong somehow. I loved that class. I got to work with just one adult, and the other kids in the room had their own teacher. I would work on the sounds that I couldn't say without lisping them out as esses. Working on reading words slowly and distinctly and with clear and careful enunciation. I'd had tympanoplasty surgery down in Little Rock at the Arkansas Children's Hospital some years previously to correct a hole in my eardrum that I was born with, but the doctors kind of jabbed around in there and I had a lot of scar-tissue damage. I didn't hear very well, and as a result some of my speech was a bit slurred and off the mark. But I didn't care about any of that. I loved the class because it was on my home's side of the school, and the door let out directly into the parking lot. I could be halfway home before the other kids had navigated the crowded hallways to their locker cubbies. And those special classroom teachers never hit me.

Once the school day was done, we were free, and encouraged even, to "go play in the street." That was my mom's joke, like her allusion to punishments not leaving a mark, but there was a palpable truth to her statement. We did play in the street, and we always had a sense that if we lost one of us four to a benign accident, well, it would certainly make things a little bit easier around the house. More room and food and resources available for those of us left. We played baseball in the street, always enough kids to play, with the chorus of "CAAARR!" about as regular as church bells on the hour in more civilized places. Sometimes when Papa was visiting, we ran around the block hurdling trash cans put out by the gutter. When the rains came heavy and quick and the bayou near our house overbore its banks, we'd slosh through the flooded neighborhood poking at floating colonies of fire-ants. We were always outside. We lived in the street, because it was easier than being in the house.

Mama was busy working on her PhD in Germanics. As she had with her undergraduate degree in fine arts, she played to her strengths, and language was one of them. With her movements around Europe after the war and her extensive travel, she spoke four languages, two fluently. That made her a killer in Scrabble and gave her a new path toward an academic career in linguistics. She was in a hurry and would finish her MA and PhD in the next five years so that she could finally begin earning a living and living a life. We had no such time constraints. With no one at home, we had the run of everything around us. Plenty of time to get into trouble. The first time I ever got drunk I was nine years old, and we found one of the neighborhood duplex apartments empty and unlocked. We opened the sliding door and immediately headed for the refrigerator, boys that we were. Inside was a bottle of Boone's Strawberry Hill wine, and we took swigs of the sweet stuff without knowing the power of cheap booze. We never got caught because there was no one to catch us catching a buzz. It wasn't a habit. The only good thing my brother John ever did for me, that I can think of, was beating the crap out of me for smoking a cigarette from a pack that I found on the ground by the school. The pack of us found an alligator snapper turtle on the street one day, and we wondered what would happen if we put a lit firecracker in its mouth. Alligator snappers bite anything you put near them, and he chomped down solid as we lit the fuse and stood back. I was always the youngest, whether in Arkansas or Texas or Connecticut, and I wasn't really responsible for the carnage, but I felt sick after the firecracker went off. That might be the only other regret I had from my childhood. But as it turned out, my childish penchant for harm was another habit that didn't stick.

We only had a few rules at home, and I think we really did try to follow them. One was not to touch Mama's Pepperidge Farm chocolate cake, which was one of the few luxuries she allowed herself. We became adept at scraping frosting from the inside top of the packaging, a kind of DMZ of the chocolate cake: a no-man's land of shared and prohibited access. And we learned the art of the laser-thin slice. If you took a regular-enough and thin-enough slice, no one was the wiser. Really, we didn't win, and Mama didn't lose in that exercise, because if the slice was thin enough to be unnoticeable, it was also unsatisfactory as a bite, even if stolen.

The other rule, really the only other rule that I'm aware of, was no ball-play in the house. Aside from chocolate cake, Mama's only other luxury was her art. She played at the piano until we shouted her down to quit "making so much noise!" And then she kept playing. She threw clay pots at the university and did some pretty amazing ceramics. She made me a beautiful piggy bank for my birthday, with a fanciful scorpion, my birth month sign, as the lid and I had it in my hands for two whole minutes before I tripped and it shattered into a million pieces on the kitchen floor. She picked it all up and glued it back together, and I still have the truncated, misshapen piece. She also made Klimt-inspired stained glass reflection boxes that she hung on the walls.

On a day when we forgot the only rule, we three boys were jumping from couch to chairs throwing a football, shouting and showboating like our NFL favorites, when a throw went errant and made a direct hit on a stained glass piece. Shards of colored glass and mirror rained down onto the carpet. That avocado shag, so good at hiding mistakes. It couldn't hide this. We feverishly cleaned at first, then painstakingly, picking up the pieces by hand, vacuuming, and throwing all of the evidence in the outside trash can. When Mama came home in the evening, we were all in hiding. Silent. A silence that made her delayed reaction, sometime after her arrival and noticing the blank space on the wall, all the more hideous for us. Because she started wailing. A high and keening and seemingly interminable scream of pain and loss and agony. Mama put up with a lot, both at the university and at home, but she held it all pretty close. Until she couldn't take it any longer and she wailed for hours. It happened only once every couple of years, but it is seared into my memory. We quailed in our room, and if we were hungry and wanting dinner, we just stayed hungry. On the verge of finishing her PhD, with four kids of her own now and just like in her childhood, with no one to lean on, she cried like she had as a child in the Austrian countryside while a World War crushed everything she knew. For just a few times as an adult, crushed by the injustice of her circumstances, she allowed *das shreindes kind*, that screaming child, her voice again.

Our subdivision was built, like much of the rest of Houston, on land prone to flooding. Nearby was Sims Bayou, although I never knew its name when I lived there and just called it the bayou, and all around us were oxbows and swamps and small lakes fed by the Brazos River and a high-water table. We would often cross the few blocks of backyards and school playing fields and busy arterial streets to get to the bayou, another one of the small remnants of a former world, from before suburban growth paved every inch of ground, that allowed me to feed a sense of connection and wonder for the natural world. The bayou was deliciously full of danger, and it was real, not imagined. The canals were dyked with old fill, from concrete and rebar chunks to barbed wire and other old rusty metal fencing, with broken bottles and nails scattered liberally underfoot. We might have been wearing shoes by this time, but their soles were no match for this landscape, and we got our tetanus shots religiously.

The water was full of things that could bite and sting and, to our kid brains at least, devour us whole. Alligator snapper turtles were commonplace and fascinating, with their chisel-shaped heads and snake-quick reflexes. The easiest way to play with them was to get a stick and put it in their mouth: they would chomp down and not let go and you could carry them around wherever, their tender and vulnerable little tail hanging down from inside their armored vault of a body. Water moccasins and copperhead snakes were always around to stir up that ancestral fear and attraction, winding their s-curves over the surface of the water and making us jump when curled like rope right where our next footstep would fall. We were like cats with our midair adjustments. I never got bit by anything worse than ticks or chiggers, and that was bad enough, but the stories from the *Reader's Digest* "Drama in Real Life" kept our fears well-fed. Walking on the bayou made you alert and alive like school or church or home never did.

Papa was ahead of his time in his running and fitness practices that he kept up throughout his life, even as his treatments and drugs to combat his mental illness took a toll on his physical abilities, and he instilled them in us so that they have stayed with us as well. Not only was he encouraging us in turkey trot races early on in the seventies, before running was as commonplace as it is today, but he was pushing yoghurt, social justice, healthy brain/healthy body mantras to us. One way to combine all of those was our annual participation in the March of Dimes fundraising walk in Houston. We would spend weeks gathering pledges of pennies or dollars from church members, neighbors, school adults, and far-flung family. We'd anxiously watch as our pledge page slowly filled with names and potential donations, and our excitement built towards the day itself when ten thousand people would meet outside the Astrodome and walk twenty miles for charity. I think we tried to stay together during the walk, but twenty miles with small kids (I think I was ten at the time) can take a while. I think during one of the years we participated, I had to hit the medical tent for heat stroke treatment and care, an event that reminded me closely of being left at daycare in Denton. A day spent woozy in a hot tent with strangers is unpleasant. But I still remember that sense of purpose and pride in accomplishment that walking twenty miles can give you. That and the sore feet and blisters and sunburn. We had the idea set for us, instilled with the logic of miles traveled and feet like hamburger, that doing important stuff was supposed to be difficult and painful. That you didn't have to wait until some certain age or stage of life before you started doing good works. That you didn't have to wait until you had something before you gave something. They were good lessons to learn.

Even if our twenty-mile walks and penchant for reading might have set us apart somewhat from our friends and kid-cohort, we were still products of popular culture just like everyone else around us, and we were sports crazy. It might be a Texas thing, but we could be Dallas Cowboys fans and still hit the gates at the Houston Oilers training facility to get glimpses of Dan Pastorini flinging the football a mile. We were Astros fans, our favorite player the amazing Cèsar Cedeño, whose name was poetry filled with alliteration and assonance, a sibilant susurrus of a name, and whose game and personality were equally as sweet. But we'd also go to our first professional game at Arlington with Uncle Bill and cheer on the Rangers and their star Bump Wills. At one point we had maybe forty plastic bread loaf bags full of baseball playing cards. During one move we had to give them away, because they didn't meet Mama's level of necessity. We kids barely made that threshold, so we weren't going to argue. And when I sometimes wonder about whether a few of those cards had historical and monetary worth, just one or two from the thousands, I always come back to the realization that with every move we always lost so much more than simple items of monetary worth: we were losing friends, continuity in our education, a sense of home or place. Some hundred-dollar card seems like a pretty small loss compared to all of that.

Our Uncle Bill, Papa's oldest sibling, was a tax lawyer for the IRS in Dallas, and we would visit his ranchette in the nearby community of Plano, Texas, a couple of times a year. All of Papa's brothers and sisters pitched in by various ways and according to their abilities to help their youngest brother's kids, once it became clear the family was in serious disarray, but Uncle Bill chose his spots well, and so we always remembered him fondly. We would all make the short drive from Denton and, later, the much longer drive from Houston, without Mama, and be met with an opulence that astounded us. Bill and Norma and their daughter Pam had a pool table, they had horses and stables, a house with two floors of palatial space, and twenty acres of pasture land to roam. Usually, we were there for the big Thanksgiving meal, and Aunt Norma would make a huge turkey, pumpkin and pecan pies, potatoes and gravy and stuffing. Three kinds of stuffing! I don't remember us missing meals at home, we weren't poor like that, but this kind of groaning table spread, the abundance, was outside of our regular experience, and we tucked in, ravenous. Uncle Bill stood at the head of the table using an electric knife like a hedge-trimmer to cut the turkey. Afterwards, we'd camp in front of the TV to watch the Cowboys and the Redskins play, and while we drowsed and groaned from the food and the Cowboys' mistakes, the dishes would get done.

At night, all of us kids would pile downstairs in a big mess of bodies, on couches and hide-a-beds and quilts and blankets and end up twisted up and tangled like laundry coming out of the drier. We'd wake up late, in the dark, to yelling and screaming and crying and harsh words. I could hear the older kids talking, but I just remember being alarmed and confused and then falling asleep again, wondering in the morning if it was all a dream. Norma, after a long day of cooking and smoking and, quietly, tippling, and then washing up after everything, would fall spectacularly into her cups. It wasn't something that was talked about, and the next morning, wan and tired-looking, but with a strained smile, Aunt Norma would cook us breakfast. And off home we'd go. I always wondered what it would be like to live in that huge house, all that space, with just three people. When I got old enough to understand such things, I was always amazed that during my whole childhood, at every family gathering we had, the women would quietly sit in their spots, watch us watching football, and quietly get drunk. Mama never touched the stuff, but then again, she wasn't a Riley.

At least once on every trip, we'd all pile into Uncle Bill's big station wagon, and he'd drive us around to see the sights of Plano. There wasn't much, but he'd take the long way, and it would seem more impressive after the back roads full of nothing. A few miles away was the ranch where they filmed the TV show *Dallas*, and we'd always slow down and take in the big white house and columns across the big green lawn that might have been a pasture. We'd drive past the hometown high school, and he'd crack the "It's just a Plain-o' high school," and we'd always laugh. It was pretty funny for an uncle joke, and he had a good delivery, anyway. Years later, the school and town would be famous for a mass-student-suicide event in which nine students copycat killed themselves, and a mass-shooter event that's now lost in the haze of so many of them. We were all shocked when that news came out, because Plano was such a safe and wealthy suburb in our minds. The only big thing there was the Dallas Ranch. But by then, the city's growth had pretty much swallowed Plano, and it was really all Dallas now.

Uncle Bill's house was surrounded by grand old pecan trees that would litter the Bermuda grass lawn like acorns from an oak: if you loved tidiness, it was just an unsightly mess of them. We were living in times when folks had little use for what they could more easily buy in the store than harvest from their own yard, but when free labor in the form of Riley boys showed up, we were offered the opportunity to pick pecans for a nickel a paper grocery bag full. We leapt at the chance. I remember having fun with the task, but as with any small fruit wildcrafting, it took a lot of work and time. Like our mother before us in the Austrian fields, we'd spend hours under the massive old trees, separating the whole nuts from the stepped-on and cracked, the squirrel-damaged, the worm-weevilly ones. In the end, we'd get our quarter or thirty-five cents pay and go inside and crack the walnuts they always had out on the tables, carefully removing the woody growth between the segments, avoiding at all costs biting down on the small, sharp shell fragments that would make your gums bleed. They were days where we had time to burn, and the detail work was a blessing. We finished a lot of jigsaw puzzles.

The ranch had horses that our cousin rode competitively, named Pepper and Major, and they were a mystery to me. Big and scary even in their condescension, once Jesse got his foot stepped on, I never went around them again. I was scared of just about everything. Uncle Bill had a few cattle that he'd run, but he wasn't a natural cowhand, and I would watch him trying to round up a few errant head of stock on foot, his big bullwhip snaking and smacking around, only to have a bull turn and face him, charging right into the whip's crack and Uncle Bill sliding his considerable girth between two stock trailers just in time to avoid being ground into paste. But I wasn't scared of the purebred collies they raised for sale. They were the princes and princesses of the whole place and got more care than the rest of us put together. When we moved into the Houston duplex with a fenced backyard, Uncle Bill gave us a puppy. His full name was Princely Caprice of Houston, but we just called him Prince.

The Riley boys and Princely Caprice of Houston
(1971).

Prince was long and tall and pure beauty, but not the sharpest tool in the shed, truth be told. On arriving in our yard, he immediately got his head stuck in the space between the wall of the apartment and the end fence post. No wiggling or pushing or pulling would work, and after a space of a few hours, a neighbor came over with a big crowbar, maybe a chain and a truck hitch, and bent the metal post so that we could pull his head out. We would take him for walks most days, even though he had a good run space where he'd make beaten dirt paths along the inside of the fence, and one day a neighborhood dog came at us barking and gnashing his teeth. We let go of the leash as soon as they started fighting, and after a few rolls and bites and legs raking with claws, the dust settled and Prince was standing over the other dog, growling menacingly. The other dog ran off and we cheered! Prince, our kindhearted, clueless, glossy-haired beauty was a badass! At some point it was noticed that Prince wasn't spending much time in his dog house, so as the smallest, I was sent out to investigate. Before I even had my head in the door I could hear a faint buzzing sound, and when I got my head through the aperture, I was greeted by the quiet roar of a huge wasp nest. We got cans of wasp killer and sprayed them all out, and Prince could once again rest in his house. Prince maybe wasn't the only one among us lacking in sharpness. But he and we were smart enough to live through Texas summers when just about everything wanted to eat or kill us, so that was smart enough.

One day a person driving by recognized Prince's better qualities and stopped to ask if we would be willing to let him out to breed his girl collie. Mama's jaw dropped when he said he'd give us fifty dollars if the meet-up was successful. Money for him to do his thing? It sounded just a little illegal, but we were impressed once again with our dog: not only was he the friendliest badass in the neighborhood, now he was a gigolo as well! The date was set up, and Mama drove him over to meet his playdate partner. He got into the yard and frolicked and ran around with a goofy grin on his face but never got to the stage where he earned his pay. He wasn't disinterested, Mama said, he just didn't know what to do with this fabulously scented vixen. We didn't get paid. She drove him home, and we all had a laugh about his noble and chivalrous behavior. But really, isn't that just like a Riley boy: clueless of his beauty, worth, and purpose.

In a couple of short years, Mama had typed thousands of pages of other people's writing to help pay the rent, taught her classes and done her research, written her dissertation, and was about done at Rice University. She had so many odd jobs we didn't even think of it as odd, her coming home, making a quick dinner we probably refused to eat, and then sitting down by her typing corner a few feet from the kitchen and flashing her fingers across the keyboard of her trusty IBM Selectric typewriter for hours into the night. Papa wasn't much help to himself, much less providing for us, so Mama had to go it alone. A few weeks before she went in to defend her thesis, another woman walked into her committee on campus and pulled out a gun. "If you don't pass me on this work, I'm going to kill everyone in this room." Mama always said she felt thankful for that woman softening her own committee, because she passed without much discussion or balking and she now had her PhD. Not many other women in Texas did. With her terminal degree in hand and a quick job offer to a young and upcoming German scholar, we were moving again in a hurry, this time to Connecticut, a place none of us had really heard of before. Mama's ambitions and hard work were starting to bear fruit, and she wasn't going to let any moss grow—she kept rolling.

We didn't know anything about Connecticut, still true Southerners to the core at that point, but Yale, we'd heard of that. We proudly proclaimed the fact. "We're moving because my mom is going to teach at Yale University in New Haven,

Connecticut," us kids told everyone we met. It turned out that Prince wouldn't be making the trip with us. I think maybe we gave him back to Uncle Bill, because he really was a pricey gift, and we just didn't have room in the Ford Pinto wagon for us and the loyalty and companionship of a beloved friend. When we left places, we did it with a quick finality. You didn't look around and stay vigilant; you might get left behind. We'd seen it happen to plenty of others.

Papa was one of those we left behind. He had moved to Houston to be nearer to us and would sometimes pick us up and bring us by a fraternity house on the Rice campus to shoot pool and hang out. He was a member of the Sigma Alpha Epsilon fraternity at Harvard, and I guess once you're in the family, you get visitation rights. It was always awkward, a few college frat brothers making room for us, vacating the premises for the professor and legacy weird dude who sometimes showed up. His apartment in Houston wasn't much different from the frat house, a motel-looking room with a sliding door that accessed out onto the swimming pool. One time I was laying down on my stomach, looking down into the deep-end water, when someone, let's call him John, pushed me in. I had never learned how to swim, and wouldn't for years afterward following this, and I sank slowly down until I settled on the bottom. I'm not sure if I was a Zen kid or just used to being passive in bad situations, but I didn't struggle and thrash, and I definitely didn't swim or float. In my mind's eye, or maybe just the watery, wavery truth, I see Papa dive into the water, his newspaper separating away from around him, his big black eyeglasses falling independently from them both, and he snatches me up and rescues me back into the air and out again onto the hot concrete pool deck. Like Atticus Finch, who Harper Lee says, "could get up and down from a chair faster than anyone I ever knew," Papa could get his glasses knocked on the ground by a cop's billy club or lost at the bottom of a pool in an instant. He had that maladroit superhero trait deep in his genetics, and I was always most proud of him when it was on dramatic display.

Father and son in good times (nd).

Little Rock, Arkansas, Summers, 1975–1980

I don't know if it was part of the divorce procedures or something they just baked up among themselves, but once we moved to Connecticut, us four kids spent the school year, mostly the winter months, in Hamden (a working-class suburb of New Haven) with Mama, and the summer months in Little Rock with Papa. And when he really couldn't take care of us, with our Grandmother Riley or our Uncle Pat and Aunt Martha and family, who also lived there and could take us in.

Aside from the obvious downside that we experienced all of the extremes of the New England winter and the hot Arkansas summer (I was never interested in trying a Baked Alaska, because I already knew what it felt like to be burnt and frozen by our parent-imposed seasonal round), it really was an inexcusable and unsustainable construct. As when Mama sent us off to spend the summer of '72 with Uncle Rudi, Papa was unable to care for a family of young children. His mental illness, some untreatable variation of bipolar disorder, was part of what brought about the end of my parents' marriage, the other part being Mama's driving ambition. Really, both of those parts were what got them married in the first place, I think, so the fact that my father's flame was finally guttering and my mom's was suddenly leaping couldn't have been too much of a surprise. They were like the moth in Don Marquis' poem, who says, "It is better to be happy for a moment and be burned up with beauty than to live a long time and be bored all the while." So for us kids, caught between madness and ambition, we inevitably got neglect from both.

If they'd thought about it a little more clearly, or at least more emotionally and empathetically, a little less like the woman in King Solomon's court who wanted to split the baby in half to settle a custody issue, it might have worked out better than it did. Had we stayed with Mama in the summers, we might have been more able to sustain friendships in our neighborhoods, and we definitely would have enjoyed the weather more. Connecticut summers can be bluebird skies and mild temperatures, but Little Rock was just an unrelenting heat and humidity that could wring the starch right out of you. To be out from under the parental gaze for three months in Connecticut, we would have been less susceptible to missing meals, because even if she eschewed eating anything other than bread and chocolate, Mama knew that she had to provide for us breakfast and dinner at a minimum. And if we'd had our schooling in Little Rock, we could have at least been assured of the school providing a meal or two. Papa was less clear on that responsibility. Sometimes, if the church ladies or our distant childless cousin who was angling to adopt us boys didn't show up with food, we didn't eat. But I guess there aren't always good solutions to difficult situations. We survived it.

The first time I remember making the trip down on the Trailways bus, I think I was eleven and Jesse was thirteen. Mama bought us our tickets and saw us to the bus leaving for New York at ten o'clock at night. Schatzi and John were older, and they had separate lives and plans. I don't know how they got to Little Rock, but it wasn't with us. So it was just Jesse and me, and that was okay, because we were pretty much best buds. We rolled into New York City's Port Authority bus station sometime after midnight. It was a cavernous building, dimly lit and with a feeling of the underworld about it, a purgatory you were delivered to at an inconvenient time and were hoping to leave soon for pleasanter climes. We had a few hours before our southbound bus loaded and left, so we walked the tiled hallways watching this unfamiliar world and its denizens. At one point, a guy tried to sell us a Walkman, the ubiquitous marker of wealth and teen with-it-ness at the time, and we refused. "We don't really like to be plugged-in like that. Not so into music." He was flabbergasted. "What are you two, Amish or something?" Jesse and I laughed. No, we knew, just Rileys with a gift for being out of tune and time with the zeitgeist. Another, older, man asked us where we were going. "Let me see your tickets," curious-like, and we handed over our packet of slips in the paper envelope, New Haven to Little Rock. When he handed them back, they felt bulkier and different somehow. He was already walking away, and we shouted and chased after him. He stopped and sheepishly gave us our tickets back saying, "I must have mixed that up somehow." We were barely into our teens, barely into the trip, and we'd already narrowly avoided being robbed. Bus trips had a way of getting interesting in a hurry, and for me and Jesse, the learning from the cultural, geographical, and socioeconomic lessons that were a cross-country Trailways bus trip was just beginning.

On a bus, you always see the bad side of a town, and only the bad-sided towns, down on their luck and earnestly hoping to be something other than what they were. Towns like Harrisburg and Philadelphia, Pennsylvania; Roanoke and Charlottesville, Virginia; Bristol, Knoxville, Memphis, Tennessee; and finally, to Little Rock. The early part of the trip was always a bit of a blur of fast-moving changes of states, but by the time you got to Tennessee, you knew you were on a long trip across a long state. Each town had a bright, prosperous-looking kind of welcoming sign, either Las Vegas lighted-up-style or with pretty flowers and white-painted rocks, but when you got to the station, got out to find a greasy-spoon early morning or all-night breakfast spot, there was nothing much welcoming about the places. I guess those greeting signs were for other people arriving by means other than the Trailways bus. Jesse and I would walk through the broken streets and shuttered businesses, sometimes a couple of miles, to stretch our jangling leg nerves and to get away from the bus station institutional fare they served, and we'd find a place that fit our needs and budget. Every meal was breakfast, it seems to me now. Always eggs, over easy, greasy sausages, white bread with a stain of yellow margarine. Again, there was that feeling of being in limbo, and if you didn't know what time it was or what state you were in or when your next meal might come, it was probably better to go with breakfast.

Our childhood of middle-class poverty made us familiar with cheap knockoff brands and food like Tang that had only recently become food, but we did have some brand loyalty. One was that we were red Trailways bus riders, not Greyhound Gatsbys on some fancy, expensive purebred ride. I can remember when the tickets were fifty-nine dollars anywhere in the states, and even back then that was a deal. We were growing up on food stamps and off-brand cereals, ice milk instead of ice cream, and granulated, dried "blue" milk. Those choices, based on the necessity of very little choice, were influential in making me enough of a snob later in life that my wife and her fishing buddies call me "The Arkansas Prince." Brand awareness and price blindness are part of my life now, but once upon a time, it was just about loyalty, and we rode down south on a Trailways bus.

Early on in this yearslong experiment in parenting and child-rearing, if that's what it was, we at least had a firm and settled home at the end of the trip. Grandmother Riley had moved out of the White House a couple of years after Grandfather had died, her businessman son Pat noticing with a real estate speculator's keen eye that the neighborhood was changing, and he had sold the place and moved her into an apartment on Cumberland. Near downtown, it was just two blocks from the Second Baptist Church, an anchor space and abiding passion of hers. Papa had slowly fallen from his academic perch as his unpredictable and alarming behavior from his undiagnosed bipolar disorder caused his marriage and career to sour and end. He'd become pretty much unemployable by this time. Now he was living with his mom in a large, comfortable two-bedroom second-floor apartment, and what could it hurt to add his four children to the mix? Grandmother took it in stride, as she had taken in Papa and Mama and Schatzi and John when they stopped their world traveling, but it must have been a challenge for her. She had quiet and sedentary personal habits, and we must have done our fair best to displace her from those in the summer months we were with her.

The apartment didn't have air-conditioning, so the windows were always open, trying to draw in a breath of breeze in those hot blacktop and concrete summers. I have a picture of me in a light-colored T-shirt, I think it was light blue, and even from the zoomed-out perspective of the family photo, you can see the dark concentric lines on the sleeves, a topography of perspiration, from where I was constantly wiping the sweat from my face. On the really hot days, Grandmother Riley would wear just a slip and a camisole, sometimes even just a bra, and I struggle to think of her in such informal dress, for she was a proper woman, well-versed and a true believer in modesty and decorum. But the Arkansas heat was a plague of Old Testament vigor, and not to be easily dismissed or assuaged. One summer it stayed over a hundred degrees for more than thirty straight days, and older people died in droves.

ARTIFACT: A MEMOIR

Cumberland and 9th Street was a busy intersection, and the traffic noise, although not usually loud, was constant. On a fairly regular basis, often it seems in my memory, there would be a crash outside and everything would stop. There was that time-wrinkle loud bang, that once started seemed to drag into a zone of slowed-down, of elongated impact, and the accompanying loud silence. A crunch of soundwaves that bounced off the buildings, the heat, our bones. And then the after-commotion as everyone rushed to help, or we and others to their windows. Soon there were sirens and more busyness and thus was a morning or afternoon hour whiled away. We were saved from any memorable scenes of violence by the relatively slow speeds and a disinterest in blood or suffering. The scattered glass and oil-pool stains on the roadway afterwards were enough for us. After a fair show, it was back to reading or solitaire and the clock set ticking for the next accident.

Grandmother Riley was a great cook. She had a great big dining table, a monstrous round that sat twelve easily, but the apartment had a tiny and dark little kitchen, which seems incongruous to me now. When it was just Papa and us kids, and by kids, I mean me and Jesse, because I don't remember the others around much, she would make simple things for breakfast like poached eggs cut up over buttered bread, and somehow that would be magically delicious in the way Lucky Charms never were. For Sunday dinners, which would have been lunch after church, she'd often have other family over, and she'd make a spread for that whole big table, food cooking confidently and well-behaved by itself while we were listening to Dr. Dale Cowling preach to us down the street at Second Baptist Church. We'd get back and be greeted by the smells of cornbread and roasts in gravy and vinegary green beans with bacon. She could command the table, too, in her kind and exacting way of serving. There was a gravity to the ceremony until the prayer was said, the pace was anticipatory but not urgent, and there were glances around to see that plates were full before the cutlery started clicking in earnest. On one special occasion, she cleared the plates and then set down a tall, beautifully frosted layer cake on the table and said, with her understated humor and slow drawl, "Well isn't that pretty? How about we just look at that for a bit?" I can see it still, that tower of high Southern confectionary skill, the slight curling smile at the corners of her mouth, and my restless outrage at seeing the prize but having it tantalizingly withheld. A lot of folks think they had the best grandmother in the world, but I knew it. I told her it often.

The pace of a summer's day was pretty slow in that apartment, excepting the occasional car crash, and we had a regular and unextraordinary menu of diversions. Grandmother would watch *Dialing for Dollars*, a locally produced call-in money-giveaway show, and some other few programs I don't recall. We read quietly. I would draw pictures and write letters. There were decks of cards for everyone to play Solitaire, and once learned, it was a hard game to forget. I rarely won. Maybe I never won. But the tactile and manipulative labor of drawing and stacking the cards, the thousand "ahas" as you built your lines by number and suit. It was self-mesmerizing. It was a peaceful existence for us, if Papa was well, and there was a marked lack of tension, which I've always kept as close to me as I could. I've never been a fan of drama. Quiet and aloneness are my friends. A little of something is worth more than a lot of anything.

One day when Papa wasn't well, he ran downstairs and stood next to a car stopped at the light outside the apartment, ranting and rambling and upset and unintelligible, worked up by the demons in his head. He dropped down to the ground, crawled under the car and spread-eagled himself so that the car couldn't move without running him over. I'm glad that driver didn't just drive forward. But instead, they just waited while my dad lay there, cars piling up in a line talking and waiting for the police to show up. When they did, a couple of patrol cars' worth, they too stood around figuring the situation. After trying to talk to Papa and coax him from beneath the car without success, they finally got on their knees and dragged him out and stuffed him in the back of a squad car. They were doing their job, and they didn't do it with any excess of violence, but I was on the sidewalk just a few feet away, watching. And listening. And when the cops stood around after their brief work, brushing off their pants and laughing about the "looney-bin, crazy, wacko," I was angry at their lightness and humor. Their easy forgetfulness that I was right there, and that this man in distress was still a man. It wouldn't be the last time I saw him arrested, because like the people he taught us to respect, from Muhammad Ali to Martin Luther King, Jr., he was often the target of violence. That incident was the end of my ability to see the police as simply a force of good, serving and protecting. My eyes were opened, and they stayed that way.

Before his mental illness really kicked in at full-power and his alcoholism habit started up to compound the problem and really destroy him, Papa's incidents were on-again, off-again affairs. While he could no longer work and hold a job, he could do normal things and be a normal dad. Sometimes he'd be reading and I'd go over to hug him, and he'd look at me with eyes that were in the process of changing their vision. It would make me cry sometimes, when they would intensify and grow dark, and I would feel like he was a werewolf in transition, their gaze predatory and unpredictable. He would laugh and shake us both, and he would be back again, but the fact that there was a process, a continuum of changing from one thing to another was unnerving for me. We would walk the half mile to the Little Rock Public Library, and while Jesse and I would go our own way among the huge shelves and multiple rooms, Papa would camp out in the dark off-entryway and peruse the new acquisitions on the rolling carts and then go into detailed searches for arcane political and cultural tomes that he would always carry home by the armload. Reading was a contact sport, a lifestyle, the air we breathed. Books were a survival strategy that we all employed.

⸙

It was on one of these forays to the library that Papa caught a headful of fear and paranoia and hustled us around town, telling us to hurry because "They're moving in. They're going to get us if we don't move faster!" We walked quickly past the Barber School where we got cheap haircuts from people learning new ways to make mistakes on people who didn't have money to have good hair. We walked past the Big and Tall Men's store, where my Uncle Ed worked and might have been quietly locked away in the bathroom, replaying some scenes of his own demons before going back to smiling and joshing and fitting other big men into big men's clothes. We walked through parts of town I didn't know about and finally ended up in a park near the War Memorial Stadium, not far from where we would later spend bad years in the Arkansas State Hospital, he incarcerated and my brother and I visiting. We huddled up and cowered in fear as he talked and worried and cried. That's all I remember. We got home to Grandmother's apartment, obviously. She probably fed us. We probably all lay down for a nap. Forced or faked or just really a necessary short-term removal from consciousness. Naps have always been my flip side to my imaginative reading, the physical escape from mind and body.

I had forgotten over the years how funny my grandmother was. I remember her as gentle and loving and quietly powerful, in her eighties able to endure her youngest son's epic downfall and make a small place for him to be grounded after the crash. Able to put up with his four kids in a small apartment and sacrifice the peace one might want after a long life of caring for others and denying yourself. I was always very loving to her, calling her, it seems to me now with an irritating ad infinitum quality of overuse, "The Best Grandmother in the World." I was probably her favorite grandchild from her favorite child, so maybe that keeps any kind of love from growing old. I know that on one wretched morning I told her that she wasn't the Best Grandmother in the World, and that I hated her. She'd raised four boys and two girls, and I was the last of the grandchildren, so I doubt that she was overly shocked or disturbed that we were having a bad day, but I was devastated for years remembering my rude and hateful words. After giving away all of her stuff in her last will and testament, from coffee spoons to artwork to linens, she arrived at the grandboys and discovered there wasn't much left. "When it comes to them, the cupboard's bare." I got a paperweight, without description. When my dad died twenty years later, I got a check for fifty dollars from my Uncle Pat. Well-meaning, but demeaning. It turns out that when Rileys die, all they leave you is alone.

In what all of us siblings seem to acknowledge as the worst year of our lives, we once spent an entire year with Papa. After Grandmother Riley felt she was no longer able to take on providing for her son and his family, we lived at any number of bombed-out, crappy apartments that Uncle Pat would procure for us, each one a new necessity when Papa fell hard into his bipolar illness and had to be incarcerated at the State Hospital for a few months, or leaned into his alcoholism and got kicked out of even the most meager of living situations. Papa took up a lot of time and space and care. He still wanted a lot, even as he gave less and less. But this once we got a nice-enough, nondescript house in a middle-class neighborhood not far from the mall and across the street from the Wilbur Mills freeway. It was just kind of a regular place. There were no dead animal carcasses smelling up from under the floorboards; no avalanche infestations of cockroaches to haunt our toilet time or meals; no neighborhood shootings. Just Papa dead-drunk on the couch and not enough other distractions to keep us from seeing him. We were alone in our own little hell, window shades drawn, grass mown, left mostly alone. Schatzi was tasked with the cooking, because she was the teenaged girl, and we mocked her mercilessly for messing up spaghetti and canned chili or, really, anything she managed to put on the table. We hated her cooking without ever questioning why she had to be the one to provide it. Who else? When she'd had enough, she would open her bedroom window and run away. Then dinner would be Papa giving us five dollars at the grocery store and telling us to buy what we wanted for dinner. For me, that was a LOT of ice cream. It was better than my sister's cooking.

Our house on Marguerite was just less than a mile from the school I should have gone to, but with the integration project that Daisy Bates started with the Little Rock Nine still a work in progress, I got bussed four or five miles downtown into a mostly Black school to help balance the enrollment for the district. I was shy, greasy, obviously forsaken, and I stuck out in a way that made it easy to hammer the sore thumb. Packs of kids would walk around and say, "Is today your birthday?" and if it wasn't they'd beat you up. I imagine they would if it was ironically your real birthday. My teachers, all Black, were kind to me. They took extra time to make sure I knew the procedures, found pockets of calm where they could have conversations with me since I wouldn't talk in class, and helped me feel cared for and seen. I was pretty much a ghost, so I appreciated their vision and belief in me. I made it through without too much damage.

Even though we never knew a neighbor, never made any connection with a person or family on that whole street, we did have visitors caring enough to make calls on us from time to time. There were the Welcome Wagon folks, who showed up with coupons for local businesses and a gift basket to help welcome us into our new home. It was a one-shot deal, but we moved enough that we came to look forward to the free snacks. At Thanksgiving, there were the church ladies who showed up, somehow knowing, and delivered us a Tupperware turkey feast. If those women hadn't shown up and fed us, we wouldn't have got fed. It was a big deal. It was a once-a-year benefit, a small contribution to us making it by, but pumpkin pie can hold a place in a kid's imagination for a long time. Our second or third cousin Hunter Douglass, who was old enough to be an uncle, would also visit on occasion. His presence was a conspicuous bright spot for us boys and yet, somehow, an indefinable mixed blessing as well.

ARTIFACT: A MEMOIR

All of us kids had been neglected and left alone and been around enough to have a pretty good spider sense of the up and up, and if there were not alarms ringing, we definitely had a sense of a second-scene overlap with our experiences with Hunter—like the blue and red paper 3D glasses, where things were fun and fuzzy and a little disorienting until they came into sudden focus. Hunter always took us three boys out and left Schatzi home alone with Papa. I'm not sure if she was happy or miffed by that, but it was a fait accompli, a predestined and not spoken-of part of our interactions. We'd leave Papa at home and go out for a weekend with Hunter and his wife Martha and do rural Arkansas stuff. Hunter had this seriously cool country-cred six-wheeled all-terrain amphibious vehicle, and we'd go mudding with that. He had beagles that he hunted with, and he'd do homemade surgeries on the dogs after they got messed up by barbed wire or a particularly vicious varmint, first sticking his fingers deep into the wounds and scooping out the maggots that had found their way into the flaps between their muscle and skin. He'd take us on drives in his eight-miles-to-the-gallon RV bus that he got in trade as a part of his successful mobile home business. Martha was quiet and kind and always made us great food. I remember her as a thin and wispy blond, soft-spoken and easy with a smile, and passive to Hunter's bold and bulldozer ways. He was a Christian man and a Gideon, and he reminded me a lot of the vehicles he drove.

All that year, Hunter would invest time and money in us, and we appreciated the breaks from days with Papa. There was not a lot of doing things as far as Papa was concerned, at this time, and so getting out felt like a good freedom, even if we were always kind of like, "Now how are we related to Hunter again?" Our relationship seemed . . . unexpected. When we moved up to Connecticut at the end of that year, we'd sometimes get letters from Hunter, until that stopped. When we came back down for another summer with Papa, we never saw him. And then we learned that after years of trying, he and Martha had finally had a child. A boy. And as the years passed, we heard through the family grapevine of other children, a growing family. I don't know if I talked about it with Jesse or John, but I remember having that realization that we had been auditioning for a new family, he was trying us out and having contingency conversations somewhere about adopting us or calling CPS and being a wholesome alternative home for those nice boys. Girls need not apply. I met him years later at my Uncle Pat's funeral, and we had a nice talk. No rancor or hurt feelings to express or share.

He wouldn't recognize the need for regret, actually. His gun shops were thriving in three locations, and his boys were mostly running the business by then. He was a Confederate history buff, and I was a middle school history teacher. I skirted areas that needn't come up when he introduced them. He was a man my Grandfather Riley would have recognized as successful. I felt a little happy for him that his life had worked out in a way that he appreciated, a little sad that our blood connection had been so finite and ephemeral. Family can be an anchor that weighs you down close to drowning you, and it can be the knife that cuts you loose and frees you from the burden of your shared history. But when it's a thin veneer, a magic trick prop that's there one moment and gone the next, then it can leave a scar so fine that you can't see it to remember. It's tough for me to think that a family member might see our family, see only my father's life in that present of drunk and mentally ill, and see the potential in us. An opportunity that he could take advantage of. And then decide that he didn't need us after all. And then leave us stuck in the worst year of our lives. Did I say there were no hurt feelings?

When my oldest brother, John, was in his teens and a seemingly good bet to be the best of our litter of kids—athletic, good-looking, outgoing, and interested in bettering himself in the way ambitious young people are—our Uncle Pat took a particular interest in him. Most of our summers John stayed at the Pat Riley house next to the country club, with the cool cousins, in the mix of that wealthy, Southern, monied, upwardly mobile lifestyle that felt like a kind of nobility.

John would live with them, get clothes and shoes and food and all the things that weren't a part of life with Papa. Uncle Pat gave him a blue Toyota coupe that was a castoff of Pat Junior's, and he was living the life. I was jealous, of course, because I liked good stuff too, but really, I was pretty glad that he wasn't around, because that meant I had his cloud of mental and physical beatings lifted from me, and just had to deal with physically surviving. At one point, Uncle Pat kind of tried to call the debt due, and asked John if he'd be willing to change his middle name so that it would align correctly with John's grandfather, John Rutledge Riley, thereby keeping the name and honor alive. Pat had named his second child after himself, back when he could reasonably expect another male heir, but his line ran high to girls, and he lost his chance to honor his father. In maybe only the second thing I can remember of being thankful for John, he refused. There was some money to sweeten the pot, but John remained John Edward Riley, honoring my father's older brother who had died in childhood, and my father himself. I got the Rutledge, and I wasn't sharing, especially with John. The idea died, just as Bill and Papa and Pat followed their father, but it wasn't forgotten. It was a small gall of disrespect, an irritant like sand in a clam's soft parts, but it yielded no pearl. I used it as wisdom for when it came time to name my own boys: the only family name they bear is the Riley surname. They're named for their mom's family, my stepdad, and a good friend. The ones that are easier to love.

Of all of the places we stayed with Papa, I think I remember the one that was in the shadow of the stately capitol building most of all. It had the stench of death overlaid with bleach, two smells that I would correlate with each other the rest of my days. The roaches. They were a problem. A horde. They would come out in the daytime, so sure were they of their mastery, and they would harass us in any forum of the apartment: kitchen, bathroom, in bed. We kept a big open used jar of peanut butter on the kitchen table as a trap, and it was a kind of terrarium of life and death, a Dantesque jar of the concentric rings of hell, as the bottom level was weighed down into a roach sludge, the middle layers still had some shape and, upward of middle, still some movement. At the top of the death jar, vigorous movement and climbing the slick and sticky walls, still full of life and the expectation of continuing life, the day's catch. Schatzi had a place of her own nearby, when she was working for a crisis center, and I would walk up there to her place to get away for a while. She was always running away as the oldest child, but she always managed to be a refuge for me, too. She was always my hero, maybe in large part for her resourcefulness at leaving.

Papa had a big old red Cadillac Eldorado with a white soft-top and a hood about a mile long, a hand-me-down from Uncle Pat, and he would roll that bad boy down the hill until it was half a car's length past the stop sign and into a lane of busy traffic, before slowly entering traffic and heading down to the Pop-a-Top package store. Every trip started with "Oh my God, we're totally going to get T-boned and die," and ended with, "Papa's on a drunk again, I wish we would just once get T-boned and die before we had to watch this again." I hated that Pop-a-Top store. It had friendly neon graphics that moved, a bottle expressing a cork like a champagne bottle, and a convenient drive-through window. Except no one bought champagne there. Papa would get a bottle of something brown and go back to that rancid apartment to drown. We went somewhere else, sometimes touring the capitol and looking at the portrait of our Uncle Bob, a former lieutenant governor who was governor for a day a few times when the governor was out of state. A reminder of how far we had fallen, and yet so ironically nearby. I always counted it a sign of my recovery from that place that I could listen to Bobby Jimmy and the Critters rap "The Roaches" in college and laugh. But it was laughter with remembering. With a little bile rising. Accompanied by the smell of death and bleach.

The last summer I spent in Little Rock was in 1983, just after I graduated from High School in Washington State. I stayed with my sister Schatzi at her place up on Wye Mountain, an unincorporated community about forty miles northwest of Little Rock, and had what I called in my journal, "a tick-infested summer." I was in between big life events, having just finished school and soon heading out for a fall monthslong solo grand tour of Great Britain and Ireland. After that was yet to be settled.

Little Rock, Hospital Slippers, 1970s

One night when I was still quite little, maybe eight or nine years old, driving home from Uncle Pat's in the big red Cadillac, Papa told us he had big news.

"You have a new baby sister!"

I couldn't for the life of me see how that could happen. It was way outside of my ability to conceive of such a possibility. But Papa was excitable, and I, as the youngest, had always wanted a baby sibling to be better to than mine had been to me, so I was excited, too. Papa had always loved to travel, and after his divorce and termination from his university job, he had more time to exercise that itch of constant movement to new and interesting destinations. On one of his trips to Samoa, he'd spent quite a few months with one group of native folks and told us he'd been initiated as an honorary chief. He'd also gotten a woman pregnant, and so I now had a sister somewhere out in the middle of the Pacific. When Papa would go on these trips, he'd always bring us back a present of some trinket or representative gift from the place he'd been. Once we'd asked him to bring us stuffed animals, and on his return, he presented us each with a taxidermied animal. Mine was a squirrel. It wasn't quite what I'd meant. And now Papa was bringing us back another surprising present in the form of a new sibling. In the kid-logic of the bird in the hand, I might have preferred the squirrel, because even though that was quite scary, teeth bared and crouched on hind legs, clawed paws extended outward, at least that one I could actually hold in my hands. I never got to meet that little sister.

Purported Honorary Samoan King, Ed Riley
(1970s).

I don't really know how mental illness feels, because the big question of my childhood of who's going to get what Papa had was finally answered as everyone but me. All of my siblings struggled to find their way through the diagnosed or not reality of depression and bipolar disorder. But I know what it looks like. And for Papa it was increased agitation, a rage against taking his lithium and other medicines, and an event to spark a trip just down the road to the Arkansas State Hospital. The lying down under the car at the stoplight was one such incident. Another was when Papa was planning a trip to Hot Springs and was getting super worked up and excited. We shared his excitement because he was so charismatic, and Hot Springs was a hallowed tourist destination we'd heard much about but never experienced. The morning of the trip arrived, and having breakfast at Uncle Pat's house, we were interrupted by the arrival of an altogether different sort. The state police came to the door, put Papa in handcuffs, and took him away. We weren't going anywhere, and Papa, he wasn't going to a resort. Uncle Pat had perhaps rightly made the decision that this brief escape my dad had planned might not be a good choice and had called the police on his brother. There was a hullabaloo and some chaotic moments, and then Uncle Pat's lawyer took me to a back bedroom and tried his best to put a careful spin on the events: "Your dad is going to be alright. He's going to a good place where they'll take care of him. Don't worry about all of this. It'll all turn out okay." I was such a waif then, such an overlooked and underfoot, underappreciated, underachieving kid, but I know I met his smiling, well-meaning gaze with steel and hatred. It was not going to be okay. Nothing about your dad getting arrested in front of you was alright. Things would not be getting better any time soon. Papa, it's fair to say, would not be going to a good place.

After these events inevitably happened, as the inexorable march of brain chemistry and my dad's lack of personal responsibility and the problematic options available to the medical practices of the time took their toll, Jesse and I would incorporate walks to visit Papa as part of our weekly activities. Whether we were staying alone in the apartment, or just a few blocks away with Schatzi, or three miles away up in the Heights with Uncle Pat, it was just a matter of a few miles to go see him. All miles were a few miles for us, because that's just what Jesse and I did. We walked. It was always near a hundred degrees out, and when we got to the State Hospital, it was blessedly cool. We'd wait out in the corridor while Papa got into some semblance of clothes, sweats and pajamas mostly, and then the locked door would open and Papa would shuffle out in his hospital-stock slippers, crazy hair and stubble, slurred speech and a smile, and we'd go for a walk on the grounds. Sometimes Papa would want to get some exercise, so he would cock his arms, throw them up and down as he pulled his knees up a few extra inches, and we'd shuffle along in a pantomime of running, the world's slowest jog. He always wanted to be an exercise role model for us, except when it came to him having to take lithium or needing to self-medicate with alcohol. When we had done a few laps, listened about who had stolen what from him that week, we'd head back inside and drop Papa off with an orderly, and then head back to the place, stopping on the way for an ice-cold frosted mug of root beer at the Frost Top. Add a big scoop of vanilla ice cream. If life was a long, hot, difficult road, full of emotional slights and feasts of swallowing pride, we were going to do a bit of self-medicating ourselves along the way.

On Sundays when Papa was around, we'd always go over to Uncle Ed's house. Papa would navigate the mile-long Eldorado into the precariously small driveway, and we'd pile out for an afternoon of living large. Uncle Ed would greet us with his perennial large smile and jocularity, while Aunt Sister, Papa's oldest sister, would smile thinly from her seat at the table, and then he'd usher us into the living room where they had chairs and a couch arranged around a huge TV screen. Uncle Ed would ensconce himself in his big La-Z-Boy recliner and grab big bags of chips, survey the room to see who wanted what, and throw us each our choice. We would spend the next four hours watching football, Wide World of Sports, golf, whatever was on, getting Cheeto dust and Funyuns crumbs all down our fronts and keeping a lively conversation going. After the games were done and it was closing in on dinnertime, Uncle Ed would get all of us kids piled into his car, and we'd head out to McDonald's or Bimbo's Burgers for take-out. It was such an extravagance for us, and he would add to the anticipation by counting down the time as we drove: "Three minutes to BIMBO'S! Two minutes to BIM-BO's!" When we got back to the house, we'd set up TV dinner trays and have our meal watching the last show of the day, usually *60 Minutes*. We would leave with regret and glowing from calories and bonhomie. Uncle Ed was everyone's favorite, if maybe not Aunt Sister, and we always had a brief inoculation of joy and hominess to see us part of the way through our trying weeks until the next Sunday. They were the best of times.

Uncle Ed in his charming mode, with his wife, my Aunt Sister, and her mother, Grandmother Riley (1974).

There was so much going on in that room, unbeknownst to me. So much replication of hurts and ailments and sorrow. Not only was it a room of Ed, Ed, and Eddie (my cousin Eddie and his wife, I kid you not, Betty, would visit sometimes, and he was full of energy and positivity like his dad), but all three of them had serious mental illnesses that they were struggling with, and both my dad and uncle had endured high electric shocks as part of their treatment regimens. Both would attempt suicide, and one of them would accomplish it. Aunt Sister, while quietly sitting at her own table away from the circle of TV watchers, smoking cigarettes nonstop and drinking tea, was really drinking hard alcohol and silently getting stoned amid our sports passions and loud chatter just across the room. I wonder if they would have recognized themselves and their lives if they had seen it before Sister ran off and eloped with the big star quarterback on their high school team. Before he went to war and came back changed and she went to work alone in an insurance office, cut off from family for her choice of a husband and coworkers because she was so damned efficient that she could do the work alone.

As the years went on, summer after summer, Uncle Ed would have to rock and rock and rock until he could get enough lift to leave his big La-Z-Boy throne, making the process an object of humor, playing for laughs. He had a frailty and pallor about him that conflicted with his big body and personality that had made him such a good salesman at the Big and Tall Man's store in downtown Little Rock. He husbanded and sealed off all the pain he felt and left for us all of the joy and gaiety and love that he had in such great supply. He gave it freely to us kids those years when we really needed it.

When Jesse and I were sixteen and eighteen, we visited Uncle Pat at his Riley Building and were offered a job to work at one of the nursing homes that was a big part of his business empire. He always felt the need to share his business exploits and hard work and money-matters values with us, because he knew we wouldn't get it from his bookish youngest brother. Mama and Papa were never much interested in overtly teaching us a work ethic, neither forcing us to get jobs or good grades, but apparently, we'd soaked up the lessons through watching Mama raise the four of us kids alone and climb the career ladder in academia, doing every kind of odd job to help us barely make ends meet. Mr. Trickey, the old school maintenance lead, was a character of the south: gruff, slow of speech and slow with praise, tall and intimidating and skilled at everything having to do with how things were put together and how they fell apart. That meant tools and machines and people, too. When he said to pick up a "slang," a bow-shaped blade on the end of a long wooden handle, he had to show us the tool. When he said to "slang that patch of tall weeds outside the back of A-Wing," we said, "yes, sir" and got to work. He had us change light bulbs in the residents' rooms, paint hallways that seemed to stretch for miles, and wash windows outside the hundred-bed facility in the deep heat of Arkansas summers. He would appear over our shoulders, tall and dark with his own shadow he carried with him, and say, "Ye boys take your break now, hear?" And we would quickly answer with a "Yes, Sir, Mr. Trickey!" We didn't have watches and didn't care much to look at clocks, and he would always have to tell us to stop working after two hours had passed. I think he was curious about our lack of energy in pursuing the mandatory fifteen-minute rest. We finally figured out that it was disrespectful to the other workers to not take advantage of that one benefit. All of them were veteran hourly workers and well aware of the few modest perks of the job, and as we were part of the owner's family, and only hired because of that reason, it wouldn't do to put on airs. We took our breaks.

At lunch time, we'd go through the patient lunch line and get a hot lunch, and back in the break room, all of the maintenance guys would pull out their lunch pails, full of fried cornbread hush puppies, ham and pork chops and wax-paper wrapped sandwiches and, most interestingly to me and Jesse, cans of potted meat. Mr. Trickey would always eat a raw onion at his desk. We were well-versed in poverty and knew Vienna sausages floating like fingers in clear gelatin and the paper-wrapped canned Deviled Ham as a sometimes treat, but potted meat was an altogether 'nother thing. We asked the guys what it was and, nonplussed, they said, "Well, I don't rightly know. It's potted meat." So they handed it over, and we read the ingredients list of meat byproducts and unpronounceable chemical additives and concluded that it was what we would colloquially call "lips and assholes." Tripe and toenails. We passed on the offer to try it and stayed true to our nursing home hot lunch.

Mr. Huskins was our big boss and Uncle Pat liaison and was altogether different from Mr. Trickey. He was a nice guy who wore cheap suits in beige and gray and seemed to know that nursing home administrator was not what he'd dreamed of as a career growing up. Jesse and I called him Mr. Husk-of-a-Man and felt genuinely sorry for him. He was always harried and rumpled and sitting down or nervously moving around, while Mr. Trickey was country to his core, and was like a rock in the river: things either brushed by or broke on him. I think Mr. Huskins probably did a bit of both.

All day painting inside and washing windows outside, the intercoms would blare out for "Janitor needed immediately on A-Wing" or "Our afternoon activity is now happening in the D-Wing rec-center. Please get yourselves down here." There were names for the wings, for differentiating the letter sounds, but the only two I remember were "B-Wing, Betty-Wing" and "D-for-Dummy-Wing," which was only what Jesse and I called it because it was where the least capable residents stayed. There's gallows humor in a nursing home, a laugh or cry mentality, because there's a lot to wrap your brain around. One of the residents would always follow me, earnestly saying, "A who and a who and a who and a who," and look expectantly at me for a comeback, to which I would reply with, "That's right, sir. That surely is right," and we'd both go back to our work. The jokes and needling went both ways. Once, slanging weeds outside of one room, we hit a bees' nest, and they swarmed out on us. Jesse and I ran with our hands swatting them away from our heads, zigzagging and panic-stung. Whenever we'd see the old guy whose window we were outside on that day, he would gesticulate wildly with his arms and roll his eyes crazily, laughing until he had tears in his eyes. All summer long after that, whenever we'd get stung, Mr. Trickey would recall the memory and say, "He knows 'e." At home, we'd answer any request under our breaths with a quick and panicky "Yes, Mr. Trickey" mimicry. At the end of the summer, he told us to work hard on our studies so we wouldn't have to work jobs like this, and said that other than our older brother, John, we were the best summer workers he'd ever had. The most anticlimactic high praise a baby brother could ever hear.

Hamden, Connecticut, First Snow, 1974–1981

When we arrived in Connecticut in the late summer of 1974, I felt the importance, the strangeness, the vast difference of a family move for the first time. The summer of Vienna two years earlier had been a change, for sure: there were language, geography, cultural differences galore. But that had been a visit, a jump into the new with a time stamp seasonal boundary of summer. And growing up with Mama speaking German to us and feeding us on chocolate and pancakes, reading us *Struwwelpeter* and Goethe, we knew the shadow of Austrian culture, and the changes were like a sleepwalk memory, half-remembered and familiar in our subconscious. And Little Rock to Denton to Houston, well, there were subtle regional differences, but by the time we were growing up, the South was beginning to be a monoculture and there was a comfortable sameness from place to place, with no particular learning necessary. Hamden and New Haven were not like that. The trees, the houses, the language, the weather: every single aspect of daily life felt new and, somehow, onerous. At one of the first places we stopped upon our arrival, a ubiquitous convenience store called Wawa, I picked up a few things and paid at the counter. My request for a sack to carry it in was met with incomprehension.

"You want a what?" the clerk asked.

"A sack, please."

"A sack. You mean like a potato sack?! What for?"

"Nah, you know, like, a paper sack. A bag. To hold all this," I said, pointing at the Funyuns and Snickers bars and Corn Nuts.

"Oh! A paper bag! I didn't know what you were saying. Where do you come from?"

"Arkansas. We just moved here."

"Oh, well, that's why. Here you go."

We were going to have so much to learn. We were different. And the people around us were going to make that very clear.

High Top Circle, our new street and neighborhood, was geographically and socially different from anyplace we'd ever lived before. We lived in a row of townhouses at the top of the hill, with rows of townhouses stacked below us. Above, to the south of us was a thin belt of grass and weeds and then a tall chain-link fence to keep kids and dogs from falling down a steep cliff into the artificially blue waters of a rock quarry pond far below. To the east of us, an area of cratered and mounded earth where they had stopped building, and then a thin strip of trees to hide another cluster of apartments. The center of the circle was a grassy sward, one of those suburban greenspaces that remains open and unused until the population pressure and home prices rise enough to put it to more profitable use. So, it existed in summer as a hide-and-seek grass jungle and in the winter as a top-notch sledding hill. To the west was what were called the Projects, some low-income public housing. We didn't go down there much, and our friend group was all from our side of the Circle. We were more of the married, young academic family dynamic on our side, and the lines were indefinable, but clearly drawn for us kids to see. Where you lived mattered, and in that way, we had our first common point of reference with this new place. Because wherever we'd lived, where you live always mattered.

I was painfully aware of the stigma of my parents' recent divorce and felt like it was a scarlet letter and character stain all my own, but almost every other family in our row of dwellings was a biracial family, single-parent family, second- or unmarried family. I should have felt right at home in the mix, but I held my hurt close to myself and didn't open my eyes, ever, to the reality that it was the same common hurt shared by all of my neighbors. We were all a rich mix of Italians, new to us, and Columbians and Black folks and highly educated young people. There were always kids to play pickup games of baseball and football with, and we formed a close bond with the neighbor kids and their parents: it seemed like Mrs. Little next door fed me every day. I'd be out playing with David and Kato, and then, it was time to take a break, and she'd ask me once, "Michael, do you want some lunch? There's plenty." "No, ma'am, thank you, ma'am. I'm not hungry." Then she'd ask a second time and, after the third time, "You sure?" I'd finally say yes and chow down ravenously. I was skinny and Mama was seldom home, and everyone knew I was going to eat, once the polite niceties had been observed.

It would have been a great place to grow up if I hadn't kept that grudge of moving away from Papa, moving away from what I'd always known, and always been waiting for the inevitable next move. We didn't get around much except for occasional weekend trips to New York City, and I can count on my hands the time I saw the ocean there. I was shocked years later to learn that New Haven was a port. You couldn't see it from Hamden, that's for sure. I wasted quite a few years there, in what I found out later was quite a beautiful area, while I waited, year after year, for that move to happen. The way it always had before.

That first fall, the landscape and weather changed like that in all of the books that I'd read, but that I'd never experienced in person. When the chill hit the air, so like air-conditioning that other people had in their homes in Arkansas, and the leaves changed into startlingly bright colors and fell to the ground, so that I could kick my feet and swish-swish-swish through the leaves, it was like the *Hardy Boys* stories and *Charlie Brown Christmas* show come to life. These things really existed, and they were amazing. All around, there were stone walls that I walked atop, balancing and watching my feet and giving purpose to my walks to school, trudging along towards days full of people that I experienced alone. I was a quiet and lonely kid, and I had always padded my spending money by walking, head down, finding other change and, occasionally, bills, that other people would pass by while happily taking in the world and talking with friends.

The first snow hit, and I was shocked at the sudden pristine quality of everything it touched. Overnight it became a land- and human-scape that was spotless, washed in the blood of the snow-white lamb. It was a scriptural epiphany. The thought that I'd have months of this, a whole season, filled me with wonder.

Early in the school year, a Nor'easter blew in and changed all of that. The storm dumped tons of snow on us, and after helping with our daily chore of clearing snow and ice from our red Pinto wagon so that Mama could get to work, we trudged out through our regular shortcut down the fissured field that led down to Pine Rock Avenue, where Jesse and I would part ways to our different schools. The path that we normally followed was obscured by feet of snow, and at one point I fell deep into one of the runoff-water gullies and went into the snow almost up to my head. I got coated in powder, and as I walked it melted and made my sneakers and the socks I wore over my hands as gloves wet and cold. By the time I'd made it the mile or so to school, I was crying and in desperate pain from the cold. I sat on the stone steps, locked out of the school building until the bell rang, and I was a pitiful thing to behold. A teacher let me in and exclaimed over the fact that I had no boots or gloves or snow pants, and she helped me thaw my frozen hands by running them under warm water. The pain was exquisite. My views on snow and winter changed dramatically from that day forward, and by the end of the season, my lasting memory would be of the black piles of rock-hard iced snow berms on every roadside, a feature that would serve to remind me that even if the lamb started out white as snow, it wouldn't take long for the world to make it black with sin. I got good at holding grudges, and Connecticut and my life there became a litany of disappointments and wrongs.

I'm not sure whether it was because of the industrial, blue-collar, Italian-dominant culture of the town, where the town and gown of Yale University and a blighted downtown area of nearby New Haven overlay and made the working-class outliers feel less than, but Hamden taught me a lot about taking a beating. Arkansas and Texas had their teacher-whippings, not to be easily dismissed, and the occasional incident where my older brothers' gang of friends demanded a correction, like when I wrote "Phil is a Homo" in big letters with chalk on the brick siding of our duplex facing the arterial street and I got roughed up by brother John's friend. But in Hamden, there were circles of influence of bullying, and if I escaped from one circle of hell, there was still another to endure or fight my way out of.

At school, where I was the quiet, smart, greasy kind of kid who showed up to picture day in his sister's orange zip long-sleeved turtleneck and wore it backwards all day long, I was an easy mark. At Helen Street Elementary, I found myself under the protection of one of the tough kids, a guy much like a young Arthur Fonzarelli, who had a cool and calm threat of violence about him and kept a retinue of minor toughs and followers. I was kind of the court jester: I could sing a mean version of Peggy

Lee's "Big Spender," could wiggle my tongue to make a sound like a tuning fork, walked on my kneecaps across concrete, and was a walking encyclopedia. His second-in-command, a wizened little yes-man, would needle me mercilessly, day in and day out, whenever we were out of the safety zone around our leader. Pick pick pick pick pick all day long. One day I snapped and kicked his ass. Left him on the ground crying and bloody, kind of like me when my older brother John was done with his periodic beatings. After that, I got messed with less.

Michael wearing his sister's shirt, backward, for school pictures (1973).

On the walk to school, I had to watch out for Dina Ruggerio and her girl gang. I wore my target solidly front and center, and Dina, a big girl on a fast bike who lived near us, was a consummate bully. I would be walking to or from school, head down and kicking through the piles of leaves or balancing step after step on the curb, and I would sense her. Looking up, I saw the gang of five or six bike girls, big Dina at the lead, and would take off running, bobbing and weaving through yards and across the busy traffic on Pine Rock Avenue. Inevitably they would drive me to earth, encircle me, and pepper me with punches. I got a black eye from one of Dina's lieutenants once, and the school was full of talk and merrymaking that I'd gotten beaten up by a girl. Notwithstanding that everyone else was afraid of Dina, it all left a mark. After many times of them riding, chasing, and beating me up, I managed to square up and deliver a strong right hook to the eye of the girl who had blacked my eye earlier. Her mom called mine, and my mom threw down and shut her up. It was okay to hit a girl second, if not first, and my mom was okay with me fighting back against my oppressors. She had needed to do it a lot herself. Again, for a while, I was seen by my enemies in a new light and left alone: an easy mark that had proven himself a bit less easy.

John was the one constant in this regard. He was four years older than me, and we shared the same house. He was one denizen of the beat-down underworld that I wasn't going to escape from. Since my earliest childhood, he'd sat on my bed and told me scary stories before bedtime to give me nightmares. When we went on trips to strange places, he would prepare me for the most preposterously inconceivable violent occurrences so that I would dread the upcoming vacation. And now that I was in elementary school, it was time to take out his demons on me in a more age-appropriate manner. John was an intensely physical, competitive, athletic person, and even the neighborhood kids like Kato Little, who was quite a bit heavier and bigger than him, struggled to tackle him in our pickup football games, where he would keep his legs pumping and churning and to tackle him necessitated being relentlessly kneed in the face. He was tough.

When we would play baseball, over the hill by the Projects in the open field there, I would have to play whether I wanted to or not, because having players, even one as bad as John told me I was, was nonnegotiable, and coin of the realm in the neighborhood. You needed bodies to play the game. If I could plan it correctly, and wait until John was up at bat and I was in center field, as far from the action as possible, I could sometimes drop the pretense that I was playing and book it as fast as I could across the field, up the short hill, and make it to our house, the first townhouse in the first row, and escape a serious, public, shame-ridden beating. But John had that former Texas State record-holder-in-the-mile speed, and a tenaciousness to not let me succeed in my transgression, and like as not, he'd catch me, tackle me to the blacktop or the grassy weeds of the yard, which was almost as hard as the asphalt itself, and wait for the rest of the kids to show up. Then he would hit me and hit me and hit me until I was a crying and slobbering mess. The others were mesmerized. Probably they were glad that John was someone's brother other than theirs. He would taunt and gloat and laugh, and it was neighborhood drama of the highest order. Escaping that particular hell was going to take a long time.

While I was quietly earning my bruises and facing the desolation of a friendless newbie, my mom was undergoing humiliations galore herself. Junior faculty pay at Yale at the time was barely enough to cover one person living alone, much less a mother with four children, so Mama got other jobs to make sure the bills got paid. The car paper route job was the one I remember best. Even as a grade school kid, I knew that a Yale professor with a paper route was unusual to the point of irony. But I was my mom's son, and I knew irony: she kept her PhD hanging in the downstairs bathroom, she said, "To remember all of the shit I had to do to earn it." Prepping the huge stacks of newspapers was a family assembly line project, each kid with a station, and then Mama would drive the route in our Pinto wagon, and I would throw the folded, rubber-banded, plastic-sleeve-clad newspapers onto porches and walkways and lawns. When it came to collecting the money at the end of the month, she'd drive the route, get out and ring the doorbells and talk to the customers, and collect dollars and coins and checks backed with insufficient funds. The money was the hardest part of the job, and after pleading with some of the subscribers, she'd laugh and make stern talk and cry and have very few options. I was the last resort, and she'd send skinny, clumsily dressed, greasy-haired innocent me to seal the deal. The closer. "My mom says that we won't have food for dinner tonight if you don't pay me now." The people at the doors were Italian and

Eastern European immigrants, working-class poor, just like us. I usually got us paid.

Mama had an office in Harkness Hall at Yale, and I would sometimes visit and help her run copies with the mimeograph machine, watching the German tests or worksheets or writing assignments spit out from the mouth of the copier, and the endlessly rotating wheel of hot, wet, ink-sponged packet that you changed without permanently inking your clothes and skin only with the greatest luck and skill. Once, while occupied with one of these mundane tasks, she had her purse stolen, and I looked everywhere until I finally found it outside, down a dark, dogleg mechanical alley, contents scattered on the ground, the wallet missing only her cash and credit cards. A small win not to have to replace her license and other non-valuables. When visiting, I was introduced to colleagues, nameless and affable, and one who stood out: the department secretary, Mrs. Houda. She was a dour and sour-faced woman who was the bane of everyone's existence but perhaps more so than anyone else, to my young, beautiful, and arrogant mom.

The cultural and personal contrasts between the battle-hardened department fixture, who in the end, though, was still just a secretary, and the newcomer junior faculty Frau Doktor Professor Riley, could fill a German opera. Disadvantaged by professional degrees and schooling, Mrs. Houda had boxed-out her office space like an old Dennis Rodman, and if you went in there in confrontation mode, you were going to feel pain, win or lose. She had set down roots, invaded every facet of the Germanics program to make herself the necessary person who held the keys, passwords, and institutional knowledge. She had the old-school tenure of a civil servant, and she'd seen faculty come and go. But no one could remember a time when she hadn't been there. Mama, in the other corner of the ring, had the titles and the glamour. Even with her waist-length black hair tucked up under a more professionally acceptable bobbed wig, she was beautiful. She also had the collateral as the newest young and upcoming published academic, and she was going to enforce that Germanic reliance on standing, title, and rank: she had left Vienna with my dad in large part because the position of secretary was about the highest she could achieve there, and her ambition demanded more. Now that she had it all, and a paper route to boot, she was not going to be subservient to anyone like Mrs. Houda. The game was on.

Helene, all of her long hair hidden beneath a short wig, with her mother, and her brother, Seppi.

My sister Schatzi had been running away from home off and on during the whole of her teenage years, and she was always willing to take a certain amount of risk just to physically get out and create some personal space for herself. In Connecticut now, just about finishing school, she found a perfect solution to the inherent dangers of running up for a day or two to New York City and breathing the fresh air of freedom: the Stephanos brothers. The twins were huge, six feet seven inches tall and with thin, muscled bodies; they made a striking contrast with my skinny, five-foot-tall badass sister. She was smart and sassy and Southern, and the guys were Northeast, mafia-looking protection, with long, curly black Peter Frampton hair and the dispositions of golden retrievers. One morning when Mama was teaching, Mrs. Houda fielded a call from the Connecticut State Police, and could they please talk to a Mrs. Helene Riley? Mrs. Houda burst into my mom's freshman German classroom and announced to everyone, "Frau Riley, the State Police have your daughter arrested for running away, and they would like to speak with you urgently right now." Mama left to take the call and was livid with Schatzi and Mrs. Houda for making her look ridiculous. But I like to think that even in the midst of crisis and concern and embarrassment, Mama must have thought in the back of her mind, back behind her fury and damaged reputation, "Well played, Mrs. Houda. Well played."

In spite of the enforced frugality of our situation, Mama always managed to find ways to gloss over our poverty and allow us to forget for a bit that we were poor. While we were growing up on a diet of alternating nights of meat and nonmeat dinners, cartons of dry, powdered milk and ice milk instead of ice cream, Mama figured out a plan to give all of us something that was immensely valuable and in short supply: alone time and a feeling of satiety and abundance. Once a week, she would take one of us four kids out to dinner at the Bonanza or Sambo's or, back in Houston, at Wyatt's cafeteria, and we could have an all-you-can-eat buffet and an all-you-can-ask conversation with Mama. By the time I had filled my stomach to the breaking point, and my pockets were full of stolen coffee-cream and buttery crackers from the condiment bar that I could eat at my leisure later, I was always ready to go home. Mama would dawdle over her unlimited refills of weak coffee, making that time where she had a fair shot at relaxation last as long as possible. In our latter years in Connecticut, when the other siblings had graduated and moved on and we finally had some disposable income, Mama and I would eat out more often. Saturday mornings were for eating Egg McMuffins in the car at McDonald's, and we would often go out for Chinese food, where Mama would order duck and feel like a queen of America, with only one easy kid, tons of books published, a house of her own, and enough freedom to even start dating again. Things were looking up.

Middle school is supposed to be tough, and after the relative ease of elementary school, Michael J. Whelan turned out to be a toxic place for me. The kids were older; they'd sharpened their meanness and humiliation skills to a very fine point. And we were no longer just content to be told what to do and when. We wanted to learn something worthwhile, and we questioned why it never happened. We didn't know it at the time, and no one made any noise about it, but the school really was toxic, built upon a foundation of industrial waste and clean fill dirt to cover it up. We could have laughed at the irony if we'd known, but instead we just got headaches and accumulated reservoirs of carcinogens in our bodies.

There were all sorts of new embarrassments to endure. Every school day morning, we'd rumble up to the drop-off, and I would have to stay seated for a minute or two, my coat over my lap, as the deep engine grumble and the vibrations of belts, wheels, and shafts brought my nascent sexuality into a horrific physical reality. My balls were always sore from so much raising and lowering of the flag. Then I'd get into class and get into trouble. Art, where the teacher gave me a detention for stabbing a kid with a pencil (even though I always contended that a poke is not a stab); history, where I had to beat the crap out of another kid for mercilessly and carefully bullying me nonstop; English, where we were reading *To Kill a Mockingbird* and I was made to read out loud often because of my Southern accent, and where I picked up the nickname "Boo Riley," one that I kept for myself; and German, where despite my mother being a German professor at the big university nearby and my advantage in having a native-speaker at home, I generally ended up with a C- and was lucky to get it. I was used to slipping into cracks and going unnoticed, and middle school was where I got my first F in math. I would not get any other grade in that subject for the rest of my school career.

ARTIFACT: A MEMOIR

There have always been incentives added by schools or parents to try to keep kids interested and striving through the slow and brutal onslaught of their never-ending education, but food has always been my main motivation for success. Not the school food, of course, which was as brutal as the hallway interactions and middle-level curriculum. But outside food, real food, was and always has been the lingua franca of kid rewards. In Texas, we used to get a free cheeseburger from the local McDonald's for A's. Teachers could give out pencils or stickers or their own handmade coupons, but an Otter Pop beat all of them any day of the week. At Whelan, on my bus, the driver would pay for a pizza party for kids who had the most improved grades, and I always appreciated that measure of success because I had a long way to go up. I won a place at the table one month, and after the driver had dropped everyone off, he took five or six of us to a local pizza place and ordered us some ginormous pies. I think we had some feeble sort of parental contact for the occasion, and while it might have turned out to be a horrible chance for kids to be abused instead of just bussed, it turned out to be a highlight of my middle school experience. Pizza, a little recognition, a kind old guy doing more than just his job. The things that help struggling kids get through their long childhoods.

Mama knew how to use the power of food, too, and would have fancy faculty parties at our house a couple of times a year. We were strictly forbidden to show ourselves during these coworker gatherings and were basically locked in our rooms upstairs until the guests left, hours and hours later. I'm not sure if Mama was just being very solicitous of her colleagues, but it was definitely true for her that she could have a much better time if we were not around and so, the temporary banishment. She would serve chocolate covered cupcakes filled with whipped cream, rich beef Stroganoff, sangria that she made especially for these occasions, and other food that just didn't appear in our lives, ever, unless there was this party. The table would be set with special linens and silver silverware, the wedding china made its only appearance, and she threw quite a soiree, even if the venue was rather modest. When the faculty finally left, we helped ourselves to the leftovers, gorging on our rich favorites. Jesse was a famous eater and was known to lick his plate clean when he got a chance at the good stuff. Mama had a few friends from her work, some of them lifetime people, important to her, and lifelong correspondents. But we were never invited to meet them. In the German language, the Das noun indicator can be used for animals and small children. I'm sure she never thought we might have something to add or take away from her gatherings, and therefore we didn't, apart from the scavenger feast at the end and a sense of being unjustly imprisoned.

High Top Circle was a neighborhood with a lot of diversity, which brought me opportunities to learn about compassion and cultural norms and that walking-in-someone-else's-shoes lesson from others. We were always outside, always playing with whoever was outside, too. One game was King of the Hill, played on the unclaimed construction leftover grounds, and it pretty much entailed all of us heaving stones over the big pile of unused fill dirt, trying to claim the high ground by keeping it unoccupied. On a memorable occasion when my stone found its mark, evidenced by a loud wail of pain, our side set up a big yell of celebration. Then one of the little kids, a Black boy, came tottering our way with a big gouge in his forehead and blood running down his face. I walked him back to his apartment, and his dad was furious at me, a white Southern boy damaging his son. I tried to explain the game we were playing, and the fact that we all had equal chances to be bloodied like he had been, but he was still loud and glaring and angry. I told him, "I'm sorry I hurt him, sir. I didn't mean to. We're not like those bad Southern people. My dad always taught me to be nice to Black people. In particular." And whether that was the right thing to say or not, I didn't ever know. I just felt bad.

One of my best friends from that time was Albert. He and his brother William, who was my brother Jesse's best friend, lived in the row of townhouses just below ours, and they were both big, kind-hearted, smart kids. In a rough-and-tumble kidscape, they were the eye of the storm. I didn't really like visiting their home, because their dad was a scary, white-haired, Australian man who swore a lot, and their mom was a Colombian woman from the housekeeping school of wrapping everything in plastic to keep it clean. Since I was kind of a Pigpen Charlie Brown character, carrying my own cloud of dirt with me everywhere, I felt out of place if not unwelcome. We would take off our shoes outside, walk on the hard, clear plastic runners into the living room, and sit on the plastic-encased couch, trying not to crinkle and skid and stick too much and draw attention to ourselves. Outside, though, the rules of spotless cleanliness were suspended, and we were free to run around and get into trouble without any supervision, just like every other kid in the neighborhood.

In the woods near the apartments to the east of us were some big, chain-link enclosures for two huge and wolfish German shepherds. They were dogs of childish myth, ferocious in their barking and gnashing of teeth whenever we took the shortcut near them to get down to the closest Wawa store and the playing fields at the nearby junior college. Stories were told of their viciousness, and we all believed them without question. Except for Albert. Albert one day went up to the fence and poked at the dogs with a stick. "Don't do that!" I yelled. "Those dogs are murderers. They're PROFESSIONAL guard dogs!" I didn't need to test any myths about German shepherds, because of the deep-seated fear my brother John had instilled in me prior to our childhood trip to Vienna. They even had a jingle worked up for me and my notable fear of dogs, sung to the tune of the Chicken of the Sea tuna commercials:

Who's the biggest Chicken, you ever did see?

Chicken of the dogs, Michael Riley.

Well, fear and myth and truth were scrambled that day, once the poking sticks came out and one of the dogs, displaying epic athleticism and little inclination to myth-bust, flew at the gate and scrambled over the eight-foot-high cyclone fence and attacked Albert. I ran home screaming bloody murder, and Albert was left with the German shepherd. The dog savaged him badly, and after some days in the hospital and extensive stitching around his chest to close the wounds, we heard that what saved Albert's life was his fat. Biting and tearing easily through Albert's shirt and going straight for the heart of the matter, the dog faced a daunting girdle of blubber to get through first. By the time help arrived and the dog was dragged from him, Albert was covered in blood and had a gaping wound in his chest. After the fact, once he was all well and sure to live, we'd quietly laugh sometimes about his fat saving him. I did a mean Bill Cosby Fat Albert impersonation, and the "Hey, hey, hey" would get us laughing every time. Albert knew he was fat; it wasn't a surprise to him. And if it was something he felt bad about, hey, it was also the reason he was still alive.

Another lesson was girls. I always struggled with the girl issue, even though, or because, I was raised by strong women. I was getting beat up by and was, myself, beating up those same girls, and Mama's rules about fighting were unclear. Generally speaking, a "If they hit you, you can hit them" rule applied to both boys and girls. There was a neighborhood girl I liked in sixth grade. She had long red hair and a fascinatingly large pair of breasts. Curious in the special way of a sixth-grade boy, one day when we were at someone's house and listening to records, I handed her a stack of LPs, and once her hands were full, I filled my own. I reached out in a two-handed, two-breast honk. They were soft and squishy, and for a moment I was full of joy and amazement. Then she dropped the records and screamed. I ran. She was not a former Texas State mile-record-holder, so I beat her in a race to my house and slammed and locked the door. When she repeatedly rang the doorbell and banged on the front door, I briefly opened it and yelled, "Go away, you

BITCH!" My mom rocketed out from somewhere and told me to apologize and then go to my room. She stayed at the door talking to the girl a bit and then came up to see me.

"Is it true, what she said, that you squeezed her breasts?" Mama asked, with barely controlled anger.

"Yes."

"Why did you do such a thing?"

"Because I wanted to," was my lame but truthful response. I was having trouble coming up with a good reason for my behavior on every laddered step of the process that ended up with her on my doorstep.

"Where did you learn the word *bitch*? Why would you use such a word? Do you even know what it means? It's a crude word for a female dog, not for a young girl!" My mom was almost crying in her anger and bewilderment. I was her good boy, the quiet and forgotten and trusted one. The one she wasn't supposed to have to worry about. "You listen to me. I never want to hear you say that word again. I can understand you wanting to grab a girl's boobs, but you don't get to do that without asking first. And if you do it without asking, you DEFINITELY don't get to call her a bad name for your bad behavior. Now go to your room and stay there."

I think I had to write her a letter of apology, and that was the end of my budding feelings of romance toward her. I kept my word and never said the word again. When you upset Mama that much, got her in the moment, parenting and in your face, you remembered. Disappointment ultimately was a much stronger punishment for me than physical violence, and unlike the toy rubber bat of our younger days, this one did leave a mark.

We had lived in Hamden for maybe four or five years before Mama was finally on a good enough financial setting to buy the deep-red brick house on Pine Rock Avenue. Saying goodbye to the High Top Circle life wasn't hard to do. We had a garage now, so no more early mornings spent defrosting the Pinto's front windshield. The new house was closer to the library, which was really my home away from home, a comfortable place that neither school nor my house ever were. There was our own backyard to play in, although I remember it mostly as a playground for squirrels to plant acorns and grow oak saplings, a state of affairs that brought Mama constant frustration. "If you would play outside more, the squirrels wouldn't make such a forest of our lawn!" She probably wanted to tell us to go outside and play in the street, like she had when we were younger, but Pine Rock was a busy arterial, and it was probably best not to encourage us. Often on my way to school I would pass road-killed possums and squirrels and an occasional cat or dog. For the first time we were living in a place where kids didn't rule the road. But there was no doubt that the Pine Rock house was a step up. Schatzi had dropped out of high school and moved out by that time and John had his own room. Jesse and I had a big room with bunk beds. Suddenly, everyone seemed to have enough space. Even Mama.

When I finally made it to high school as a freshman in 1979, I found it to be a new and different educational space, but still not a pleasant one. Hamden High was huge, with almost two thousand students. We had security guards in the hallways and, unknown to me at the time, a prostitution ring running out of the cheerleading squad. It wasn't a dangerous place, except in the sense that there were a lot of moving parts, but it was easy for me to lose myself in the crowd, once again, and underperform quietly and without recourse. We had some amazing curriculum choices, including the Latin language classes that Jesse threw himself into, body and soul. I had a health class taught by a former Mr. Universe, who'd been in *Pumping Iron* with Arnold Schwarzenegger and who always seemed ready, like the Incredible Hulk, to burst out from inside his button-down shirt and tie. But my favorite class, my favorite teacher, and the first time I think I ever excelled in school, was Environmental Science with Mr. Calvin Haseltine.

Up until this point in my learning career, I'd had some good teachers who helped me get through my days under their care. The preschool teacher whose summary reports of struggles and improvements showed that she saw and valued me; the inner city Little Rock teacher who gave a little extra time and care to the poor white boy bussed into a school outside of his neighborhood and cultural security; my fifth grade teacher, Mr. Baldwin or Balducci or something altogether different, whom I liked and therefore, when called to serve a wrongly meted out after-school suspension in his room, stared him down without speaking or answering or blinking for an hour until he sighed and said, "I guess that'll do, then. Go on home." But I wouldn't say I was inspired by any teacher, except for maybe some of my many library folks who fed me sustenance in my lonely and grim early school years, until I met Mr. Haseltine. He was a short and stocky Vermonter with brushy, long Robert Frost hair and big Popeye forearms that spoke of hard manual labor who taught a biology class that emphasized the natural world around us and our context within it. We went outside on the school campus to identify flowers, we got extra credit for bringing in fresh roadkill for dissection, and we had, an experience unknown to me before his class, discussions on real processes that affected us. He talked with us, not just to us. To me, he seemed like the writing in an Ernest Hemingway story: short, strong, real, and his words hit above their weight-class. He would take us on nature hikes Saturday mornings, and he might have been the only teacher my mom ever met, dropping me off to go on a hike at Sleeping Giant State Park. "So YOU'RE Mr. Haseltine. My son speaks very highly of you." I was a devoted fan, and not just of him, but of what and how and why he taught. He was a person who was well-suited to do many things, but because he had the knowledge and the care and actually liked working with young people, he chose teaching. I put that lesson away for later.

Mama was slowly and surely building her academic vitae and gaining for herself a measure of comfort. She was an associate professor at Yale, promoted without tenure perhaps because she was a woman, or maybe more because she was an extremely sharp woman, and had wounded many while making her way, finding fewer friends than enemies. She had a killer publishing record and was officially down to working just one job. She was a homeowner. Her kids were getting old enough to leave home, and finally she had disposable income time and wherewithal to reward herself with some bad habits, whether by drinking a bit or having a boyfriend. She was feeling the confidence of her success. My mom had always avoided alcohol because she disliked losing even a modicum of control, and whether she learned that behavior from hard lessons or just knew it from her own self, she abstained. The same was true of men. Now, in the largess of her situation, she would have a nightcap of some viscous yellow BOLS liqueur in the evening and would find a man now and again. One of her good-looking guys would take us all out to play tennis, and afterwards he would drive us to Baskin-Robbins, where I'd get a French vanilla shake on his recommendation. It was good, and I'm sure he was fine, but we kids kind of grinned and knew he'd better get what he could get, because Mama could do better than him. Not like there was a parade of men, no debauchery of drinking for Mama. She would have one, sparingly, and then again, after a while, another. As a child survivor of war and a young woman survivor of divorce, she was sober and calculating and never a spendthrift. She built up a margin of safety and then took a little pleasure where she could find it. Unlike my father, who took William Blake's poetic advice and followed everything to excess, Mama had ambitions that she never stopped striving towards. She made more than a pretty good life.

After ten years at Yale, she faced up to the knowledge and truth of the matter that the university would not be giving her tenure, and she went to look elsewhere again for work. A tenure-track position opened at Washington State University to be a German professor and Chair of the Foreign Languages, and she accepted. We were moving to the Evergreen State, just me and Mama now, and before long I'd start my junior year of high school in Pullman, Washington, wherever that was. I learned that the Snake River was nearby, and just that name alone, and the images I associated with the West, drew me into looking forward to that long-awaited next move. When I looked back on my time in Connecticut, it was hard for me to feel bad about leaving. I'd always been a Southerner biding his time, somewhat different and unwelcome, and going West was a logical solution to where next, a place new enough that everyone was from someplace else and where there hadn't been enough time and homogeneity for language to harden into accents and ancient family stolidity. It felt, without me ever having been there, like I was going home.

Albert

Albert was the fat kid.
Not like Kato,
who was large,
but picked-on fat.
Chubby fat.

Albert always called
Weeyum! Weeyum!
When tired of the tedium
 the teasing.
And William,
six foot three William, always
came running.

But William did not come
when the fierce German shepherds,
penned across the bulldozed field,
crazy with the teasing
of a chubby kid,
broke their fence:
nearly broke his heart

His fat is what saved him,
his doctor said and we would repeat.
His fat is what saved him.

And there was no William
when Albert found his father
dead
by the basement stairs
alone.

Did he scream *WEEYUM*!!!?
Did he whisper *weeyum*???
Weeyum, please?

When I met him again,
much later,
he said to me,
I'm going to be an EMT.
And I knew then
that he was way beyond me.
Beyond Weeyum.
Over the fat of his baby years.

Part III: Seeking

Lake Folk, Nisswa, Minnesota

No great distance separates them
Midwest-Northwest divide
For these two:
there is no away.

Ten thousand lakes to choose from
and this one will do.
Shallow enough to walk to the center
deep enough to contain thirty years
and not cloud the waters.

Water and dock-wood murmur
Loons laugh hysterically, appear and reappear
Friends share in the tone
Human nature.

No musical confusion,
just wood wind
Heart-stringQuiet. Joy. Voices in unison:
the things we weren't taught to yearn for.

Wye Mountain, Arkansas, Parking Lot Stripes, 1979

The summer I was fifteen and a freshman in high school, Jesse and I left Hamden to stay with my sister, Schatzi, and her husband, Larry, up on Wye Mountain. Only an hour in time and distance from Little Rock, it was so much further in terms of culture and landscape and lifestyle from the city. I'm not sure if it was because Papa was in the hospital any one of those innumerable times or whether she just wanted to help us out and give us some positive life lessons in the country, but those couple of months were filled with memorable times. There was the community daffodil field just down the lane, three acres of flowers planted just so the scattered neighbors could come together once a year to celebrate their blooming. And a further walk to Little Italy, a wide spot in the road that no longer had anything to do with Italy but was a definitive example of little. And Schatzi and Larry's place alone was special. Both of them were in construction, and the house they built together for themselves was a beauty. With high, airy ceilings, large windows and skylights that let in lots of light, and unfinished wood everywhere to make it feel like what it was: a cabin in the woods. There was a big organic garden and chickens and guinea hens that ate their weight in ticks every day. Picking fresh vegetables and warm eggs from underneath a chicken was an Arkansas that I'd never experienced. I kind of liked it.

Larry was a Vietnam veteran and a rough, bearded, tall, slow moving and speaking guy with the broken body of every roofer and carpenter. He shambled. I never knew much about him and Schatzi together except that they made a cute couple because of their size differential, she barely reaching five feet and Larry a good bit over six feet, much like the dynamic of her and the Stefanos brothers some years before, and that they'd made a good life for themselves up on the mountain. He smoked a lot of pot and built a lot of houses, and when they split up some years later, they remained neighbors on friendly terms. Schatzi could give a lot of love and put up with a lot of shit, but she had limits, and Larry would finally exceed them.

Of course, Jesse and I were teenage boys, and suddenly for Schatzi, it was two more boys sitting around waiting for the next meal to appear, just like the bad old days, and she got tired of us needing instructions to do any of the chores and work that needed to be done right in front of us. I was afraid to go outside much because I'd always been afraid of bugs, and out in those woods they were fierce. The worst were the seed ticks and chiggers, both so small you couldn't see them burrowing into that vast well of blood that we appeared to them. Gasoline baths to kill them were as bad as the terrible itching, and I was enough of a classist to worry about the optics of the headline "Arkansas boy self-immolates while taking gasoline bath." There were rattlesnakes, too, and Schatzi's dog got bit on the snout once. His whole head swelled up like a balloon full of Jell-O, and he jiggled and stumbled around for a week, overbalanced on his forward end, and then the swelling went down and he was fine. He was never a smart dog, but the venom didn't make him any dumber. That summer, I felt a lot of kinship with the snakebit dog. In the end I wasn't much smarter, but I had some memories to take forward with me.

Schatzi and Larry had some side gigs, like most rural folks do, and one was their parking lot striping business. Some nights they would hitch up the painting rig on the back of the Datsun pickup, and Jesse and I would pile into the bed of the truck, and we'd head off to Jacksonville or Stuttgart or Searcy and spend the night under the bug-clouded lights of a Walmart or grocery store parking lot putting down chalk lines and filling up the sprayer hopper with more yellow paint. Some of the old boys who would hang out or help or just stand and watch the paint dry would talk about various local points of pride, like the guy who told us in Jacksonville, "You want to watch out for these mosquitos. They're full of all those PCBs up from the Air Force base, and you get enough bites you'll swell up and get all purply." They were hot, sweaty nights, and there wasn't enough DEET in the world to keep the bugs off you. When we were finished, maybe four or five in the morning, Jesse and I would ride home in the back of that truck, cool wind floating over the cab to kiss but not chill us, the stars burning up the heavens, and it was good. We'd stop somewhere at a greasy spoon and get a working person's breakfast, and it tasted better from having earned it.

Schatzi was a Jill of all trades, and she did plenty of stints at all sorts of work, from carpentry to working the suicide help lines at a crisis center, and always, the fallback of waitressing. We'd stop in sometimes and visit her at one of her restaurants, have a lunch and have her serve us. She'd introduce us to the waitstaff, invariably gorgeous young women who called us Sugar and Baby or other terms of Southern endearment that could make an old lady sound sexy, and from the mouth of a young, pretty one, well, we melted. Schatzi gave us lessons in the hidden economy of waitressing and told us how little she made per hour without tips. Tipping was not a choice, she'd tell us, but a mandatory practice that showed respect for anyone feeding you and trying to feed themselves and their families at the same time. Once I asked about "that girl" who had just come by to top-off our sweet tea, and Schatzi said, "That wasn't a girl." I was shocked into speechlessness for a minute, going over in my mind the cogent points I'd noticed that seemed to very clearly point her out as a girl. She continued, after a short pause for emphasis, "That was a woman." I was mad at her the way a boy would be, might have given her a bad tip, and felt like the dissonance she'd given me was unwarranted for the honest mistake. But Schatzi wanted me to know that there were too many people covering up disrespect, misogyny, stereotypes, and racism in a white sheet of honest mistakes. She wanted us to be better, and because of her lessons, lived and spoken, we were.

144

Pullman, Washington, High School Dances, 1981

After a four-day cross-country bus trip in which I slept through my stop in LaGrande, Oregon, and went all the way to Portland, which added another ten hours to my trip, I finally arrived in Pullman on a hot August day where the sun was burning down with an intense heat on the empty and near-treeless streets. The town was dusty and quiet, and the monochromatic light made everything flat and drab. There was not an evergreen in sight. Mama came and picked me up in her light blue Ford Fairmont and brought me to the house we'd be staying in for a month until the place that she had rented was available. She'd just started at the university and already found herself unimpressed with the library and the four steep hills that made up the town and provided a foil to pedestrians, bike riders, and drivers alike. Her office in Thompson Hall, one of the original buildings on campus and impressive with its red brick, wide windows, and slate-capped cupola, was more than sufficient.

When I opened my suitcase and unpacked my few things, I was horrified to see some cockroaches scurry out of the satin lining and onto the carpet. That this scourge of the southlands had hitchhiked along with me for my long bus trip, and I was repaying the kindness of a colleague of Mama's to lend us a landing spot, immediately tortured me. Roaches played a long game, I knew, and give them an inch, they'd make a beachhead a mile wide. I hurriedly threw the suitcase outside under the carport and hoped fervently, with a deep and abiding loathing, that the cold night air would kill them and that I had not infected this new place with a non-native pest. I didn't know it yet, but the Palouse was a Goldilocks zone of extreme heat and cold that made it a difficult place for vermin to survive. No roaches and kudzu, few ticks or poisonous snakes. It was the anti-Deep South.

The first folks I met were the next-door neighbors, Ken and Marge Struckmeyer, a kind and physically imposing couple, both well over six feet tall, who worked at Washington State University and for the Pullman school district. School was starting in a few days, so Mama and I did the back-to-school shopping, which necessitated an eight-mile trip across the border into Idaho, where there was a shopping mall. In all of the years of schooling in all of the different places, this was a constant: pencils, spiral-bound notebooks, carryall binders with Velcro fasteners. Exploring the two-block Main Street of the Pullman downtown didn't take long. Other than the old-school White's

Drug Store, where they still had penny candy, there wasn't much there. The university was out of session, and there were no summer school classes, so there was the feel of a ghost town. It had all the makings of one of those "Great town to raise a child" places. Ugh.

Somehow, I'd gotten caught up in a bait and switch scheme, because this pathetic place was definitely not the snow-capped mountains, the foggy conifer forests, the waterfalls and seashores that I had always been told were part of the Evergreen State experience. I didn't realize it, but every bit of that was right here, in the geologic sense, with silt-covered mountains, dry waterfalls, and inland seas from the great Bretz floods, or nearby, in the Western sense of six hours as nearby, if you had the eyes and the patience and the creativity to see them. Most people didn't, so the majority of students from western Washington left Pullman whenever possible, and we had the place to ourselves. Not much of a win, really, but an empty small town felt better to me than one crowded with people. Pullman was a boom town on an academic schedule, and I never was much of a fan of school or crowds.

My first day of school, I had to cross a wheat field to get to the high school, and halfway across, I first heard and then saw a flock of geese, heads down, loud honks and fierce hisses issuing from their beaks, menacing from the end of their long necks, wings flapping madly as they hurried towards me. I ran. If I needed a reminder that I wasn't in Connecticut anymore, that worked. Pullman High School gave me plenty of other reminders as well. A modern jumble of blocky, jutting, fat-bricked classrooms, the legend was that it had been designed by an architect who specialized in prisons. It certainly had that brutalist look and feel. It was also tiny compared to Hamden High, with a hundred and sixty-six kids in my junior class, whereas there were five hundred where I came from. I'd recently learned that there was an expectation among kids my age for daily showers and washing your hair, so I was able for the first time to blend relatively easily into a population used to the comings and goings of university families. I was a new kid among many new kids. I had the feeling that I might have finally thrown off the chains of childhood and come into an age where I had a modicum of control over my life. That I might survive that imprisonment of the very young, where others define you and the safest place to hide from the world was inside a book or your head. I started to take the baby steps of growing into myself and interacting with the world around me.

In my first semester at Pullman High, I took the required Washington State History with a bunch of freshmen, because I'd missed out being on their curricular schedule. I'd taken Texas State History, endless accolades of insurrectionist white men and heavy on feeding that monstrous pride they have down there on being a big, rebellious, violent state, and light on the facts pointing to their ill-gotten gains of land. The stupid egoism of the Alamo and the fact that Sam Houston was ridiculed as a coward and faced mounting threats of mutiny before he finally faced the enemy and won at San Jacinto was not in the curriculum. Just the winning, so much winning, and then the naming rights as their spoils. In Connecticut I faced the same state-pride requirement, but I fail to remember a single element of it. Puritans and patriots, I'm sure. Now, a new state and a new set of self-satisfying propaganda factoids and figurines. Small history for the local crowd.

Mama and I did a few of the things that were necessary to enjoy living in a town like Pullman, namely getting out of it from time to time. We traveled up to Spokane with a colleague of hers to see the falls and eat at The Flour Mill, the tourism-required restaurant built right over the river. We would travel a few miles to the north to hike at Kamiak Butte, the top of an ancient mountain buried in wind-born loess soil that gave the Palouse its iconic wavy hills and deep reserves of dryland farming productivity. Because of that rich soil, the wheat barons made Whitman County at one time the richest per capita county in the nation. It didn't feel rich, though, and there was little obvious evidence of it. We took a weekend class in mycology and headed an hour eastward into the Idaho forests and had a mushroom scavenger hunt with other students and faculty from the university. We even took a weekslong hunter safety education class, for what reason I can't for the life of me fathom, because there were no less likely gun owner, animal killing, put-meat-in-the-freezer people than Mama and me. This brief moment in time was what I thought maybe other families looked like. We were at the end of the real family time, before I was all grown and gone and we'd all left her, and it was a sweet glimpse of what our childhood might have been if everyone had been able to pull forward on the same rope together. But that's more easily done with two than with six. We enjoyed our companionably quiet time together.

Mrs. Yount, my Washington State History teacher, was a soft star of a teacher, and she saved me many times from the kind of prejudice I'd faced in so many different classrooms where I was different. When I said "sal-mon" instead of "sam-un," she told the haters, "That's the British pronunciation." When I wanted to study the far off, unpopulated, unknown Clallam County for a research project, she made sure I got what I wanted, and I paid her back by learning it and vowing to visit someday. To see otters at Shi-Shi Beach and the rainforest in the Hoh. She had a quiet individual smile for me and a loud, screeching shout for the wild young ones.

I took Vocal Workshop as one of my electives, and I was one of the few boys in the class. Definitely the only boy who enthusiastically, voluntarily, and loudly, with the assurance of someone who enjoyed what they were doing, sang with a voice that was nice to listen to. I had no idea that this was a high school boy superpower. I probably could have leveraged that into a date or a first kiss on the basis of my singing alone, let alone my tall and skinny unbowed frame, clear complexion, and Ed Riley's devastatingly dark and glowering eyebrows. But I was clueless and thus unable to turn that goodwill into any kind of the physical affection that I was profoundly wanting, needing, groaning for. I made do with having friends and people who were generally nice to me on a regular basis, and that was pretty close to enough. Closer to enough than I had experienced up until that time.

I had absolutely zero coaching or mentoring in my life on the art of making myself available to the pursuit of asking a girl out and making a romantic connection, or for in any way breaching the vast abyss that lay between me and any object of my desire. Papa may still have been fathering children on far away islands in my childhood, but he left me on the island of myself when it came to sharing any of the smooth moves he might once have had. The only advice on the subject that I remember him giving me was, "Women are a gift of God. I hope you won't turn out to be a homosexual, because they miss out on the best part of this life." I had no idea as a kid what being a homosexual meant, or how girls were a gift, because girls were yucky, but I remembered his words. Mama brought home an occasional boyfriend, like tennis/Baskin-Robbins guy, but how they met or what they did and why, well, that was behind the parent veil. Neither Jesse nor John or Schatzi ever had a boyfriend or girlfriend that I met, so the whole process was a mystery that I carried alone.

Mama told me the rage she felt as a child from having to learn about the mechanics of sex from watching dogs in a Viennese alley, and Papa talked rapturously of the joys of the opposite sex, but all those years later, I was still as clueless as an eighteen-year-old boy as she'd been as a young girl. Providentially, though, I found a paperback book on our basement shelves called *The Happy Hooker*, by Xaviera Hollander, and that, coupled with my newly acquired habit of daily showers, informed me about a whole new range of experiences from the perspective of a young Madame and allowed me to relieve some of my built-up frustration. I never asked about or commented on the pink-covered memoir of *Her Own Story*, but I do wonder who bought that and put it where I could find it. In any case, I was thankful.

There were mechanisms in place in a small rural high school for boys in just my state of insecurity and know-nothingness, as I found out when posters went up for a Sadie Hawkins dance. A Finnish exchange student invited me. Fortunately, I at least had the correct insight to say yes, because how rude would that be to say no, but I can't say I enjoyed the experience. I was terrified of the smart, tough, cool, short-blond-haired girl and what might be expected of me, and so instead of enjoying my good fortune, I went through the motions of dancing and talking and being a date, whatever that meant, and hoped only not to damage either of us in the process. Not reputational damage, because we had none to damage, and not physically because we weren't going to do anything, were we? But psychic damage was a clear and present danger, and I totally felt the pain of it. I was a terrible date. Such a loser. Sigh.

I was desperately in love with Gail, one of the girls in my class, a friend of mine and the girlfriend of one of my other best friends. I would sit behind her in the big lecture classroom with amphitheater seating and draw pen and ink sketches of her in an Argyle sweater vest, her black tresses cascading over her shoulders, while I was instead supposed to be taking notes. Creepy, I know, but a drawing consisting of long hair and plaid, with nothing more risqué than the architectural arch of her sleeveless vest goes a long way to show how pure and intellectual my longing was. At the end of the year, she would write in the front page of my senior yearbook, "Thanks for letting me read out of your books all semester and hope you have a memorable life filled with love, ladies, and kelp." Her boyfriend wrote a note about me having to work on not working too hard, and added with a postscript, "Maybe we can make the beast with 17 backs someday." They were kind of perfect for each other, and I was kind of just not. But the heart wants.

This paragon of young womanhood with whom I was desperately in love had a best friend, and to make my nonexistent love life even worse, she and her friend met me in the halls one afternoon and asked me to go to prom. At first, I was like, wait, who's asking me? I recovered quickly because, duh, Gail was already taken, and I exhibited the wherewithal to know that this hideously uncomfortable and untenable situation could only be answered with a yes, lest I hurt the feelings of the friend of the friend that my heart hurt for. It was a plot of Sicilian complexity, and I felt helpless again in my lack of gamesmanship in these affairs of the heart. This girl who asked me was a perfectly nice person and someone who, in different circumstances, might have helped me make some positive steps in the direction of being a person of common experiences with the rest of society, but since she did not conform to my ideal of physical beauty or, being fair to me, have a good range in her conversational repertoire, I didn't give her much notice before or after the dance. None of the girls who were actually interested in me were ever very interesting to me. I got dressed in the only nice clothes I had, some ill-fitting hand me downs, bought a corsage, had a double-date dinner at my date's house, and slunk through an evening of dancing and ennui that was underwhelming for both of us. Or what I always think of as a regular old date.

Mitigating my lack of romance and general loneliness and self-loathing, though, was a newfound cadre of friends. People in Pullman were nice. I got invited to the Nazarene Church and found there a social structure and homeyness that helped settle me and the overactive inner life I'd grown used to and cultivated from years of being alone and immersed in hundreds of books, mostly science fiction. Every Sunday the Emersons would pick me up, and when we got to the church, I was the kid designated to swing the little ones around until they were dizzy, sit down and listen to the old folks share their remembered wisdom, and quietly critique the beliefs and practices of the church while checking out the scary dentist's gorgeous daughter. My eyes, like my stomach, were always hungry, which I almost recognized as a sin, unlike the strictures against dancing and going to movies. Afterwards, there were potlucks and volleyball at church, or meals with the Emersons at their double-wide trailer home in the nearby bedroom community of Albion.

One night I stayed out late with a couple of friends. Not the Emersons, because they were aware of the common courtesy of bedtimes and parental consent and curfews: normal parent values that I was unaware of because I'd never had to make use of them. I wasn't out late doing anything bad, because I didn't have rowdy friends who partied or broke necessary laws, but it was one o' clock when I let myself into the dimly lit living room of our house. Mama stirred on the couch as I came in.

"Where have you been? It's late. I didn't know where you were." It wasn't a scene of drama or recrimination, but as I went to bed, I was dumbfounded and amazed. I was eighteen years old, and for the first time in my life, I was aware that my mom worried about me. In her sleep-distressed state, deep in the night, I saw her unsettled and vulnerable in a way I never had: the caring mother, waiting fretfully for her youngest to return home. It was so unlike her. I felt a phantom shift, a bit of knowledge imparted, a lesson learned. My world was changing.

Although my first year in Pullman was a step up for me from Connecticut, and I settled into the school and friendships like I never had before, for Mama it was more of the same lack of academic job security, and her stint at Washington State University didn't work out as she'd planned. After a year in Pullman, she still didn't have the promised tenure that was her whole purpose in going there. And there were other reasons for her dissatisfaction. Trying to research pre-internet at the middling state university's middling main library when she was used to the deep trove of manuscripts that was Yale's Beinecke Library, a car crash while attempting to navigate the steep hills of the Palouse in deep snow in winter, and a man she'd met in New Haven three thousand miles away all made her itchy to leave.

She invited my brother Jesse to live rent free with me in the same two-story house we already had and left for New Haven. It was my senior year of high school, and although it was an important milestone and a precarious time to leave two teenage boys alone, Mama was consistent: she had needs, and she was going to make sure they were met. She found some loophole in her contract and inserted herself, uncomfortably for all parties involved, back into the Germanics department at Yale for what she and her superiors all agreed was absolutely her last year. Perhaps another factor in her decision to move was her correspondence with a student of hers from that previous year in New Haven, an older man who had taken her class to brush up on his German so that he could better work on his retranslation of the accepted works of Freud in English by James Strachey. He was tenacious in keeping their connection alive.

That summer, I mostly lived out at the home of my best friend, Shawn. Verne and Windy, his parents, and all of his numerous sisters had their individual ways, but Shawn was out there on a limb that they must have struggled to support. He was into black leather jackets and all of that great music of the time that I'd never heard: the Ramones, the Dead Kennedys, Ric Ocasik, Boomtown Rats. So much music all the time. We'd sometimes walk the eight miles from Pullman to Albion on the defunct railroad tracks, seeing country no one else saw, like the dilapidated abandoned farmsteads where the daffodils still kept righteously springing up, untended, every year, and discarded old rail machines from a time when America was a different country. I'd go climb the hills with the littlest Emerson, Shae, and when we'd get up by the rimrock, she'd sigh and say with wonder, "When you get up here, Albion looks like a kingdom!" I laughed and agreed. A kingdom of trailers and dead cars. A playground and school and library that were no longer open to being what they were originally purposed for. It was a poor and almost forgotten little place that had been rendered obsolete by the bigger anchor towns of Pullman and Colfax, but it still had the Emersons and some other pretty good folks to boot, so I loved it.

Partly out of a sense of paying my fair share, as well as doing dishes and going to church, I also helped the Emersons with their part-time business of cleaning one of the grocery stores in Pullman after hours. We'd roll up in Vern's awesome old rounded '50s Ford panel van, kind of an Appalachian Escalade, and own the store in the deep hours of the night. I would clean the toilets and pilfer the "Grown in Arkansas" stickers for chicken in the meat aisle to send to my sister's husband who liked them for his pot stash, while Vern ran the big squeegee floor cleaner machine. It took a few hours at most, but the feeling of being alone in a space meant for crowds, like being in a church on a Saturday, matched well with my inner solitude and was a balm to my soul. Being alone with a few good people was always how I wanted to be.

Vern and Windy were parents for me the way other people had parents. Vern was an auto parts salesman and one of the sweetest-natured men I ever knew. He spoke slowly, smiled often, and counselled on occasion with a native intelligence and well-meaning advice. Vern didn't make you do anything but instead offered up a logical and common-sense option for you to follow, and you did it. He had a degree in geology, and he was a granite outcropping himself: upright, a bit worn by the elements, but strong and solid and staying the course as the landscape changed around him. Windy was more mercurial. She could have a temper, but she fed me and her four kids and other ragamuffin foundlings like me on good country cooking and sharp and playful conversation. She was engaged and present and aware of the kids around her in ways that my mom, and certainly not my dad, never were. And since I never refused to rub her gnarled and calloused feet in the evenings when she asked, she loved me. Junior year in high school and finally I almost felt like I had enough love and care. It was a powerful new feeling.

When Jesse arrived from Arkansas to be my older brother minder, I moved back from Albion and into the house where I'd lived with Mama. We had the whole place to ourselves for my senior year. We didn't take advantage of our sweet crash pad and party house opportunities because we weren't rowdy boys, and I guess we lived up to our mom's trust in us. Or didn't take advantage of her cluelessness. I would walk to school every morning, and Jesse would begin his own walking on the long, elevated entrance deck that ran the entire length of the front of our house. His pacing, as I called it. With his food and rent paid by Mama, and without great physical or social needs of his own, his job was to see me off to school and greet me when I made it back from school. Otherwise, he paced the porch. When I came home in the afternoon, he was still at it and would cease and desist and come in and we'd hang out and talk about my school day for a while before we made our dinner. Like Uncle Rudi, our menu was routine. We were spartan in our ways.

High-school-aged Michael, Jesse, and a friend in Pullman, WA (1982).

Jesse and I had always walked a lot, and sometimes in our Arkansas summers we'd get up to thirty miles in a day, if we were correct in putting together the distances. Jesse was a wizard with maps and numbers, so I believed him. The day after he graduated from high school, Jesse donned the Roman tunic and some sort of skullcap that he had fashioned in his Latin club and literally walked away from a couple of free-ride academic scholarships that he'd earned from some prestigious eastern universities. I think he'd been headed for New York City, and he was picked up by the police fairly soon after starting, maybe twenty miles down the road, for whatever constitutes the illegality of walking in the breakdown lane in a tunic and not much else. I think he was being authentic and thus, was sans undergarments. Police don't like that sort of educational passion, and so his walkabout was cut short. Now in Pullman two years later, there was no one to stop him, and he walked and walked and walked, back and forth, wearing out a path in the waterproof stain of the decking boards. If there was anything weird about his habit, I don't think I mentioned it except for some mild comments and responses now and again. We had enough weirdness in our family that it wasn't worth thinking on too much. Just a Riley boy thing.

At school I had people and classes that I didn't dread being around. My English class had two of the things I'd always loved most, reading and writing, and not much else, so that was always a safe place. My history teacher, Jerry Harms, was a former Peace Corps volunteer in Central America, and he would regale us with stories of how the well-meaning corps members, tasked with decreasing chicken mortality, were given a debeaking machine and made to force feed heads into the steel knife chamber for hours on end, with the inevitable results that some chickens lost more than just their beaks. A significant amount more. The bloody ridiculousness of it, along with his other tales of American historical snafus and the dunce-like behavior of men in power throughout the ages, made the ideas and ideals of our country more real to me.

Of course, I had to have math. The porcine and dismissive teacher told me if I couldn't do better than that to leave, and he dropped me from the class. Not an incorrect assessment of my skills or effort, but a strong reinforcement for my math phobia. And there were the everyday dangers of using the bathroom, where the stalls had no doors so I always had to wait until I got home in the afternoon to poop, and traversing "Jock's Landing," where if you didn't acknowledge the primacy of the sports figures who ruled the atrium, or loitered a bit too long without leave, you could get pushed or pummeled or have random shit dropped on you as you walked the hallway below. But generally, the daily grind was okay and felt doable. A manageable regimen.

I had started to get the fitness craze from some minor successes in my weight training class and in PE, where I was starting to outrun some of the better, hence lazy, athletes who ruled Jock's Landing. Mrs. Melhart, our PE teacher, would give us a hand-drawn map of our running route, often a couple of miles up and down the unavoidable and omnipresent Palouse hills, around the school and through the nearby subdivisions, and turn us loose, absolutely unsupervised. It was 1983, and there wasn't much of a running shoe boom, so I just wore tennis shoes. I ran fast and long enough for a couple of students to ask me whether I ran cross-country, but since I'd never done an organized sporting activity in my life, it wasn't in my mind to join a sport. It never occurred to me, and by the time it did, the opportunity had passed. But I kicked butt on those runs. Like Jesse, I picked up some repetitive movement myself, and every evening I did sets of push-ups and sit-ups. As I grew accustomed to the work, my sets and reps went up, and by about a hundred push-ups and five hundred sit-ups, I'd be tired and bored. Afterwards, I would read or do writing homework for English, which had a yearlong journal assignment of writing a page per day and, like the sit-ups or Jesse's pacing, gave me something positive to do.

Jesse and I, without having any philosophical rationale for it other than a childhood of surviving on simple fare, were monkish and ascetics in our cooking as well. Every morning that year, we had oatmeal for breakfast, and for dinner, we made hamburgers with instant mashed potatoes burnished to a shining radioactive yellow glow with the addition of copious amounts of butter. At the store, we would buy in bulk. Five-pound plastic logs of ground beef and large paper canisters of desiccated oats and potatoes. It was cheap and filling and, at least for me, made the school lunches and Sunday suppers with the Emersons just that much more appealing. The Emersons loved Jesse, too, and he was an accomplished eater. Windy would "ooh" and "ah" over his ability to put away helping after helping of Yankee pot roast and potatoes, real potatoes, and trifles and pies and cakes. Jesse and I were just grateful. I don't think Jesse ever went to church with us, but his religious practice was in the church of repetitive movement, in the cycle of doing, and he already knew Jesus well enough from Papa's teaching. He didn't need to sit still in a pew to find God.

English was always my best subject in school. I enjoyed writing the poems that my teachers required us to write, but when it came to reading them out loud, I always refused. It was maddening to me and my teachers, both, because I liked my work, knew it was good, and would nonetheless have to take a reduced grade for not being able to share it. Speaking and writing were clearly two different skill sets, and I didn't like being held accountable one for the other. When it finally came time for turning in my journal notebook, it was heavy with ink, every page chock-full of words and without the shortened sentences, line skips, and white space of the other students. It was intimidating even for me to look at. I got back a grade and some comments, but mostly what I remember was a feeling of relief. That task was done. Jesse read the teacher comments and became incensed at Mr. Akin calling my words "trite." Other than the calloused pad on my left ring-finger, I didn't have a lot of ownership in the project, but Jesse was up in arms:

"You can tell that guy from me that he'll never be the writer you are, Mike. He gives out a trite assignment like that and gets all that work only to denigrate it? He's not worth what you gave him."

Jesse always had my back. He was there so much more than any of my other family. He was a good brother.

New Haven, Connecticut, A Pennsylvania Quaker, 1982

When Mama left Pullman, a big part of the reason was to be closer to a man she wanted to be closer to. At Christmas break, my brother Jesse and I traveled by bus to New Haven to see Mama and meet her new guy. After three days on the Greyhound bus, slogging our way through the big empty spaces and small, wasted, empty towns of the Northern route, places like Minot, North Dakota, where Jesse and I coined the tourist gem, "Why not in Minot?" but never got paid for it, we arrived at midnight in New Haven, having burned a quarter of my vacation just getting there. We walked the last couple of miles from the bus station to Loomis Place, relying on Jesse's innate map reading skills, and arrived at the house, a tall skinny old place reminiscent of Luna Lovegood's house in Harry Potter. They'd left the door open for us, and as we walked in, there they were coming down the stairs to meet us, dressed in almost matching nightgowns and bathrobes, weird and cute at the same time. We said hello, were shown to our rooms up on the third floor, and conked out to sleep for twelve hours.

Jesse and I knew that the purpose of the trip was to meet this important person, to make a connection and support Mama in a relationship that was immediately, clearly, unlike the brief flings she had engaged in every few years after her divorce. But for me, the task turned out to be an easy one. With a Harvard-educated dad and a Yale-educator mom, even in our lowest times, in our meanest living arrangements, I always felt confident and comfortable in being wealth-adjacent. With all our family history in Arkansas and growing up on food stamps and stories of my mother eating boiled nettles in the Second World War Austrian countryside, I knew what poverty felt like. But I also knew we weren't trash. And I knew that we might have been dirt poor but not piss poor. I knew we were from good family stock on a break. At a brief generational downturn. I knew we were as good as anyone else. But Darius's wealth and intelligence, his soft-spoken kindness, the flavor of his wealth, were all much more attractive to me than that of my rich uncles with their houses on the golf course in Little Rock.

It turned out that it was easy for us to like Darius. He was a small, lively, balding man of great intellect and character, and my mom had fallen head over heels in love with him. And he with her. He was a psychiatrist, a Pennsylvania Quaker, and a divorced and longtime bachelor who lived in an ancient five-story home with slate roofing tiles in a stately old neighborhood that was losing its battle with the encroaching modern world. He drove a stripped-down Chevy Chevette with no radio, and he left it unlocked year-round so that no one would be tempted to bash the windows in to steal things that weren't there. He was a pragmatic guy and a romantic as well. When my sister, a carpenter, later saw how well he cared for his hammers and chisels and screwdrivers, oiled and each placed where they belonged, she told him that when she died, she wanted to come back as one of his tools.

Maybe it was his Germantown friends background, or a reaction against his dysfunctional doctor father and Darius's own early divorce, but the house was comfortable and homey in a way that was new to me. It was also cold as hell, because the stonework and multiple stories were a nightmare to heat. He kept the thermostat at fifty-seven degrees, and every chair and couch had a lovely tartan plaid wool throw blanket which you either used or, instead, faced Jack Nicholson's end in *The Shining*. It was a frugality that wasn't parsimony. The kitchen was big and dark, and Darius made a few good things: lentil soup and pot roasts. There was an old, narrow servants' stairway that felt like a secret passageway maze that his housekeeper used to get to the third-floor study, where she pretended to fold laundry while watching television game shows all day long. She was about eighty years old, and Darius paid her to come and have a place to stay during the day; when they were both younger, she had actually cleaned and cooked, but that was no longer an expectation, and it didn't happen. Darius showed me that wealth didn't have to come with a moral caveat.

I finished my senior year and graduated high school, and no family but my brother Jesse showed up to watch me walk across that big Colosseum stage rented by the school district from the university. It was the typical affair, a blur of lights and action and done. In our family, these events were not celebrated, because they were expected and necessary, like getting your teeth cleaned was for other people. My friends thought it odd. I left Pullman as I'd left every other place, with an ease and familiarity that leaving so often ingrains in a kid. I wasn't sure if I'd be back.

From there I went to Arkansas for a last summer of sweating under the home sun, and then back to Connecticut to fly out for a grand tour of the British Isles and Ireland that I'd planned as a graduation gift to myself. By that time, Mama and Darius had married. For the occasion, she wore an outrageously red sheath dress to announce her fallen nature and her pride in the accomplishment. None of us kids were invited or showed up. It was their marriage, after all, I guess the reasoning went. And a second one, so why make a fuss? But Darius was the real deal now, and so, for the couple of weeks before I left on my trip, we studied and measured each other up and tried to be careful in our words and comportment. It was not hard to do. We were similar in our natures, and we were both beloved to Mama, so the obvious thing to both of us was don't screw this up.

Helene Kastinger Riley and Darius Ornston, Jr on their wedding day (1983).

Upon my return to Darius's house from my trip, the vibe was distinctly different. Not unfriendly or unwelcoming, but expectant. I went about my plan of signing up for the Air Force, and when the day showed up, I went downtown in New Haven to the recruitment site. We'd already done the preliminary work. I'd already taken, and scored highly on, the ASVAB test, the Armed Services Vocational Aptitude Battery, during my senior year, so that day I was to get my physical and sign the papers and literally wait for my orders. But the process was done very quickly. After the exam, the doctor said, "You know your hearing is atrocious?" and I was like, "Yeah, but I'm going to be around jet engines so that won't be a problem, right?" He laughed and told me I'd failed to pass muster. I went out and got my one free Air Force meal in the cafeteria and headed back to the house and an uncertain future.

While I was deciding what to do next, and decision-making was something that had never been a strong point for me, Darius put me to work. There was snow shoveling to do on his lengthy and steeply sloped driveway. Leaf-raking and wood-piling and stone-moving tasks followed. But what we finally settled on and settled into was me painting the interior rooms of the house. Darius was not a harsh taskmaster, but he had high expectations, took pains to do things correctly, and was persnickety. Again, that Philadelphia Quaker work ethic and his demanding father showing up in him. Mama had almost refused to marry him based on his religious background, because the only Quaker she knew before him was Richard Nixon. He was able to convince her that Nixon was not a great exemplar of the Quaker way. So he bought the different brushes and grits of sandpaper and spackle and then showed me precisely the level of exactitude that he would accept. Relative perfection. I quailed a bit at the imposition of values that were not my own, but I was a slow and careful worker, despite rarely having ever been forced to work, maybe because of that, and I set to work resolutely.

It was clear to both of us later that this shared project, this compact of work, was when Darius began to love me, and I him. Day by day, I would set the drop cloths carefully to protect the floors, tape the windows and moldings to prevent paint runs, spread spackle to fill the dents and divots on the walls from the decades of daily living, sand them when dry to a satin-smooth texture, and paint the study, the living room, the upstairs bedrooms, indeed much of the lived-in spaces. I used careful dips of paint; I rolled and brushed out errant excesses of paint. I did a yeomanlike job. Darius gave me regular, but not effusive praise. He examined my work daily, pointed out mistakes for me to fix, and told me when I had done something particularly well. We got the work done, and, as it turned out, the work was not painting so much as building a strong bond of father and son. Something new for both of us.

While I was painting, I was also mulling my options. What next? I had been convinced for a while that I would go into the armed services precisely so that I wouldn't have to answer that question; for at least a few years I would be told what to do and when and how to do it. A life without the necessity of thinking for myself. If I'd known about the Peace Corp, I would have jumped at the idea, but I wasn't qualified yet, without an undergraduate degree, in any event. In high school, I had applied to work on trails for the Youth Conservation Corps and, inspired by a vapid performance at a spring assembly, tried out for the Up With People program, so I was obviously a young man searching for structure. Just as obviously, though, I couldn't paint Darius's house forever. I searched around for clues. Ever the impatient one, my mom got tired of hosting me in her fabulous new life, because what was the point of raising your kids to adulthood if you didn't get to be apart from them? She gave me an ultimatum, that I could either get a job at the local grocery store and start making some money, or she would pay my way to go to a college I could get into. I sent out applications to the few universities that might accept me.

I got rejected by the University of Washington and the University of Connecticut. I didn't apply to my relative hometown school of Southern Connecticut State College in Hamden, but I did get accepted into the University of Arkansas at Little Rock and Washington State University. For years afterward, I got literature from UALR, and their loyalty and need warmed my heart, for no one had ever competed so diligently for my heart, my dollar, my choice, as they had. I decided upon Washington State and made preparations to leave for an intermediary destination to live for a summer in Key West with Jesse, who was living his best life in our southernmost American city, running for hours each day nearly naked through the streets and supporting that habit by working in the hospitality industry.

When I left, I called Darius my dad. It felt natural to do, was fitting, and pleased both of us. He wasn't the first father figure that I would often find myself searching for, and he wouldn't be the last, but he was and would remain my second dad. He enjoyed receiving the title as much as I did bestowing it.

Pullman, Washington, Sagebrush Navy, 1984

When I came back to Pullman for college, it looked different. There's something to be said for going places and doing things and making decisions based upon what you want to do, with your input and choice, as opposed to just tagging along or being dragged along. From two years of high school, I knew that Pullman was more than just a sleepy little wheat town with the state agriculture university. I liked that there were four seasons and few bugs. I liked that it had a small-town rural vibe, but it also had access to the arts and culture and entertainment that universities brought with them.

After crashing out of my planned military service and using up my allotted time with Mama and Darius, I got an acceptance letter from Washington State University and started my undergraduate education. I had already exchanged many letters of correspondence with the admissions department over my status as an in- or out-of-state student, so when I showed up one day to the French Administration Building and went in to argue my case, it was an open question which way it would go. Fortunately for me, it was 1984 and there were real people to talk to. I had an appointment. I met with a university admissions representative and discussed my time in town, how I'd left to travel the world, and had always meant to return and attend this fine place of higher learning. They said, "Okay. That sounds about right. Now go to this floor and that office to get this done. And then go to this office on that floor to get that done." And I did. I was in. Over the next five years at the university, I'd always remember those interactions and hold a warm place in my heart for an institution where you could talk your way into an education you could afford. My tuition that semester was $690.

On the day we picked up class schedules at different parts of the athletic complex, there were thousands of young people crowding out into the late summer sunshine, and every organization on campus had a table or poster set up or various eye-catching displays to lure new meat to their cause or group. The most impressive of these was a sixty-five foot long, wooden eight-person rowing shell. I'd known a little about crew from being in New Haven, at least in the same town as Yale's famous rowing squad, but it was a surprise to me that there was rowing in landlocked Pullman. They even called themselves the Sagebrush Navy and rowed thirty miles away on the Snake River. The wooden lacquered boat, a thin splinter of speed, complete with sliding seats and tulip-shaped oars, called out to me as much as the oarsmen, who waved me over and gave me the spiel. There was history and beauty and craftsmanship in the tools of this trade that spoke to me with loud immediacy. I took the paper that had the signup meeting information and didn't throw it away like the others that were shoved into my face by other enthusiastic young hucksters.

My dorm room was basic. The skinny room on the fifth floor of Streit Hall looked out over the Mooberry Track and Fieldhouse, two desks and storage closets mirror-imaging each other, and two twin bunks on casters so that they were couches by day, with room to unfold your legs without kicking your roommate's bunk, and by night swung out so that there was about twelve inches between the beds. If I'd had a coach who told me, Hoosiers style, "I want you so close that you can tell me the flavor of his chewing gum," I could have told him Stuart chewed Juicy Fruit. Stuart was a good guy, a military brat from Oak Harbor, and we got along pretty well because we didn't spend much time together. The room wasn't big enough really to hang out, and I didn't do much studying, so we would have breakfasts together sometimes and neither of us had any bad habits or hygiene issues that were deal-breakers. We shared the room that first semester and then went our separate ways with a warm, if vague, remembrance. My kind of roommate.

I had wanted to be a forest ranger for as long as I could remember, so in my first semester I took Forest and Range Management, Chemistry 101, and the general university-required classes that my advisor helped me choose. I had an English class and PE and whatever else gave me enough credits to start, and I was instantly amazed by the ease of the schedule.

Time off during the day! Tuesdays and Thursdays almost free of any entanglements whatsoever! It was not the public-school grind that I'd experienced in elementary and secondary schooling. My chemistry class at Pullman High had been rigorous, and I would have bombed it completely if not for my lab partner, Vu Duc, who shepherded us through all of the difficult procedural steps and rule-following that I was incapable or unwilling to do. Chem 101 was easy in comparison, and after doing well in my forestry class too, I was confident that I could do the science of forest rangering. I got to skip English 101 based on my SAT scores, the first class I'd ever tested out of in a good way, and the one I took instead was a favorite of that semester. Reading books and dashing off first final drafts of essays was what I was born for, and suddenly I had things to say about the literature and a voice to say them with. I was liking this college thing.

It was good that my academic schedule was going smoothly, because I had a new passion that was taking every bit of my free time. I had dutifully gone to that first rowing organizational meeting and was surprised to see someone I knew. Up on the stage in front was the familiar, unmistakable, six-foot-seven-inch, three-hundred-pound frame of Ken Struckmeyer. He'd been our first neighbor and, along with his wife, Marge, the first Pullmanite I'd met when I first arrived in town. After the blah blah blah requisite with every information meeting, I went up and introduced myself as his one-time neighbor and was immediately taken by his charm and humor and kindness. I had always looked askance at organized team sports and had a deep distrust of coaches and police officers for the same reasons, in that inflicting pain and disrespect in equal measure seemed part of their jobs. Struck wasn't like that at all. He was a self-deprecating gentle giant who wore loud wide ties and mismatched socks. He was a landscape architecture professor, and as such, he was a part of a grounded and creative academic discipline that might embrace some of his nontraditional behavior.

A few days later, I found myself waiting in a crowd of sixty or seventy people at the meeting spot, a concrete wall outside of the anthropology lab, where the rowers gathered every day at 3:30 to board dilapidated vans and drive the thirty-five minutes down to Boyer Park on the Snake River, right below Lower Granite Dam. After a few hours on the water, getting slugged in the back by a new rower's errant oar, and splashing ourselves into a sodden mess, we'd head back to campus just in time to stack plate after plate of food from the dining hall onto the table in front of us before service closed at 7:00. I was 145 pounds of raw excitement and gung-ho true-believerness. The fervor I wasn't allowed to invest in the Air Force went instead into crew. It turned out that you don't have to hear very well to pull hard on an oar.

One thing you did have to have, though, was the ability to swim. Just like I'd made it through school without passing a math class, I'd managed to graduate childhood without the ability to swim. Coach made it clear that if I wanted to row, I had to learn. My second semester, I took a PE beginning swimming class and threw myself into mastering the skills of dog paddling and treading water. My swim teacher was a sweet guy who knew he was dealing with oddballs if they were adults who didn't know how to swim, so when I asked him, "Can I use earplugs? Swim goggles? Nose Plugs?" he finally answered with a bit of exasperation, "Just plug all of your holes, already, Riley!" Once I'd got that settled, I lost some of my fear of water and drowning and managed to pass my test at the end of the class, treading water for fifteen minutes and getting my certificate. I didn't find that I needed the swimming skills much after all, because unless you're a terrible crew, most of your time is spent above the water. But on a few occasions, when we won a race and all jumped in after we tossed our Coxswain in or had a rambunctious dock sweep scrum on a hot day, where everyone grabbed a body and cleared the dock, it came in handy. On one memorable dock sweep, I ended up underneath Struckmeyer in the breakwater and had to swim for what seemed an eternity before I got clear of his big Wisconsin frame and saw sunshine again. I did my swim teacher proud that day.

The crew became an immediate outlet for everything I'd never been able to put into action. I became a monster workout machine. I worked diligently on technique and style and learning the rowing stroke and quickly became proficient. In rowing, we were nearly all of us doing something completely new, and I found myself on an equal standing with my peers. I made quick work of rising above. I had this huge group that I hung out with five hours a day, and it was just natural to fall into some powerful friendships. I hadn't found myself with a range of friendships before, usually soldiering through with one or two at the most, and even with those, light on the shared time and purpose. Here, after rowing together, we'd drink and party together, both firsts for me. We'd hang out on couches and drive around in cars doing absolutely nothing other than talking shit and listening to music. It was all a new and exciting and rewarding glimpse into the world I'd been self-partitioned away from. And family. Every one of my friends had awesome parents, mostly because they weren't mine, and they all loved me. Again, because I wasn't theirs. Because we didn't have to.

That first semester Thanksgiving break, I'd been working hard and proving myself an up-and-coming prospect, and the O'Dell boys invited me home with them for the week since I wasn't going home. I'd never been into the North Cascades and the upper Columbia Plateau, so the scenery around their apple and pear orchard in Omak was stunning to me. Great blades of sheer rock walls surrounded us, mountains behind them in every direction, with a calm, wide river cutting through a valley mixed with a patchwork quilt of open sagebrush desert and verdant plots of fruit trees. It seemed like a Johnny Appleseed spaghetti Western wonderland to me, who'd mostly lived the suburban kid's life. Jess and Thad, my upperclassmen rowing buddies, took me around the farm's landmarks: the pear orchard, the oldest trees on the place and a solid spread of thick limbs that could be counted on to make a modest profit when the apples took a dip, and vice versa; the hangar, an old airplane and storage shed that housed owls and equipment and that stood tall and straight in a landscape prone to swaybacked and broken down abandoned structures; the warehouse, a cinderblock building where they stored produce from their diversified farm, whether it was bunches of dried baby's breath flowers from the previous summer or milled lumber from old apple trees that they'd pushed out with tractors after they'd failed to produce or old vehicles and implements used to scavenge parts from; the pond, set up on the western hillside in the trees, for skating in winter and swimming in summer; and the old house where their migrant workers sometimes stayed and kept goats in the basement.

Winter was the one time around the orchard when there wasn't a lot to do, so we would get up late and hustle downstairs to the smell of Madre's fried bread. We'd slather it with butter and homemade raspberry jelly and then tuck into the second breakfast she was preparing for the houseful of family and guests. Carol and Al, Madre and Padre, always showed up to our races with boxes of apples for us rowers, and they had a soft spot for wayfaring waifs and strays like me. The kids with an upside that were used to being castaways and misfits. The O'Dells liked a project, and I wore that label directly across my forehead. Me and the boys would go for runs on the lightly traveled county roads and drive around exploring towns and points of interest around us, but mostly we sat near the fire and played cards. The game was No-Trump, in which you tried to predict how many tricks you'd take and, if the cards were good, shoot the moon and try to take them all. We played for hours and hours. It was another new experience for me, sitting around a table with friends, competitive play and compelling rivalry, and just wasting hours together. If I was used to wasting time, it was with reading and it was always alone. This was different. I quickly realized that I hadn't come visiting the O'Dells because I wasn't going home, but I was visiting to learn what home was. And I'd found a good one.

Something I immediately noticed in my second semester was that classes weren't as easy as I thought. While I did well in Chem 101, in 102, suddenly, there was completely new and difficult material, and I floundered again as I had in high school. With some input from my advisor, upon fully realizing that forestry was a science and not just walking in the woods and writing down my thoughts, I took the Frost and Thoreau road instead and changed my major to English. I immediately knew it was the right choice. Even if I didn't always do well in my classes, far from it, I was buoyed by the knowledge that it was my effort and strong skills, not a deficit in logic or scientific reasoning, that determined my grades. I was also needing this curricular cure because rowing was taking up every bit of energy and effort and thought process in my life.

I threw myself into the crew life with every bit of untapped athletic and religious fervor that I had stored up throughout my nineteen years. Suddenly I was weightlifting, using light weights and high reps, three times a week at five in the morning. Conditioning with winter workouts or on the water later in the spring for four hours a day. Running up the three-mile eight-percent grade after practice or running eight to ten miles out toward the river before practice. Sometimes Struckmeyer would put the van in neutral and we'd push him and his van up the steep hill. When we moved into our new shell-house above the dam at Wawawai, we rowed six eight-oared shells up the Snake River into the locks of the Lower Granite Dam. We started down below, oars locked and all eights side-by-side and began to float up in the giant concrete canyon looming above us. After twenty minutes, the gates opened and we were suddenly in a big lake and rowed the last couple of miles to our new building. The change was a huge one for our team. Instead of rowing in a quickly moving current below the dam, now we had flat and calm waters almost every afternoon. On race mornings, though, we often faced choppy water and wind gusts that we were unfamiliar with. Not a great recipe for success. The shell-house was physically much bigger, the parking lot at the Corps of Engineers breakwater more than sufficient for all our vans and the vehicles of the upperclassmen, the docks were capacious. It was so much more than just a venue change. We felt like we were hitting the bigtime.

We had rowing ergometer tests in the WSU Fieldhouse, the results of which helped make the decision about what boat you made it into. I was skinny, six foot and 145 pounds, but I made the first Frosh boat on my rowing and tenacity. After every two-thousand-meter erg test, I'd roll onto the hard, rubberized indoor tennis court floor and get myself to a trash can to barf my guts out. It was a physically and mentally taxing task, and I loved it. Our Frosh coach was Kash Van Kleef, a former rower not much older than us. Kash was a real redneck country boy, crude and intimidating and funny as hell. He would follow our shell on the water in his little putt-putt Thomas the Tank Engine leaky coaching launch, all the while spitting tobacco juice over the side and telling us to keep our dicks over the keel.

We worked hard, learned to row with fair precision, and had some modest successes. At our final meet of the year, the PAC 10 Championships on Lake Natoma in Sacramento, we won the third heat and got shirts off the backs of the crews we'd defeated. The huge USC freshman who gave me his sweaty double-XL shirt looked down at skinny little me, and I could tell he was thinking that, maybe, this wasn't the sport for him. I, on the other hand, had the conviction of a true believer. I'd been sanctified.

The next three years were full. In the mid-eighties, the choice of most English majors at Washington State for favorite author was Stephen King, and I was more of a James Joyce kind of guy, so I mostly hung out with my crew friends. My roommates, my band of brothers rowers, all of the crew women who got me through my romanceless years on friendships and hugs, the father-figure coaches, rowing was an instant and all-absorbing life choice. One-stop shopping for a kid intent upon growing into an adult. I had some amazing teachers who inspired me, like Bruce Anawalt and Alex Kuo. I loved Bruce so much that when he died years later in 2013, I visited him in the funeral home viewing room during a lunch break from my work at the nearby middle school. I had expected family to say hello to and exchange pleasantries with, but it was just me. And him, on a tabletop. So instead, I had a conversation with him, ranging from how much he'd taught me about the milk of human kindness in Shakespeare class to his lesson on "not peaching on a fellow" from our study of Joyce. Professor Kuo introduced me to writing poetry, and introduced me to my classmate, Sherman Alexie, and I felt like a real adult in his classroom. It was not the English class for video-gaming, Stephen King reading students, but real people who loved words and sought to use them powerfully. We went out drinking after class and after poetry readings, and it was the education that I'd thought college could be.

Along with my great learning experiences, those classes that helped me determine who I would be in the rest of my life, there were the maddeningly boring and calcified literature and composition classes where the professors and I shared our mutual contempt. There was the professor who told me I couldn't write an essay about a mouse, because the reader didn't care about such a common thing. I needed to choose a more charismatic animal, one that would inflame the reader's compassion and imagination. I'd broken the body of this individual mouse in a mousetrap and then, because I hadn't quite killed it, left it to die in a deep depression in the snow outside of my apartment. I'd heard from Jack London in "To Build a Fire" that freezing to death was painless, and although I hated mice as a broad category, individually they were pretty darned cute. I was full of remorse for what I'd done. When I refused to make the change, I took my grade and wore the F from that class with pride.

Although it always seemed an odd turn of events to me, after a childhood in the care of an alcoholic father and having never had a beer even all the way through high school, I drank way too much in college. With my inclusion in the rowing social scene, suddenly there were parties that included shot-gunning beers, beer-bongs, Jell-O shots, and Ouzo-themed dinner gatherings. We would go across the border to Moscow, Idaho, where the drinking age was eighteen, and I could always be goaded into trying to drink a full pitcher of beer. I would get close to a full-chug, I would feel the pressure inexorably building, and then I foamed-out all over the sawdust covered floor. After that, I was the wasted plaything of my buddies for the rest of the evening. My good friend Scott, our coxswain, said I was like that lyric in "Johnny Come Home" by the Fine Young Cannibals: "What is wrong, in your life, that you must get drunk every night?" That, and on one memorable occasion, waking up in a friend's kitchen naked except for my pissed-wet tighty-whities, gave me pause. It didn't stop my drinking, though. That behavior was surely part of the decision that kept me out of the Varsity Light eight as a sophomore, when my height, ergometer scores, and rowing put me right in the mix of the top four Starboards. The character factor, which Coach took into account in conversations with his veteran rowers, mattered. I kept drinking, kept outworking every one of those four guys, and held the grudge. I suffered in the awful Junior Varsity Heavyweight eight instead, probably the slowest boat we had on the water, and I paid for my sins.

My sophomore year summer, I went down to stay in Pittsburg, California, with my good friend Rodney, a fellow lightweight and a happy-go-lucky ne'er do well who matched those qualities with mine. For a few years, we accomplished almost nothing in our times together except make a bond that lasted a lifetime. We'd get into his green '69 Chevy Camaro and descend into "The Rod Zone," cruising to the Beastie Boys and burning cheap gas in a purposeless drive to nowhere in particular. Rod's parents were beautiful people. Argust and Louise were good, God-fearing folks from Oklahoma, and they walked the world lightly. They didn't court drama or find fault but spoke little and did quiet good works. Louise introduced me to chocolate gravy on biscuits, which alone earns her a spot in heaven if God ever asked me for references. The hot butter, milk, and chocolate pudding ladled over fresh biscuits was unlike anything I'd experienced before—and was proof that miracles still existed. Argust would sit in his La-Z-Boy chair in the mornings and yell upstairs in his quiet voice, "Rodney Brian, get up!" Louise and I would be at the table, both of us getting ready for work, and those two would call and response for a good quarter of an hour. "Rodney Brian, I said get up now!" They were the only words I ever heard him say. He was a deacon at his church and an electrician by trade, and a beloved man in both of those capacities. He was curious to me, because I couldn't imagine a man with so few words, but he was a sweet old guy. When Rodney and I had money, we'd get out and go make some noise.

I was penniless, which was a drag on our social life and friendship, so I quickly got a job at a Togo's sandwich shop and settled into East Bay life. "The 'burg" was working class and gritty, and my coworkers and our clientele at the sandwich shop were the same. I was a bit of a novelty as a college kid, but my childhood had imbued me with the superpower of being able to fit in anywhere, and I was equally unintimidated by friends in low or high places. People were people, and we mostly got along. We would get crushed at lunch every day, four or five of us on the line making hot pastrami, meatball, cold cut subs in a dizzying rush until we slowed a bit and could breathe and talk again. I learned to slice five-gallon buckets full of onions, alternating goggles, a piece of bread stuck in my mouth, and other hacks to avoid crying my eyes out, and even if they generally didn't work, I was experiencing another helping of that Everyman experience that taught me to respect work and workers.

Unfortunately, I was weighing down my college transcript with too many prideful Fs. My junior year, after I'd finally cracked the first Lightweight Eight, our team's fastest and most competitive boat, I got my report card and had a 1.55 GPA. I was stoked. Lightweight rowers needed to weigh in at below 160 pounds and average 155 pounds among the eight oarsmen, so I figured that I was a lightweight in mind and body. I photocopied my report card and sent it proudly to friends and family. Not my mom, though, because she was paying for it, and I felt bad for her. My teammates didn't find it so funny either, after the initial shock and laugh. I was putting my boat and fellow rowers and my rowing career in jeopardy.

Michael, Dave Reeder, and Thad O'Dell rowing hard (1986).

I was disenrolled numerous times for my poor grades, a result of my poor academic work habits, but each time, the English department secretaries would pull strings and reach outside the chain of command and get me re-enrolled on their own. Nellie and Ruby saw something of value in me and, though frustrated like everyone else at my lack of classroom resolve, wanted me to finish this course of study that I'd started. They kept me in school when I couldn't do it for myself. Sort of the anti-Mrs. Houda from Yale, they were both kind and willing to take a chance on me just because I was a nice young man who was flailing and failing to thrive in the classroom. I learned from them that secretaries rule the world, and if you want to go anywhere and be proud of yourself when you get there, look to those people for help who do the important work of caring. I learned that seniority and degrees and standing, while they have their place, were less necessary for my success than the hard work of compassion from a caring office staff. I owed those ladies, and when I graduated, I brought them bouquets of flowers and my effusive thanks. I introduced them to my parents. I owed them a debt of gratitude that I could offer, but couldn't repay.

My real education, my major, my calling, was the rowing team. It's hard to put all of the hours and effort and beauty into words, but I guess that's true of every sport. For me, the sport was an amalgam of experiences that propelled me forward (or backwards, if we're being honest to the sport). The dumb workouts like pushing Struckmeyer in his Chevy van for miles up the steep grade after a hard two-hour practice. It was the five-mile pieces, staggered starts for the eights, as we rowed steadily into the coming darkness, the oarlocks thunking in unison as we finished a stroke, moving closer to the Heavy eight, the open water between us growing ever smaller, hearing Scott yell to us, "I've got their stern! Give me ten now!" and we'd move. Someone in the other boat, Bobby, maybe, yelling, "Let's GO!" while our coxswain chanted, for us and for them, "I'm on their Stroke! Six seat! Four!" and we stayed low, strong, inexorable, savage with the joy of eating them up and putting them behind us. Rowing was so many losses and those few sweet, memorable wins. It was a sport that taught me I had worth.

One Christmas break, we all headed to Mama and Darius's home in Greenville, South Carolina, to spend the holidays together. Mama was indisputably at the top of her game after a lifetime of being edgy and ruthlessly busy, producing manuscripts, art, and children, and now, free from insecurity, she had an unmistakable sense of relaxation and happiness around her. She lived in a beautiful home surrounded by urban forest, her work at Clemson University was set and settled and rewarding, and she and Darius were deep into the shared partnership that was the love of their lives. We went shopping at the mall, walked around the Furman University campus, rode around on Mama's souped-up, highway legal Honda scooter, her Vespa days long gone, and ate a lot of good food. Everybody was getting used to the new me: confident, strong, more outspoken. John challenged me to an arm-wrestling duel, and it turned out to be not much of a competition. I was 150 pounds and was bench-pressing 210 pounds. I could do pull-ups until I was bored and had the wings above my ribs to prove it. I put him down quickly, and I felt a joy and lightness and forgiveness about him. Now that I could beat him, I no longer felt the need to beat him. I put him back in the past with the rest of my childhood I didn't want to remember, and it was well with my soul.

Helene and Darius in love (nd).

Junior year, after a few short-term attempts that proved how unprepared I was for the world of women, I had a girlfriend for the first time. Pam was a Kappa and a rower, and we were unlike other couples I knew. I always expected that couples made out and had sex, and that was a real factor in the short-term nature of my previous relationships. Pam was six foot and tanned Californian, laid-back and uptight both, from a fabulously wealthy family, and I was a good-looking boy to wear on her arm at a winter formal or a lake cruise while drunken debauchery occurred all around us. I was as far from a Greek system boyfriend as it would be possible to find, but the girls in the house liked me because I was nice and didn't make demands on them or Pam. I was safe enough that they'd let me go on the second floor, which I think was kind of an unusual honor. They'd yell up "Boy on Second!" and anyone not clothed would know to get out of the way or cover themselves. I learned that a girl in a towel was my ultimate icon of longing. But Pam and I were chaste. We hung out, snuggled on chairs and loveseats, and were somehow, tenuously, connected. At one point she told me, "You know you're not marriageable material, Mike." I laughed, a bit hurt and quite a bit incredulous. "I know, Pam. But I'm pretty sure you're not supposed to say that." We were mocking, companionable, and friendly, and while I was a bit confused by the arrangement, I was a willing partner and we had good times.

The summer of my junior year, I went down to Palo Alto to spend the summer with Pam and her parents. My summers were always free, and I kind of tumble-weeded in the direction the wind blew and where offers came from. Pam offered and it was back to California for me. It would be hard to find two experiences more diametrically opposed to each other culturally and socioeconomically in Pittsburg and Palo Alto, though they were both East Bay San Francisco and only miles apart. When I met Louise for the first time, she fed me chocolate gravy. When I met Pam's mom for the first time, we had to work out how I should refer to her. We went out to lunch at Chili's, a place befitting my stature, and I asked her if I should call her Jean. She said absolutely not. By the end of the lunch, talking through the exploratory meal of establishing norms, I was convinced repeated reference to Mrs. Ware was too formal, too bulky, and she'd already made it clear that her first name was off-limits. When she told me that her grandkids called her Ma 'mere, a kind of French improvisation on Grand-mere, I settled on that as an option. She found that acceptable. Mr. Ware was quite a bit more familiar and quickly told me I could refer to him as Leo. With the Wares I was going to have to find that third way, the creative path of me being me, but with intellectual and etiquette modifications, to navigate their particular niche of northern California royalty.

The Ware and Friedenrich Law Firm was an early Silicon Valley tech law firm, posh and respected and busy. My work venue was originally the mail room, that stereotype of the corporate personnel dumping ground. I was there a few weeks, sorting and hauling and delivering, and then moved up to the photocopying center. There I worked with a wonderful older

Latino boss for a few weeks who gracefully showed me the ropes of the office and then retired. I was still in the bowels of the building, a point shown clearly the day we had an earthquake, and with no windows for context, I just thought it was a momentary dizziness or my imagination. Something I ate, maybe. But there were important documents passing through, thousands of pages that needed quick and careful compilation, and I did it without problems. I'm sure Leo was checking on me, and I'm also sure I was passing muster.

Work at first was just putting the hours in and getting a paycheck, but it quickly became a big part of my social life, too. There was a paralegal softball league, and I was invited to join. It was low-key and fun competition with other law firms in Palo Alto, and afterwards, there was food and drinks at local restaurants all on the company tab. I was a happy boy. The firm sponsored cultural events, and I got to go to museum openings and concerts and hang around with young, smart, ambitious people. This level of business was new to me, and I was quickly disabused of my impressions of Uncle Pat's wealth. Here was real money, powerful connections, and a conduit to the halls of power. Luckily, I didn't have that ambition gene, so I was satisfied if my copies were correct and I held my own on the softball field.

I had a small room off the kitchen at the Ware home, a comfortable little nook that felt like a posh cupboard under the stairs Harry Potter arrangement, and I enjoyed myself immensely. For the elder Wares, I was a bit of a plaything, an oddly intelligent and well-educated, strongly open-minded, informed, Southern white trash, handsome young man. I was a thing new to their experience. I was used to the role of entertainer, something I'd done in childhood with my more powerful peers, and I liked being the jester. As the summer wore on, I earned my way into their affections and respect, and with people of their caliber, that was something to be proud of. Leo had done photography work in the Southern Civil Rights movement as a young University of Washington Law student, and he was a quintessential curmudgeon and good guy. He told me, "Michael, never trust a young Republican or an old Democrat." I understood that as wisdom. Ma 'mere came from an influential high society family in Santa Barbara, and she had a sharp and cutting wit. She suffered fools lightly. The list of organizations she belonged to and programs she funded as a philanthropist was lengthy and impressive. She was a woman of substance and a wicked foil to Leo's confident bombast and pithy sensibility. She told me, "I married Leo for his money, and he married me for my connections, and we've both been disappointed." I understood that as the tongue-in-cheek word of God. By the end of the summer, I loved them both more than their daughter.

After that second semester of junior year, I finally became academically ineligible and was unable to row my senior year. I liked and respected our faculty advisor, Ken Abbey, for whom the new shell-house was later named. He was a Husky and had disqualified my lightweight crew on the best chance I had to win a University of Washington rowing jersey. He called me into his office in the finance department in the administration building and had an exasperated, one-sided conversation with me. "I don't know, Riley, if you're the dumbest smart guy I ever met, or the smartest dumb guy, but you'd better pull it together." I was letting people down, and if not burning bridges, limiting my ability to move forward. I ended up learning to row a single and competed as an independent in several races and called that the end of my rowing and undergraduate career. It had been a good run. I was ready to move on and be done with school, all of it, once and for all.

In 1989, five years after I'd started at Washington State, I became the youngest and the first kid in my family to graduate from college. Schatzi had dropped out of high school and joined the working world that fitted her better, and when she got her GED, I was super proud of her. John had been at various colleges for a decade or more, and had enough credits to fill three undergraduate transcripts, but no degree. Jesse had walked away from academics even though he was the most gifted student and had the highest IQ among the lot of us.

The brothers didn't show up, but Mama drove out from South Carolina and stopped over in Arkansas to pick up Schatzi. Papa made the trip from Little Rock on the bus. This occasion was a bigger deal than high school graduation, and the family rallied. I picked up Papa at the same bus station where I'd first rolled into town eight years earlier, and although his hair was lank and greasy, he seemed to have a hold of his faculties and was treated with kindness by my friends and their families all weekend long. It was the first time he and Mama had been in the same space in fifteen years, and they were polite and well-behaved.

Michael on the day of his college graduation (1989).

Schatzi had picked up a real rattlesnake head lapel pin on the long drive out, and I put it front and center on my gown, and I had a "Don't Tread on Me" smile and walk that verged on swagger. Rowing had made me strong in body and mind, completing the long course of college had given me confidence, and my family there, among my friends' families, gave me a sense of belonging. We attended a few parties and even took pictures to capture the day. Blessed normalcy. A great day in the life of the Rileys. I had new adventures planned. The door to my life was wide open. I felt good. Mama and Schatzi left the next day, and I took Papa down to the bus station and waited to put him on the bus. I gave him a kiss, thanked him for being present, and sent him on down the road, as I prepared to say my goodbyes and go down roads of my own.

But Papa had a sense of timing about him. An air and ability of extravagance and drama. He could rule and ruin a room at speed. A matter of weeks after my graduation, I'd flown up to Alaska to work a summer job in an isolated salmon cannery on the Yukon River. I was incommunicado except for the US Mail, and I started to get a slow stream of letters. Papa hadn't showed up in Little Rock after my graduation. Still no word from him. Then, a couple of months into my summer fishing session, an explanation: Papa had lost his control along the way and was picked up in Denver, found incoherent and bruised and without a wallet or identification. He'd been rolled and robbed of his money, identity, and his dignity. And me of mine, it felt, upon hearing the sordid tale. After all sorts of sleuthing and checking, Uncle Pat finally found his little brother incarcerated in the Colorado State Mental Hospital, where he'd been admitted as a kind of John Doe. He'd sent his man Friday, Robert, to pick him up and bring him home to Little Rock. I was enraged by and for him. I ranted to myself, so far away from anyone I knew.

"I put you on the fucking bus, Papa! I watched you being driven away! Christ, do I have to sit with you for two thousand miles to get you home safely? No one ever did that for me!"

I remembered the old State Hospitals, the way everything he had was stolen from him, the echo of shuffling feet in stock-issued hospital slippers in puke-green-painted hallways. I was mortified and mangled by the news, but eighteen of my twenty-four hours every day were taken up with gutting fish on the slime line, so I didn't have much recourse for mourning. I

buried my woes in cleaning coho, Chinook, and chum salmon,
a never-ending stream of cold silver flowing in front of me,
the heavy hammer-chunk of the de-header thumping along a
rhythm. Violence and things of beauty being made less than,
a recurrent subtraction that was a complement to my mood.

Part IV: Finding

The Palouse is a Big Lovely Lady

Like Marilyn Monroe
Dust devils kicking up her skirt
Or the Venus of Willendorf
Earth Mother and fertile fetish
She's chunky but funky
Large and in charge
Curvy and buxom
People far and wide stop
Passing through
And see those wavy hills swell
And swoon over the Palouse
"would you look at those!"

She isn't showy like the Grand Tetons
Who drew early trappers and wandering
Woman-less men
Fairly shouting to them, "Yes, they're real.
And they're spectacular."
No, she knows that beauty
Is more than skin deep: she shows beneath her slip

Of Hawthorne and brush and bunch-grass
The deep and abiding loess soil that drew pioneer men
To stop in their tracks
Get out of wagons and put down roots
They knew she was a volcano in the bedrock and
inspired
Passion born of fire and sculpted by floods and winds
into a farmer's wife's constant competitor.

But she's more than a tart
Not just childbearing hips and big round bottomland
But always a warm and loving spirit
She's a woman who in her old age would wear a caftan
Smother young nephews and nieces in love
and her expansive and perfumed bosom-hugs.
Her love is slow, and urgent and sustaining:
The Palouse isn't going anywhere in a hurry.

So, my love, throw a Fall quilt of tilled wheat stalks
Furrowed rows over your shoulders
For the Winter is soon coming
When down and ermine are called forth
And check that your emerald velvet dress of Spring is
hung
In mothballs and cedar hope until that season returns
For the summer sun will never stop shining on you
And you'll never stop changing
Our big, beautiful Lady of the land.

Sunshine Slough, Alaska, Slime Line, 1989

Immediately upon graduating, I hopped on a small plane to Seattle, transferred to a smaller one to Bethel, and a still smaller one to Emmonak, deep in the willow and tributary wilds of the Alaskan Yukon River outback. I'd heard about the fishing job from my rowing buddy, Jess O'Dell, and he put in a good word to the owner's son, Russ Bodey. It was a quick and simple transition. One of Sunshine Alaska's small skiffs, on the daily thirty-mile ride into town to pick up mail, collected me and dropped me at the small collection of corrugated tin buildings, ramshackle docks, boats driven up onto the shore, and the scattered shipping containers that passed for housing. One big gray fish-processing barge hugged the shoreline and overshadowed the settlement. This little flea of a community on the big dog river would be home for the next three months.

For the literature major and student of life that I was, the colorful collection of people that inhabited this space in the brief bright summer of salmon runs on the Yukon was unsurprising for me. Bill Bodey, the owner and unquestioned king of this muddy, mosquito-infested fiefdom, was an Alaskan archetype. With an eighth-grade education, a pronounced limp from a bad hip, and a snarled and scar-puckered mouth that poured out incomprehensible abuse when he was upset, he was the definition of the Old Salt. A millionaire in muddy rain-slickers. Duke and Irene, the septuagenarian couple who ran the cook shack, were kind and harried in equal measure, and fed us enough to put thirty pounds on my skinny frame in three months. Russ, the affable boss's son, was a calm and soft-spoken mirror image of his dad, and if Bill held us all in a thrall of near-constant fear, Russ had us charmed with hero worship. He was decisive, unfailingly kind, and could fix and do everything and anything in the camp better than anyone excepting, maybe, his dad. When there was an emergency fish pickup situation, Russ would hop on the Sunshine Ten, a huge flat-bottomed aluminum skiff with quad four-hundred horsepower outboards, more like the Miss Budweiser Hydroplane boat than a fish tender, literally the fastest boat on the Yukon, and he would get it done. Add in Native Alaskan and college kids, high school dropouts from the lower forty-eight and the part-owner Japanese fish masters, the only ones with access to beer in our dry part of the state, and we were a damaged and memorable group.

Once a fishing period opened, everyone waited nervously for the action to begin. Bill was on the radio nonstop, directing all of the fifteen fishing tenders to their variable destinations and usual pickup spots. Our tenders were World War II-era troop transport LCMs (Landing Craft Marine) with flat bottoms to bump over the Yukon's famous sandbars, and they had removable wooden-slat decks to carry the fish we bought from the local fisher people in the deep transport holds. In crews of two, the captains and deckhands drove their boats to their accustomed meeting places and anchored, waiting for the coming storm of activity where multiple fishing skiffs unloaded, fish in the hold were iced, and everyone worked at a frenetic pace until the fishing session timed out and everyone went back to their base camps. The folks on the slime line, like me, waited for the tenders to come in before getting bludgeoned by eighteen-hour shifts of gutting fish. We'd work around the clock, with short meal breaks and a few hours' sleep before a bullhorn and shake the bunks wakeup. Finally, the aluminum gate that let in fish from the hopper outside showed light around the edges that meant no more fish to clean. After a quick spray-down and a huge meal, we'd hit our bunks in the cargo containers for some uninterrupted hours of deep, exhausted sleep, before being roused awake to clean and do maintenance before it was time to clean fish again.

We had a company store there at Sunshine Slough, where our local fishermen could buy on credit from their catch, and it sold a little bit of everything, from mosquito smoke coils to pilot bread, tuna fish and condensed milk, nets and sweats. Backcountry merch and hardcore survival stores. If we had slow times, that's where I would hang out, on the bench out front, and talk with whoever came by. I was starved for social interaction and news from anyone. Some of the local Native girls that I worked the slime line with were pretty cute and full of sass, and there were always fishermen stopping by, so we'd sit and shoot the breeze and drink Duke's weak coffee and eat Irene's delicious leftover pancakes, which she slathered with butter and sugar and rolled into handheld snacks for us to eat in between her huge three square meals a day. One girl, in that slow and singsong Native accent that reminded me of the voices in Ireland, told me one day of how one of her sisters had doused a brother in Blazo, the ubiquitous starter fluid of the delta, and lit him on fire. "It was really sad." I didn't get a context for the story, and I didn't have a response, but it went a long way toward giving me a glimpse of how hard life could be out there in the villages and backwater sloughs where whole lives went up in flames without much attention or mention. Then a call of "Mukluk!" would come over the radio and the Native guys would pile into their skiffs and go off hunting seals. Life happened in short bursts.

I was sitting on that bench one day when a statuesque beauty, an Athena in Helly-Hansen gear, appeared out of nowhere and sat down next to me. She was built like a downhill skier, tall and big-boned, with an air of gravitas. Or, at least, gravity: she was a big girl. As soon as she spoke, I recognized her accent and asked, "*Sprecken sie Deutsch?*" *Ja.* "*Sind sie von Deutschland?*" *Nein, Österreich.* "*Ah! Meine mutter sind von Wien! Guten tag und hertliche grüsse!*" And there my German was done. She laughed at my middle school German. Her name was Liesl

Scherntanner, and I was smitten. She literally had appeared from nowhere, working in a fishing camp with a couple other guys in tents at the end of some deserted nearby slough, trying to make a killing in the salmon just like everyone else out there with the golden ticket of a fishing permit. We talked for an hour or more, and then she had to go. I never saw her again. For days and weeks and years afterward, I'd think back, remember that name, and smile. Wondering. Worrying for her and that summer on the Yukon. Sigh. What a girl she was.

I got along well with the Japanese contingent that worked with us on the slime line. Some years past Bill had sold part of his business to a Japanese company, and the rotating crew of four to six guys were the quality control element. One wore the steel mesh glove and worked the header, maneuvering the fish and pressing the pedal that took thousands of heads off salmon every day, for long hours at a time. I don't think anyone was fooled that that glove of his would save his fingers. A couple of the other men graded the fish by species and quality: King, Silver, Chum, and "Cannery" for the off-color and rank-looking specimens. They were then flash-frozen on trays and stored on site for shipping to Japan. And there was the boss man who checked our work, exhorted us to higher productivity when our efforts flagged, and gave us our cues to start and stop. "Q-K, Mikey," he'd yell, and hold his two hands together pantomiming breaking a stick. "Break!" And we'd hose ourselves off, hang up our waterproof kit, and go to the cook shack.

"Gohan and imo. Imo and gohan!" he'd laugh, and I would smile along sympathetically. Rice and potatoes, potatoes and rice got a bit dull after a while for all of us. Irene would take the freshest King salmon, a beautiful, big, sparkling Chinook that almost remembered breathing, it was so recently caught, and she'd cut the steaks and fry them hard on the big grill. Sushi grade fish rendered into a McDonald's Filet-O-Fish. It was a sin for me, but how much more so for those guys who prized it professionally and culturally. After I noticed the Japanese guys drinking on the deck of their shack, a marginally better housing arrangement than our shipping containers, I went up and asked how to ask for a beer in Japanese. I hadn't had a beer in a month on account of the dry county, no-alcohol status the government imposed on the mostly Native population, and I wasn't too proud to ask. "Birru arramasuka?" A laugh. "Birru. Ara-masu. Ka." Okay, "Birru-arramas-Ka?" "Sure, Mikey," and he handed me a cold beer. It was delicious in a way that weak coffee and hard-fried salmon could never be. I was thankful and grateful and polite. It wasn't my last beer.

Like in the military, mail call was a big part of the daily round. The boat that brought workers to camp also stopped at the post office in "Emo," and a group of hopefuls always greeted the returning skiff to get a sweet care package of illicit goods or just a postcard from someone they actually liked, unlike the people they were surrounded by at Sunshine. I was always a big letter writer, so I jumped into the initiative to get mail in the same way my brother Jesse would get his miles in on our front deck in Pullman. I wrote in any available moment. When the fish were in and I was working on four hours of sleep—and even that sleep was tortured by dreams of fish sliding by the foot of my bunk, me fingering out the thick bloodlines and yanking out the connected guts—I would have pen and paper at the ready for our twenty-minute breaks in the cook shack and write muddy-thought, rambling missals anointed with coffee stains and bacon grease and pancake syrup. Maybe they weren't my best work, but they had the genuineness and vulnerability of desperation, and I was repaid in kindness. I sent out a hundred letters that summer, more than one for every day, and come mail call, I was the envy of every lonely soul in camp. And that was everyone. I got thirty-three letters in reply, I counted, and that percentage of return mail made me happy. When some of the guys would ask me how I got so much mail, I would look at them with incredulity. "Dude! Do you see me doing anything but writing? Do your work if you want something." I wrote to rowing buddies mostly, and all of my family, even John, back when we could still talk to each other. Maybe even Papa, but I'm not sure about him; he moved so often that I never had a current address. And anyway, unbeknownst to me, he was locked up in the Colorado State Mental Hospital, where he landed on his way home from my graduation.

But social interactions aside, my time at Sunshine, Alaska, was all about the work. The slime line was all nasty drudgery, and that's why they had Native young folks and college students doing the work. The beautiful fish had their heads lopped off, had their bellies opened up, and then they cascaded in waves down to us to grip their guts and flush them into the channels of the big aluminum chutes, where they would go directly into the slough and into the Yukon. Sometimes, punch-drunk by a twelve-hour shift, we'd see daylight at the entrance gate where the fish came in, and we'd give a cheer. After finishing the remaining fish, someone would grab a handful of guts and put it down someone's slicker, and before you knew it, the air was full of flying fish entrails and whoops of exhausted laughter, and then, abruptly, we'd have to stop before one person decided to take offense and start a fight. We'd all clamp down quickly and stop our boisterousness, because Bill Bodey didn't take fighting or drugs or backtalk, and none of us wanted to get sent home early. The work was too tough to leave any of the money on the table. We worked terribly hard, had a little fun, and got our paychecks logged in the books.

Midway through the season, after staying and working and not being singled out for trouble, I was promoted to deckhand, and I got to leave camp for a while on a tender to go buy fish during the fishing period. Being on a barge pulling guts or sleeping in a container on the muddy banks of a bywater slough wasn't really being in Alaska. It was instead a kind of forced servitude. But once I got on the *Sunshine V* and we motored out of the tight willows and into the main channel of the great river, I really felt like I was in the place. I learned how to drop and pull up an anchor, how to navigate point to point in the wide expanse of the muddy river delta, how to lift and drop the big aluminum bucket into a small skiff without dropping it through the skiff and sinking it. I learned about carburetor starting fluid and tying off lines and the dark magic of mosquito coils. When we motored out and anchored at our pickup zone and cut the engines, it was quiet out there on the water. We'd swing gently in the current at the end of our anchor line and drink coffee and wait for the fisherman with catch to come find us. The liquid swirl and purl were calming. Sometimes a pod of beluga whales would pass by, their shiny white backs flashing in the muddy brown waters. Once a fisherman brought in a sixty-pound Chinook, itself as big as a baby whale, and I was awed by something that would have been commonplace a hundred years before. It was a whole lot of new experiences for me, and that's the way you pay a young person. After years of variations on the same thing, with school, school, and more school, Alaska was teaching me from a new curriculum I hadn't seen before. I appreciated the gift.

After some runs as a deckhand, I got the chance to captain a tender. The season was winding down, both in terms of the worker availability, with the end of the summer school break coming close, and the open fishing periods remaining. I probably wasn't quite ready to be in charge of the boat, but that was part of fishing on the river: you worked, learned, and left. You didn't get a lot of choices. My deckhand, a Native guy who'd grown up on a boat, was way more experienced and shepherded me through our few runs together. We motored out to the same route that I'd been on as a deckhand, so I knew the landmarks to steer on, where to pivot and mark a new course, and to always keep my eye on the depth meter. The river there was wide and shallow and mud brown, and it was nerve-racking to see the depth gauge reading go from thirty feet to ten to three feet and feel the hull bump over a sandbar. The Landing Craft Marine (LCMs) were refitted landing craft, so they had a very low draft—you could still skate over a bar in three feet of water. But there were plenty of places shallower even than that. I couldn't read the water well enough to avoid them, so when I got stuck, I got stuck good. It was tempting to just hit the throttle and grind on over the bars, which were often just small obstacles, but then you also ran the risk of seriously wedging yourself in and having to wait for the tide to shift either in or against your favor. No one kept their job if Bill had to come out and pull you off a bar. The deckhand counselled me to try reversing, and after a few hard pushes, we freed ourselves and completed the run. I learned to check myself and accept the knowledge of others. And that sometimes backwards is the way forward.

At the end of the season, when the midnight sun was finally tinged with longer periods of dusk and everyone except a skeleton crew had been sent home and the barge mothballed and readied for travel down to Dutch Harbor in the Aleutians, I was offered a ride-along as a frozen-fish nanny. It was a weeklong trip, and I was to provide backup for the engineer responsible for keeping all of the refrigeration units working. We had about the same accommodations as on shore: a storage container fitted out with a couple of bunks and some modest food stores and a table and chairs. For our meals, the tug would send back a little skiff, and we'd eat in their galley. Once we left the Yukon, the tug lengthened the tow rope until they were just a faraway speck on a big ocean. It was a new kind of isolation and loneliness, but I knew it wasn't much longer than a week's trip, so there was a time limit to the solitude. And the pay was good.

For a couple of days, the waves got so tremendously big and rowdy that we had to take shelter in the lee of Nunivak Island. I didn't get seasick, but the heaving of the big barge, loaded high with containers of frozen salmon was enough to make me dizzy and keep my curiosity to a minimum. I pretty much stayed inside and read, caught up on sleep, and wrote in my journal. The engineer would rope up when he went out checking gauges and fasteners and whatever else his job entailed. It was too rough to get to the tug for meals, so we ate pilot bread and trail mix and cereal for a couple of days. The few times I went on deck and looked at the sea and the island, I was struck with a real feeling of fear and intense aloneness. If you lost it out here, you were lost for good: solidly dead and not likely recovered for burial. It was sobering. So when we finally pulled into Dutch Harbor, it was a homecoming that every lost soul experienced showing up in their frontier civilization. We all went out and got drunk on the company dime. We avoided getting rolled and stabbed, which was exactly the lower boundaries of what we were supposed to do, so it was a successful mission. Fish delivered. When I woke up groggy and headachy the next morning, it was just the right state to help me deal with my last Alaskan adventure. The flight out of Dutch. The airport was situated on a short stretch of flat land in between towering mountains on either side. The runway was short. Our little twin-prop plane gathered speed quickly and jumped up as soon as it could, but you could still see trees and rock uncomfortably close to the belly and landing gear. Close enough to see individual branches. We made it, just like most of them do, and I was suddenly on my way back to the normalcy of the lower forty-eight and the land of decision-making. I had a check for twelve thousand dollars in my pocket and was ready to move on again.

I was in Seattle for a little while, a week or two perhaps, but the only part of it that I remember is meeting up with my best friend, Dave Reeder, and hiking with him up to the fire lookout at Dodger Point. Dave was a well-tuned hiking machine after a summer of backcountry rangering for the park service, and I was fresh off Duke and Irene's heavy and always-available fare and the couple hundred feet of Sunshine Slough's boardwalk that were my only walking options, so he hiked my ass off. I'd gained about thirty pounds in the process, and every step up the steep mountain I cursed his back. We'd been boatmates and competitors in crew, and getting beat by the cerebral head of our lightweight team wasn't a thing that came easy. We would be roommates for the first time in Boston in another month, and it was a simple test of our relationship to climb a mountain together. We reached the top, and there was a 360 view of forever over the Olympics. The Dodger Point ranger cabin was a square wooden structure with panes of glass in every direction, so the view for fires would be unimpeded. *Desolation Angels*, Gary Snyder's book of living in a similar lookout, was something we'd both read, and we enjoyed the companionable solitude of simple one-pot meals and coffee out on the benches at the top of the world. The hike and the destination seemed like a good omen as a harbinger of times to come. And if I had to say, "Fuck you, Reeder" after every step of the way down, too, my quads shaking and sore, I could leave it on the trail easily enough. He was a great friend.

Somerville, Next to the Star Market off Porter Square, Boston, Massachusetts, Wingtips, 1989

When I flew into Boston, I was a few days ahead of Dave, and we hadn't rented a place yet, so I had arranged to sleep on the floor at the apartment of a friend of my old girlfriend Pam's, who I'd met briefly in Palo Alto. Kristine and I had gotten along famously on those few occasions, poking fun at Pam's naivety and interesting worldview and connecting on art and literature and culture, as well as our shared sense of humor and reverence for a good sandwich. And our fondness for Pam. She was living with three or four other girls who she'd graduated with from Middlebury College, and I was so thankful and amazed that they would let me share their place without any obvious trepidation or concern. I was once complimented by an Episcopalian minister at the Village Cheese House in Palo

Alto for being "without guile." I guess I wouldn't put it past an education at Middlebury to give those girls a good guile-o-meter. Their place was right off Porter Square, and they were living right. They had a couple of floors of big rooms, good light, and roommates who could keep a place clean. The place and people had a kind of elegance that I wasn't used to from my time at Washington State, and I was charmed by it all. It was a great welcome to Boston and a quick shot of kindness from strangers, which was always coin of the realm and Balm of Gilead for me.

When Dave arrived, we quickly found and settled into a sketchy little rickety apartment that abutted the commuter rail tracks on one side and faced the Star Market down a short alley on the other. It was also near Porter Square, but not like Kristine's place, not the stylish part. We were within a short walk of Harvard's Divinity School, and you could see the nice neighborhoods from ours, but we were definitely on the edge and over the imaginary line of solidly working-class poor. When the trains went by morning and night, the walls shook vigorously. A marble dropped onto our living room floor rolled without pause to the northernmost wall. We tried it for laughs just because the slope was so pronounced. Our couch was big and overstuffed, covered with a carpetbag-like tapestry material, and we'd carried it a mile or so from the front curb of a house in a nice neighborhood, running the last few feet across the rails to beat a speeding commuter train. In our own way, we were representing our school about as you'd expect. I gave us some leeway because we weren't wealthy or girls, and so a few dust bunnies and some track-rattling were to be expected. Go Cougs.

Dave and I celebrated our new life with a few significant and symbolic gestures. We went out to a nice bar called the Chapter 11 and ordered a few drams of single-malt Scotch. I think it was a first for both of us, and the cache of Glenfiddich, the swank feel of an adult rite were a real bond for us. We were in Boston, of all places, and charting a new course for our lives in the famous city. I went by the Harvard Yard and walked the places my dad had walked in his own promising youth. On my Uncle Pat's advice, I stopped by the Union Oyster House, a place he had frequented in his Harvard Business days and sat at the time-worn oyster bar and soaked up the aged and present history. In Harvard Square, I bought a CD of Nat King Cole's hits and would revel in the languid rhythm and syrupy vocals. Listening to the old music was like bathing in a maudlin reminiscence of someone else's life. My father's. At a shoe store, firmly convinced that I'd soon be working in a law office or some similar job where I had to dress up each day, I bought a two-hundred-dollar pair of beautiful Cole Haan wingtip loafers. They ended up being too beautiful to wear, so I never did.

Part of my reasoning for moving to Boston was to be in the city of rowers and see if I could find a place for myself in that rank. After four years of rowing, I still had a chip on my shoulder about not winning enough races and shirts, not finishing that last year and claiming my spot in the Lightweight Eight, my introduction to sculling without mastering the boat. I had questions, and Boston, I assumed, had answers. I called up a few clubs and finally arranged to meet a coach and crew at the Union Boat Club one morning at 5:00 am. We met in the darkened shell house and went out onto the shadowed Charles River, rowing a four-man shell under a few of the famous arched bridges and scuffling through some rough pieces on the rough water. When we got back and put the boat and oars away and I jogged the few miles home in my wet clothes, I was struck by the thorough understanding that nobody in this rowing community needed me. There were rowers more accomplished than me by the hundreds, maybe thousands in town, and no one was going to be interested in my tale of rowing woes unless I spent years proving I was worth listening to. I don't know what allowed me to be so decisive, so remorseless with my premature dream ending, but it was a quick severance. The decision was immediate and final. And easy. Like the shoes I never wore for the job I'd never have, I gave up my future in rowing completely and without much undo thought. My first row in Boston was my last row.

⋘⋙

I had all of that Alaska fishing money in my bank account, but I always felt poor in Boston. When you have money going out and none coming in to replace it, it's an anxiety-inducing feeling, like watching a gas gauge wind down and you're nowhere near a filling station. I looked through the want ads and took the first position I was offered, working at a health food store on Mass Avenue in Cambridge. It was a terrible job. The drudgery was part and parcel of what grocery work is all about, so I could stand the futility of "fronting" all of the canned and boxed goods evenly on the shelves, the work of shamming unlimited supply and perfect abundance, the endless work of rotating perishables in the refrigerated section, following the helpful "Rotation makes the world go 'round" sticker, and checking in new orders from a seemingly endless bill of lading. I would find afterwards that I'd checked a box of organic refried beans as accounted for, but there were no organic refried beans to be found. That stuff, and the sweeping and cleaning, all of that was fine. I grew comfortable knowing where the product was on shelves and in aisles, learned the names of all the vegetables like kohlrabi and garlic scapes that I'd never heard of before, and even eventually learned all of the produce codes so I could run the checkout as smoothly as anyone.

What I finally learned as the particular source of the deep-seated anxiety of that workplace was that it was not a health food store at all, in the normal sense, but a vitamin and supplement store that also had some fresh food. Vitamins, in a word, were where the future of the health food industry lay, and there was a real push to force the supplements. They took up much of the aisle space, and the store layout channeled shoppers past gaudy labels and provocative signage. It was disconcerting to me and the others. Our manager, a stressed-out young guy who dressed like all managers everywhere, nicer than was needed, but not nice enough to actually be stylish, would let out his frustration by going into the walk-in cooler and screaming at the top of his lungs. The refrigerator hum and the doors masked the sound well, except for that one unfortunate time when an unsuspecting shopper reached in to grab some yogurt and got an earful, leading them to scream in response. It was a memorable scream, one unmuffled by double-paned glass doors or background white noise of refrigeration machines.

One of our checkers, an older African American gentleman, was positive to the point of desperation. I would walk in with an ordinary salutation of "Good morning" or "How's it going?" and would be startled by a forceful ejaculation of well-being. "It's a WONDERFUL day! I'm GREAT!" He would follow that with an equally enthusiastic reminder that, "I won't let Satan find me doing 'just alright' and having a 'so-so' day. No, Sir! I'm going to wear my armor of positive energy! God is GREAT! I'm GREAT!" I smiled and told him I was happy for him and went about my significantly less-great day. Luckily, neither his Satan nor the evil of the supplements religion ever got hold of me on a bad day. I was like those demigod heroes of old, mostly covered from mortality and immorality by being dipped in the waters of a happy and challenging pluralistic childhood. I did my work and got my paycheck.

Dave was working at a computer keyboard factory and sometimes substitute teaching science classes in area schools, so we didn't see much of each other. I once locked myself out of the apartment and, in the time before cell phones, managed to call him and work out a time to meet and let me in. I hung out at the nearby Dunkin' Donuts, and the time came and passed, passed and passed and passed. When he finally arrived, a couple of hours past the appointed time, I was furious. He was nonplussed. Dave had that really intelligent physics guy brain that could turn off regular emotions, and in times like this, it was infuriating. "Sorry, Michael, but I really can't feel bad about it. I was busy."

We really did get along well, though, and he was my best friend, but I stored that one away with some of the other slights we'd built up over the years. Like the time we'd been cruising Riverside Drive in Spokane in college and he'd gotten me a black eye. We were in line with all the shiny, tricked out high school rides moodily navigating the Friday night streets, the four of us rowers sunk deep into the Ford Nova's saggy old seats, and Dave yelled out his window, "Hey, buddy, what you got in there? A 357?" The high schooler was not amused, and when he came around the cruising loop, he was out of his car and at my window, which I politely rolled down. "What did you say about my car? You want to go a few rounds?" I laughed and said, "Where's the ring?" Before I could finish my thought, he'd clocked me hard and I was sitting way back, a big mouse forming over my eye. He started talking rudely to Stacey in the front seat and we all managed to get Thad, who was driving, to kindly move his chunky junk of a car. Next time, I was starting to think, someone else needs to get punched.

We didn't have much of a social life in the city, but we did have the apartment full of Middlebury grads nearby, and the girls were pretty awesome. They invited us over to a Christmas party, and their place was all lights and fresh greenery and beautiful. At our request, they came over and tried to install a similar vibe in our place. We bought cranberries and popped popcorn and strung them all on our tree, and it was a gesture that resonated and uplifted us all, bringing a bit of freshness to our stale old place. The city can be pretty lonely, and friends made it all better. Me and Dave would sometimes go out on the town, and Grendel's Underground in Harvard Square was a favorite bar of ours. We'd sip our expensive drinks and watch all the beautiful young people chat and parlay and engage in the sophisticated meat-marketry that seemed out of our reach. Not that we didn't know and want and try the dance, and not that we weren't beautiful ourselves, but the scene just crashed and cascaded around us, full of the sound and the fury and the "no soup for you" reality that Boston always seemed to be speaking plainly to me.

I did have some scoring opportunities. I know that it's crude and callous to term them as such, but I was in desperate straits and anxious about my seemingly forever virginal status and so let's call it what it was. One time I was set up by one of my coworkers with a rad and tattooed pretty market-seller who ran a booth down at Faneuil Hall selling incense and trinkets to tourists. We double-dated and all went back to her apartment, where I had the misfortune of sitting in a beanbag chair that had cupped a bladderful of her cat's pee. I cleaned up and my friend and her date went home. Even with the cat pee, it was a perfect scenario. I even knew the script. We kissed, she put on *Abraxas*, and we went to bed. She was luscious. I was stoked. And then I was unmade by my over-anxiousness and what I called in these situations, my morality-proneness, and the chance passed. However kind she was, my self-hatred was manifest. It felt like a failure and betrayal of the highest order. I was having a full meal of the many courses of young male shame and loathing, so, no, Boston wasn't going so well.

There has never been a time in my life when I didn't crave silence, and that year in Boston, it was hard to come by. On weekends, I'd ride the T all the way to the ends of the different lines and then turn back around to get dropped off at Park Street and walk the few miles home. Things to use up time without spending all of my money. But the noise and the eye contact after a while got so invasive, so omnipresent, it just about made me shut my eyes and go away. The hungry gaze in a bar felt different from the one on the subway, so I learned the thousand-yard stare for my time on trains. I spent a lot of time trying to get away from one thing or another. Once I stumbled on the cutest little French bakery and coffee shop off Harvard Square, right next to a grand old theatre we sometimes visited to watch vintage film noir like *The Thin Man* or *The 39 Steps*, and upon exiting with espresso and croissant, I found a small, green, walled garden to sit in. I was jolted by a burst of pure joy from the relative silence, comfort, and cessation. Exactly what I needed. After I had a moment to sit and settle in, the guys working on the street outside the walls broke out their jackhammers, and the moment passed. Boston often felt that way: a place that was almost made for me, but not.

I met another woman, out one night, and she was nice, tall, smart in the head and fashion sense, and she picked me up and drove me to her home in Concord. The home and she herself were a bit staid and old-fashioned, kind of like characters in the film noir movies, but she was beautiful and enthusiastic, and we were soon on the couch, kissing and twisting and turning in ways that made me laugh out loud when I saw the title of a chess book on her coffee table: *The Art of Positional Play*. She said that it was indeed what we were studying, and she led me to her bedroom. She was long and tall, and I seem to remember garters, or some such crazy things. And then, again, after rising, I had a failure to perform. A laying down of the King. Not much of a gamer, me. We slept the night, and she made me breakfast in the morning. She was desperate to have me stay, try again, and I was desperate not to shame myself again, to run away and get the commuter rail back home and wallow in my own meanness. I'd been a failure in the past, and I hated the sensation now. Not only in failing myself but failing others. I didn't like not being dependable, leaving people hanging, being irresponsible in holding up my part. I was twenty-four going on fourteen. The worst kind of insecure teenage boy in a man's body. What a mess.

Back at the health food store stocking the refrigerated cases, I saw on the back of a yogurt container some words that changed my life. I read about the biodynamic farm in upstate New York, the bucolic landscape and happy cows, and the offer of apprenticeships to learn their agricultural practices. I showed it to my buddy during our break, and she offered to drive me up to check it out. I called and they said, "Sure! Come on up! It's fall and our offseason, so we don't need apprentices right now, but come summer we'll have an opening." We drove West on I-90 across Massachusetts and then headed south on the Taconic Parkway, through green pastures and wooded verges and maple and oak forestland. When we got to the farm, it was a virtual colonial village, one main street dominated on one side by the rounded stucco architecture of the Waldorf School and, on the other, by a centuries-old three-level dairy barn and farm store. We got a tour of the market garden, the barn, an overview drive by of the four hundred acres of pasture, and then we stopped at the farm store and had lunch. We two health food store employees were awed by the fresh produce and cheeses, the farm-baked bread, the warmth of the building and the workers. It was what we might have visualized when we first started our job at the vitamin store.

Lastly, we toured the bunkhouse, the rooms over the dairy where the apprentices lived. It was a long hallway littered with rubber boots and rain-slickers and pallets of empty pristine yogurt containers. At the end was the common room and kitchen, and we talked to a couple of the apprentices on their two-hour lunch break. They were dirty, bright, and businesslike, because on the farm you had to hustle to rest, but they made a good impression. Apparently, I did, too, because Steffen the farmer offered me a job starting in the summer. We drove back to Boston listening to *Sweet Baby James* describing our road trip scenery and *Alice's Restaurant* telling us the wisdom of traveling and living and working in the rural Northeast. There was no *Abraxas* or *Art of Positional Play* or any tension, but instead just two people learning and experiencing and leaving sex the hell out of it. Or what I always called me being at my best. The friend thing.

Back in Boston, everything felt changed. Like my plans for traveling in the UK out of high school, the military career I thought would last longer than a morning of tests and a free lunch, the five years of college less so, and the three of rowing more so, the idea of having a place to go and work, to be told what to do was a freeing concept for me. And now I had another lined up. A two-year agricultural apprenticeship in Upstate New York to give me time to figure out the answer to what new thing I would be doing with my life. I could lean in and rest into that commitment. Dave was also applying for different work and scored a counselling gig at a camp on Cape Cod, which fit in better for him with teaching and outdoors work than the keyboard factory. Work was less stressfully unfulfilling, and Dave and I coexisted with ease and an appreciated lack of drama.

We didn't see each other that much with our different work schedules, but we'd go across the street to Jimmy Mac's and get incredible barbecue, hit the Star Market for shopping, and hang out with the Porter Square girl gang from time to time. We were settled in and running on autopilot, each of us with future plans outweighing our current underperforming lives.

I took a stab at a more traditional romance and asked one of the Porter Square girls out on a date to see *The Nutcracker*. Leslie, or "The Fair Leslie" as I always called her in my head, had curly waves of blond hair, a true peaches-and-cream complexion, and the lithe frame of a former collegiate swimmer. Not a waif, because swimmers have muscle, but soft and gauzy, nonetheless. Like honeysuckle and chlorine. She was fresh and lovely in a way that hurt my heart. I'd been instantly smitten with her the first time we met, and a year of casual friendship hadn't changed that. I felt like the *Nutcracker* date was a good try at something classy, traditional, safe, and just public enough to not be a pressure-packed dating event. I was a mess of overthinking and anxiety at the idea of placing myself in love's harm's way. We had a nice time together, and it was a sweet afternoon. I was tense about being dressed up and about Leslie, but our time together was not painful. A win. I think she had a sometimes boyfriend, though, and we didn't pursue a relationship. Not that it died, but we just didn't advance forward with it. Just friends. A month or so later, when she asked me to her parents' house in Concord for Thanksgiving, I was confused as to our status, but she was just being kind and offering an orphan a place at their table. There was a friendly, low-stakes vibe. We had a walk down a country meadow lane. I might have gotten a kiss somewhere along the line. I think we liked each other and decided that was enough. It was so much easier for me to remember a might-have-been than an unsuccessful one-night stand. I was grateful to remember our friendship with a golden aura of wistfulness, which seems a perfect description of her.

On that downhill slide out of Boston, I did some of the things I had left undone. I spent more time at the Boston Public Library. The entrance between the lions and the foyer smelled of body odor and piss, because who is going to be an oasis for the needy if not a library? I spent hours in the belle epoch reading room with its green-shaded lights, endless tables and chairs, and a silence that hummed with hundreds of interior conversations. I ate at Legal Sea Foods. I went out drinking at an Irish pub and stayed so late that I missed the last train back to Cambridge. Walked home, grabbed a sleeping bag, went down to the Charles, and slept on a bench by the river, my drunken and privileged homage to the homeless people I saw there every day. My idea of allyship. I bought Birkenstocks and went to the biggest Earth Day celebrations in the country, surrounded by other people who knew that they, too, were killing the earth, but feeling guilty about it. I visited the North End church and the cemeteries that dotted the older parts of town. Said my goodbyes that way. After the fact. Retroactively. I sent my belongings by bus down to South Carolina and then followed them down on the train.

Hawthorne Valley Farm, Ghent, Harlemville, New York, Root Crops, 1990

After an extended stay in Greenville, a month or so past Mama's "Two Weeks Free" rule of homecomings after our childhood upbringing, I hopped on an Amtrak train for Hudson, New York, the town nearest the farm. By that time, much of my Alaska money was gone, frittered away after a year in expensive Boston and a minimum wage job, and I was seriously needing the free room and board that the farm was offering me to learn about biodynamic agriculture. There was a nominal one-hundred-and-fifty-dollar-a-month stipend, but I would learn that would barely keep me in Ben and Jerry's ice cream. I was literally headed into my salad days: produce was free to apprentices during the growing season, so I would be eating lots of salads and stir-fries and honing my already thin body into rowing leanness again. But that was later. First, I arrived. I got off the train and onto the depot platform and looked around for my ride. A buxom young woman with bronze skin and short black hair wearing a blindingly white cotton shift called out to me. "Are you Michael? I'm Judith." I was breathtaken and dazzled and confused. "Upik?" A frown and a toss of the hair and a wince of well-exercised frustration. "You-dit. Judith. The German pronunciation of "Joo-dith." I followed her to a dilapidated Ford van that was questionably street-legal, windows blasted out and no working seatbelts, and she drove me the fifteen miles of upstate farm roads curving through forests and pastures and farms and rivers. I was suspicious of the beautiful woman welcoming committee, referencing back to the Reverend Sung-Young Moon's city recruiters and every pretty young fundamentalist church girl I'd met, but Judith was the head farmer's daughter and way more than just pretty. She was a badass woman who knew more about farming and getting shit done than I ever would. She dropped me off at the bunkhouse and went off to do other stuff more important than delivering fresh meat to the farm.

I looked around and found Steffen, the dairy manager, and he helped me get set up with a room in the bunkhouse. Once I had settled my stuff, I was to come down to the barn and find him. The evening milking was about to start, and I could shadow him and ask questions while he worked. Steffen was tall, a few inches over my six feet, and bulkier, in his mid-thirties. He had a quick, boyish smile, spoke rapidly with a hint of a German accent, and was brisk and matter-of-fact in affect. As he attached milking hoses and crisscrossed the barn floor between the two rows of stanchioned milking cows, stepping over the manure gutters and dodging swinging tails, he answered my questions. The tails? They're tied with elastic so that they don't lay in the urine and manure and then swat you in the face. It hurts. The stanchions? We lock them in during milking so that we can keep them in place. Then we turn them loose again. Each cow has their own stanchion, and they know where to go. You can see their name tags above their heads. The white stuff? We put lime on the floor between milkings. It helps prevent them slipping and is a good amendment to the manure, also. And so it went, back and forth, as he milked and a few other apprentices meted out the feed and swept the aisleways and cared for the calves and young stock.

Afterwards, as they were readying to release the cows, the head farmer came walking down the center aisle. Christoph Meier, Judith's dad, was a polar opposite of Steffen in appearance and manner. He was small and rail thin, dark in hair and dress and manner. Walking across the white floor in his signature black beret and dark barn coat, he looked like a miniscule Swiss Darth Vader, brooding and menacing. You could almost hear the villain music. He was curt to Steffen's volubility, and arrogant to the other's friendliness. I'd heard stories about him already, so it was with some trepidation that I watched him approach. He welcomed me gruffly and talked about the serious work we were doing here. How the cows and garden signified life and death, here specifically, and for the planet more generally. Even in brief, he was didactic and pontificating. He stopped in our walk through the barn, and, just as he was about to deliver another dark gem of wisdom, the cow he was standing behind arched its back and pooped directly into his jacket pocket. And the spell was broken. We all laughed and he said, "It's worse when they cough." Lesson learned.

Harlemville was a wide spot in the road a mile or two off the Taconic Parkway, a hamlet composed of former New York City Waldorf educators and the Rudolf Steiner Anthroposophists and their farming initiative affiliates. It was highbrow in philosophy and values, and as low as a manure gutter in its necessary farm practices. It was a magical place. A fellow apprentice buddy, Ted Sickles, was a descendant of the Civil War general of the same name, and he was a Chicago boy with a measured and intellectual manner, cultivated or his native state. He told me that the first time he'd driven down the Harlemville Road, little kids had been at the margins on both sides, throwing flowers at him as he passed. He felt that it was only fair that he stop into the parking lot and see what the place was about. He was offered a job as a driver for the store, and he never left. There was a gravitational draw to the place. A fair, small stream ran through the valley of four hundred acres of pastureland surrounding and nestling the farm buildings, school, and few scattered homes. The original purchasers, those city teachers, had mostly bought up all of the private houses in the twenty years the place had been operating. Surrounding the pastures were second-growth forests full of aimless-seeming and forgotten stone walls that had once designated long gone pastures and property lines of small farms. It was stunningly beautiful. Shire-like, as if pulled straight from Tolkien's Middle Earth. The human mixture of philosopher farmers and educators, seekers, artisans, and writers made it a community as complex sociologically as the varied landscape. It was a place whose potentialities were not quickly exhausted.

My apprenticeship duties started at five in the morning, when I would roll out of the rack and stumble downstairs to the barn for milking. If the cows were on pasture and it was my week to be responsible for calling them in, it was earlier than that. Our herd were mostly Brown Swiss at that time, and we handled them in an old-fashioned and individualistic way that complimented their docile manner. In the early morning darkness, I would head out along one of the farm lanes to the various pastures, yelling, "Hey, Cow," or some variant on that theme. Loud and repeated. We had a bell-cow, a leader chosen for their age and standing within the herd and a proven track-record of being responsible. At that time, it was a hoary old dame named Agawamuck, after the creek that ran through the valley. At my call, she would get up from her night's resting, shake herself and her bell, and start the herd ambling toward the barn for milking. Each step, she'd clang her bell and the group followed. My job was to open and close pasture gates, harass the slackers and collect the misdirected, and deliver the herd to the barn, where they found their individual stanchions and tucked into the morning feed. It took more time and manpower than if we just left them in a feedlot or outdoor loafing space, but the pasture was good for the cows, and the cows were good for the pasture.

Kristof, always the intellectual and spiritual and insufferable ego leader of the farm, once told me, "Milk is the byproduct of our farming operations. The real crop we are harvesting is manure." He was not wrong. Without chemical fertilizers and pesticides and very few antibiotics except in extreme cases, the manure was the key element of the fertility, productivity, and health of the farmlands and animals. We treated the manure accordingly. It was amended with dry materials of straw and sawdust bedding, the lime swept from the floor, and leftover feed from the mangers, all gathered into the manure gutters, dragged by chain and paddle into the main hopper, and driven by a mighty piston underground to the manure pile across the concrete yard from the barn. From there it was collected and made into long windrows in the far edges of different pastures for them to weather into compost. "In Switzerland," we heard, "they braid the manure piles." Most dairies today feed their herds on processed and inexpensive feed ordered in from big agribusiness chains, and the thin and watery manure thus created is pumped into vast lagoons of slurry, where it seeps into ground water and becomes a toxic waste and a liability. For us, the manure was brown gold. The biodynamic practice also included the steps of making preparations that are best described to a nonbeliever as antiquated mumbo-jumbo. There were the Horn manures and 501 silica-water sprays, chamomile-stuffed bladders, and all kinds of different ways to add homeopathic health to the farm instead of mining the soil and buying in amendments to compensate for the loss. For me, the whole process always seemed one of leaning on the old ways. Walking your land on foot, being aware of the seasons and the micro-seasonal events, observing closely. Moving slowly but never resting. Everything modern agriculture was not. The farm repaid us for taking care.

But even as the community was one of careful and exhaustive overthinking and complexity, it was never so for me in my role. When one of the older women philosopher-shoppers asked me one day why I had come to Harlemville, I told her it was because I was interested in farming and was afraid of chemicals. She pshawed and gave me an unbelieving look. "Really? That's all?" And it was an easy answer to give. "Yes. And it's enough." Milking and feeding the stock, including the pigs and chickens, had a Zen-like quality of never-ending drudgery. "Practice," I believe the more philosophically minded call it. There was time to feed the cows individual portions based on their individual milk production, and when I did barn-check at night before sleeping, I had enough energy left over after a long day to give some words and a soft touch to my favorites. It was calm and smelly and relaxing in the barn at night, all of the quiet breathing and cud-chewing and farts and plops. And then Jasper, our mighty leader of the barn cats, midnight black and huge, battle-scarred and scary, would emerge from the shadows. Stalking with a dark menace, he'd give me a fright to remember before purring on overdrive and rubbing hard against my legs. In the winter once, I lay down in the clean straw next to my favorite cow, Mieke, and drowsed next to her warmth. She was a chubby, beef-breed-looking young cow, and cute as a button. Laying there in the quiet warmth and dimness of a barn on a cold winter night healed a lot of what I'd suffered from the noise and glare of the city. All the cities.

Our barn was an amazing structure, two hundred years old and labyrinthine, sprawling over the small hill and dominating the whole village. In the lower ground level, there were two doorways for cows to go out to pasture or off to slaughter. It was where the cows lived in the winter and milked year-round. Attached, at different sides, were the milk bulk tank and the dairy processing area, where the yogurt and cheeses were made and stored. The bakery, where we turned our wheat and rye crops into fresh bread, was next to the root-vegetable washing station under an open-air shed. At the barn-end was where all of the manure processes were carried out. On the upper ground level was a big earthen berm so that tractors and wagons could be unloaded directly into the hay mow and the grain bins. It was a big, open space that had room for a tractor and an attached hay wagon. It could be dusty and stale, but there was a sweetness from the hay and grain. When shut up for the winter, it was a dry and cool space for us apprentices to huddle around a mountain of onions we'd harvested and talk sleepily and lean on each other in the early morning hours, peeling layers for enough to stock the farm store's daily sales. I always felt kinship with those fieldhands in *The Gleaners* painting, or with some Eastern European peasants huddled in the healthy squalor of their winter lives. Our lives. And on top of all, under the huge, vaulted roof of the barn, the hay mow. At the end of summer, stuffed full of many tons of hay for the winter feeding, it was claustrophobic and stifling hot, with dust motes hanging heavy in the air, the bales almost pinned against the meltingly hot wood slats and metal roof. There were spaced wooden chutes with trap doors there so that we could send hay bales directly down onto the barn floor below for feeding. It was an ingenious and efficient setup. In the late spring and early summer, the hay all played out, and it was a cavernous space big enough to hold a barn dance and play basketball without any chance that your shot, no matter how much of a rainbow arc you put into it, would hit the ceiling. And we took advantage of it for both of those uses.

I'd done a bit of gardening in my past, more remembering than doing, from the tiny strawberry patch and marigold bed in our Denton, Texas, house to the larger operation that my sister had on Wye Mountain, in Bigelow, Arkansas, where I first learned in my high school summer break about organic practices from her efforts to be self-sufficient and grow her own food. She showed me garlic sprays and companion-planting marigolds as pest-control methods. I learned what a real garden tomato could taste like, vine-ripened and sun-warmed. The deep gold of a farm-raised-chicken egg yolk. That lifestyle she showed me was one of the bugs that bit me there, among the legion of ticks, chiggers, and mosquitos, and one that eventually bore positive fruit. But the gardens at Hawthorne Valley were another thing altogether. We grew five acres of vegetables for sale in the farm store, to sell through our distribution business, and at the Union Square Market in New York City. It was a big growing operation. We apprentices, under the direction of the head gardener, were used in every aspect of the seed-to-market process. Again, the Zen of futility, the embrace of the never-ending task, and a mule-like tenacity were lessons we learned in order to survive on the farm. It was painstaking and backbreaking work. There's a certain feeling of hopelessness when you're looking down a forever-long row of leeks needing weeding, and we learned to look down, turn our brains off, and hoe our row. I had thought from Boston that there might be time to listen to music on headphones and read books once I was out in the fields doing the mindless and time-consuming work, but the first week on the farm taught me the folly of that idea. We needed to be both mindful and mindless at the same time. Focused on the task and unfocused on the hours of the same rote mechanical actions stretching before us in the hot summer sun. There was a lot to do and a lot to learn, but the learning involved actions—there are philosophies of weeding, but if you don't do the corresponding work, there's no nirvana awaiting you. Reaching the end of one hundred-yard row was enough. Those with pure hearts and dirt on their hands go directly to heaven.

Farmer Steffen Schneider with apprentices Ted Sickels and Michael Riley harvesting leeks.

A Hawthorne Valley Newsletter excerpt showing Ted Sickles, Steffen Schneider, and Michael Riley (1991).

Like almost every other aspect of the farm, the garden tasks were constant. There was the constant weeding, by means of mechanical cultivation and by hand and hoe. Planting and harvesting went hand-in-hand, of course, and once a space opened up, new plants filled the gap. We grew many kinds of lettuces, things I'd never heard of before, like Rouge d' Hiver Romaine and Deer Tongue. Since they were a quick-growing and turnaround crop, we were always on duty, at any downtime in the spring or summer, placing tiny lettuce seeds into the plastic start-trays. Hundreds of trays in the greenhouse tunnels. Harvesting, likewise, was a constant. Cutting, counting, packing out cases of produce in the garden depending upon the orders of the day, bundling leeks and kale, pulling beets and carrots, picking peas and beans. We were unskilled labor, unlike the migrant laborers who pick the produce on most of America's megafarms with speed and efficiency, and so we were slow. As newbies, we suffered the back and knee agonies of being bent for hours on end. Our bodies, hands, and minds learned, but it was difficult work at the best of times. Friday harvesting for the Saturday market was fun, because it was a kind of ending: the need and pace was more urgent, but when it was done, there was space to breathe. Saturdays in the garden were chill. Way late into the season, into October and even November, we would harvest the frost-covered kale with cold-numbed fingers. With a typical Eastern European grit, the kale refused to give in to the realities of winter, long after everything else had given up the ghost, and harvesting became a grim game of sorts, a game of survival. When the final killing frost came, we left the kale standing bare and denuded in the field, tough gray-green stalks against the iron background, and laughed and cursed their hardiness. See you next spring, assholes.

But the garden wasn't all battle. We apprentices ate like royalty in the summer, with every kind of fresh produce available and free to us for the picking. I would order ten-pound boxes of Jerusalem artichoke pasta and huge jugs of olive oil with a discount from our distribution side-business and make vegetable stir-fries and pasta primavera for dinner every night. I learned how to make basil pesto and would ride the ten-mile round trip into the village of Chatham just to buy ingredients from somewhere other than our store for a change. We didn't have access to a food processor, so I ground with mortar and pestle and rough-chopped the ingredients, and it was lovely. The wonder of cooking with five or less ingredients is a real thing.

And some of the garden tasks were a joy. We had an old root-vegetable washer, a rotating cone of long wooden slats with a sprinkler attached, and I would marvel at the process, where dull and dirty carrots and beets were fed in the hopper at one end, and slowly rolling and washing down the tube to emerge, at the end, bright shining orange and purple glowing roots to box. It was a simple and awesome alchemy. A kind of beauty so many people never imagine or witness. Another kind of alchemy was the making of the 501 Horn Manure Preparation. This involved a huge wooden barrel full of collected rainwater, a ten-foot-long wooden and twig broom suspended above it on a swivel and, after adding the dried horn manure that was buried in the ground from equinox to equinox, stirring in alternating directions for exactly one hour. That might not sound like entertainment, and in truth it wasn't, but for a former rower, the mindful practice of stirring in one direction, which we referred to as order, building and maintaining a vortex, and then holding water with the broom with all of your might and creating chaos from the disintegrating vortex, well, that was something familiar. It almost evoked in me that mythical concept of "swing," that lightning in a bottle time when a rowing shell moves effortlessly with the combined effort of all eight rowers working in synchronicity. It wasn't something that happened often when I rowed, and so I appreciated the reminder.

While stirring, with our setup, you're up on a pedestal, out in the open, working hard to keep everything in motion, and it had an appeal like that of a talented pole-dancer practicing their craft: a combination of strength, passionate motion, and exhibitionism. It was kind of fun. Apprentices who couldn't find the beauty in carrots, beets, and stirring preparations didn't last long.

So much of the beauty of that place came from being able to see the everyday as miraculous, and that was a practice I'd always intentionally tried to cultivate and preserve, that childish joy in simple things. Every late spring, we would separate and send the heifers and dry cows, young stock and older cows that were bred and growing calves, out onto the summer pastures of Indian Valley. Once we would open the gates and let them in, they would romp and jostle each other in the exuberance of new grass. We would close them in and not see them for another month. Aside from occasional check-ins to see if one had calved unexpectedly or had some unforeseen accident, they were utterly free from oversight and had the unfettered right to roam. I felt that myself on the farm at times. Walking the edges of pasture and woodlands in the early evenings, I would stumble across a margin of older, uncultivated landscape, some ancient round of earth with huge trees and wildflowers not ploughed to extinction, and be moved to dream and write bad poetry and wax reminiscent of times before me. The work on a dairy farm is constant, and the toll of incessant and repetitive chores exacted a real price, but there was beauty and quiet and some fragments of contemplative time there that I rarely found elsewhere in my life. That yogurt container did not lie. It was a special place.

Helene and Schatzi reveling in doing the barn chores during their visit to Hawthorne Valley Farm (1991).

To keep the young apprentices happy and healthy, all of us coming from different walks of life and various capabilities for feeding ourselves, the two farm wives—Christoph's wife, Analien, and Steffen's, Rachel—would feed us during the week in their homes. On the weeks we ate at Analien's, we could expect amazing meals in a formidably clean home, with pithy peasant wisdom, sharp rebukes and stinging insults, and quick efficiency. She was a true hausfrau at the top of her game. At Rachel's, we would get friendly, harried forgetfulness ("Is it that time already?!") and quick, solid meals. She had the care and kindness and sweet absence of a Waldorf elementary teacher, so that paid for the rest. We had two-hour lunch breaks, to get a meal and a short nap before tackling the afternoon, and most days I'd go to the farm store and finish the meal with a pint of Ben and Jerry's. That alone pretty much burned through my monthly wages, such as they were. I was skinny, poor, and in exceedingly good health. The farm looked good on me.

We had an Englishman, Ralph, as our lead gardener and market manager, and he lent me his ten-speed bike while he was there and even after he left. It was my one way of getting around since I had still yet to get my driver's license. Rileys walked. I biked to explore nearby towns, other organic and biodynamic farms in the area, and out for an occasional splurge meal at a restaurant. I also used it to court a couple of young women I was interested in. One was a local girl I met at the market down in New York City who was selling goat cheese and bag balm and eggs in Union Square at the stand next to ours. We talked a bit, and we hit it off well enough that on my next Saturday, I woke up at four in the morning on my off day and rode the ten miles to her farm to help out with the morning goat milking. It was an interesting field trip, seeing the stinky old billy goat, marveling at the ease of two teats over four, and scoping out the girl for possibilities. She was pretty, no doubt, and sassy and fun in an undeniably attractive way, but pretty quickly I figured out she was way too tough of a rural farmgirl for me, and I suspect she found that I was lacking in the complementary toughness as well. Our New York farms were miles apart in more ways than one. Midmorning was late enough for us to figure all that out, and I called it good and pedaled home, stopping at the Book Barn, an amazing book-hoarder's paradise in Hillsdale, New York, on the way back. The wind and speed and winding roads brushed off any regret, and I was left with a pleasant wistfulness. When I was doing well, that feeling was my default setting.

There were girls working on the farm as I was, but it always seemed a bad idea for a workplace romance. I wasn't particularly attracted to any of them, but even if I had been, the work and living and community were way too close to have a relationship go bad and continue on. And we all smelled of cow manure all of the time. One memorable day, a girl showed up from the school side of town, and I was sent to work with her for the morning hours, showing her around and doing chores, garden harvesting, the whole Hawthorne Valley orientation experience. She was gorgeous. Towards the end of our time together, she was flirting with me in a way that even a guy as clueless as I recognized as flirting, and told me, "Michael, you are an enigma." I laughed out loud. She had a wonderful form, and what I'd later learn to call a heart-shaped ass, but the beautiful lips that could utter that kind of foolishness, well, I wanted no part of them. There was never a less enigmatic person than me.

But there was this one girl. She had a hint of crazy about her, to which I was super-attuned because of my upbringing, but she had a definite pull. We met at the store, crossed paths again eating lunch on the picnic benches in front of the farm store. Soon we were running into each other more purposefully as recognition became pleasant surprise became longing. Soon

I was riding Ralph's bike twelve miles after milking to go have dinner at her place.

She was fetching enough in herself, but she also lived in the caretaker's carriage house at Steepletop, the home of the poet Edna St. Vincent Millay. The English major in me swooned. I was captivated by the girl and by the landscape and the poetry of the place. She was lovely and lonely, living way out in the country with only her small toddler for company, and we hit it off pretty well. We would take walks together and prepare meals, and I was comfortable and happy playing with her little girl and helping out with chores and enjoying the semblance of a settled life. My bike rides home, the twelve miles back to the farm, flew by effortlessly with pleasant reminiscing on soft kisses and good times shared. After a few such dates, she invited me to stay the night. She was enchanted by my body and my virginity at twenty-six years old. "That's so sweet! And now I'll know you'll never forget me, because I'm your first." After ten years of nonstop angst, I was overjoyed to finally lose the heavy weight of my virginity. But my joy was in that young, self-indulgent, guy-focused way of joy. I wasn't thinking very clearly or deeply. She was. I wouldn't learn about single moms and "Shoplifting the Pootie" until *Jerry Maguire* came out five years later, so I was confused and dismayed when she rather suddenly was angry with me for everything. I wasn't visiting enough, playing with her daughter, covering the expenses of meals. Everything completely true and obvious if I had only been a bit more enigmatic and less of a selfish boy. Rather quickly, she threw down an angry ultimatum, and I sullenly walked away. Or rode. I remember Ralph the Gardener's name. I remember the name of the poet whose home she lived in. I remembered, after some thought, our big bad barn cat's name. But my first time notwithstanding, I can't for the life of me remember her name. It is an embarrassment to me still.

Love is something that's in the air of a well-functioning, diversified livestock farm. If not love, then sex. All of those cows need to be pregnant and giving birth to produce milk, all the eggs we left to the broody chickens became chicks, and the sows, if left with the boar, would produce those cute, squiggling, ravenous little pink piglets. It made a good background for a failed relationship because you saw the joy and pain, life and death effects of the life cycle every day. You would come into the barn one morning and see a new bull calf in one of the maternity pens, healthy and clean on its spindly, shaking legs, its tail twitching vigorously as it punched its square, boxy little head into mom's udder, bringing down milk, while she assiduously licked it clean and stood patiently for it to find a teat. And the next day, you'd arrive early, a bit before the rest of the crew, and find a calf, unexpectedly early, lying dead in the gutter behind mom, drowned in manure and urine, while she chewed her cud, locked into her stanchion. That first winter on the farm was a particularly brutal one for calves, and it was my job to bury the dead. I started to feel like one of those medieval Black Plague body collectors, as I loaded a new calf into my wheelbarrow and brought it out to one of the older manure windrows and buried it to be "re-crucified in the etheric," as one anthroposophist told me with that bald-faced bullshit of the true believer. Finding Jesus in the compost pile. It was one dark winter.

That theme of love and sex and life and death was on tender and brutal display all the time. They were all flipsides of the same coin. The farm taught me that. It was where I learned that coins had more than two sides: that life wasn't lived based upon some simple duality, but in shades and slivers and unlikely events of many divergent potential outcomes. Once we stayed late into the night with a young heifer for her difficult first birth. After many hours of her fruitlessly pushing a large calf, when we became concerned that she would die from the effort and we'd lose both, we finally attached a chain to the front hooves that were stretching out and used a come-along to forcefully pull the calf out. It landed in the hay on the floor with a loud wet impact. The heifer's eyes were wide and white with pain and fear and relief from the burden. The calf was stillborn, an enormous bull calf without a well-formed bone structure. A gelatinous mass. I busied myself with the burial rites, and mother sucked down the afterbirth as she was supposed to, removing all notice of birth from predators, real or imagined. We gave her a calf to relieve her swollen udder and give her a sense of normalcy. She was ready to join the milk line.

On another occasion, we said a poignant goodbye to our gentle giant of a herd bull, Curly. At the age of three, dairy bulls can get territorial and aggressive from all their testosterone, and Curly was five. We kept a bull to catch any cows that went unbred because of a botched artificial insemination or a pregnancy that just didn't catch. We also kept the horns on our cows and bull, instead of chemically or manually removing them, as was common practice, because the Steiner agricultural philosophy said that horns helped focus astral projections and make the animals happier and healthy. All of this made Curly a bit of a hazard. We attached a drag-chain from his nose ring when we released the cows onto pasture, so that he had to step carefully and move slowly to avoid pulling his nose. But it was a terrifying sight, nonetheless, to see his huge and intimidating form shambling towards you on open ground. Christoph told the story of the time a bull had randomly attacked him in the yard, pounding him down into the cement with its massive head and horns, breaking his back and almost killing him. He'd crawled to safety under the electrified fence and survived. After months of convalescence and rehabilitation, he could walk again. The first thing he'd done was to take a hacksaw and remove the bull's horns. A ghastly and gruesome story all around. We apprentices generally sided emotionally with the bull on this one, because Christoph was arrogant and mean, no question about him deserving it.

Curly was different, though, and never gave cause to offend or evidence of meanness. But farming was nothing if not rigid in the code of following tradition, whether it was planting time, hay harvesting, or sending a bull away. And it was time. So that one day, we released the herd after milking and opened Curly's enclosure, sending him the other way, away from the farm lane and pasture and his cows and toward the open light of the apprentice's yard and the waiting stock trailer. We murmured soft encouragement and said our heartfelt goodbyes. Curly was a good guy. A gentleman. He went quietly to his demise with his impressive bulk and grace and swinging gait. I might have cried. A few weeks later, he came back to the farm, this time in small one- and two-pound butcher-paper-wrapped packages for sale in the store. Steffen brought some around especially for us. That night we had the feast of St. Curly, and one of the distribution drivers, a guy who frequented the barn and knew Curly well, showed up and had a Curly burger. He told us that he'd been vegetarian for five years and never knowingly had meat once during that time, but tonight he was going to celebrate a great life by partaking in the offering and the sacrifice. And it was good.

And then, not suddenly or from sneaking up on me unawares, because it was a long, hard slog on the farm much of the time, I'd been two summers on the farm and was heading into my second winter, and it was soon time to move on. We had harvested the corn in that beautiful little Phudd Hill field and finished the incredibly dangerous job of loading the corn silage into the silo. The power take-off, a shaft that connected and ran power from the tractor to the connected implement, speeds at a full-throttled roar to power the heavy metal fan blades that blew and pushed the heavy chopped corn far up into the three-story-tall silo tower. Any of the fast-moving parts were pure death to anyone making even the slightest misstep, and it was scary as hell. Girls with long hair working these jobs all over rural America are scalped when their hair catches in the speeding PTO shaft. We harvested the volunteer pumpkins that always grew in and among the cornstalks, and I'd been allowed to disc the field afterwards. That evening, ploughing the stubble back into the moist, dark soil, the fresh living smell that followed me on my rounds sank into my soul and remains even now. The crows followed me, feasting on the upturned worms and mice in their exposed tunnels, and I worked until I chased the light from the evening sky, deep plum above the tree lines. The finishing of tasks necessary to put the farm to sleep for the winter. And to send me on my way complete.

As the season wound down and the frenetic pace of summer and fall slowed, so did my time in Harlemville. For eighteen months, I avoided the constant danger of being kicked in the head while milking the cows; having my ankle pulped by a huge rolling oak log as we got in firewood for the farm families; and losing an arm in a tractor's whirling PTO shaft while milling grain, unloading manure, or loading silage, but I suffered a series of setbacks my last few weeks on the farm. They served as an impetus to push me out of that comfortable nest and start anew elsewhere.

In sweeping out the last of the rye from the bakery's grain bin, I'd ingested some mold that got into my lungs and significantly reduced their function. It was difficult to take full breaths, and I felt like I was drowning much of the time. I'd been to the anthroposophist doctor in town and been prescribed some tincture of arnica or some such homeopathic nonsense, but the shortness of breath continued. Not long after that, I was struck down by lower back pain that laid me out flat for a matter of days, no way to escape the blinding pain except resting prone for long, boring hours of inaction. And then I got a flu that similarly knocked me out, with a few days of high fevers and hallucinatory dreams, when I slept on a cot at Steffen and Rachel's and she patted my brow with a cool, wet towel and fed me warm broth and herbal teas to get me through the hardest hours of my dangerously high temperature. The farm was expelling me. I went.

After I recovered, for the most part, from the humbling infirmities of my conditions, I said my goodbyes and reminisced on the experiences I had suffered and persevered through. The ballroom dancing class where the cute Scottish teacher who later married Tom the Cheesemaker asked me to the final dance party and we waltzed, dressed in some kind of cobbled-together farmhand finery. I got a peck on the cheek for my pains. Our resistance agricultural philosophy study group, where Ted Sickels and I pushed back and away from reading Rudolf Steiner's dense and incomprehensible book on agriculture to study, instead, Laura Ingalls Wilder's *Farmer Boy*. It was a far more accessible and informative text which we were mocked for and smirked back at the approved study group in return. We left with so much more useful and practical information than those students who read the sanctioned and condoned biodynamic text.

There was the time I was driving the loader into the barn and, not having a driver's license or much experience driving anything motorized, drove the tractor through the barn, actually right through a wall, and the dairy manager yelling, "Clutch! Clutch! Step on the clutch!" while I stamped on the brake and watched in horror as I ground slowly forward, splintering wood and caving a wall. During that one wild storm, huge trees falling around us, when I was given the job of cutting down a limb over my head with a chainsaw from a ladder, fully aware that this, this was really not a good idea. And knowing also that it was necessary. Learning how to back a double-axle hay wagon into the barn after a million tries and never missing again. When I left, a small piece of myself remained there. I took a larger bit of that place with me. It was a good leaving.

Seattle, Washington, The Hobart, 1992

After a year's stint on another biodynamic farm in Wisconsin, I felt I was done with that for a while. Dave was back in Washington State after his East Coast work, and I decided to join him and another good rowing buddy. Coming into Seattle felt like another homecoming, even though I'd never lived there before. It was a place and people and attitudes that resonated and felt familiar to me. The East Coast and Midwest were not my thing. I was never a country boy, even if I was just as truthfully never a city boy either, and Seattle, even then, was a city of suburbs. I moved in near-penniless and immediately went searching for jobs. I got on with a Kelly Girl/day labor business, and they shuffled me around the city daily, chasing the weirdest sort of work. I wasn't committed to much but making rent, so my short-term jobs and basement room with the mattress on the floor didn't matter too much to me. Scott and Dave were good roommates, but they had real jobs and lives and things going on, and I was all fluctuations and insubstantial being-ness. I was always hard up for cash and didn't have much energy for being social or improving myself. One Friday, at a particularly grim money point, I had to borrow bus fare from my regular driver and promise him payment the following Monday. I spent my first Thanksgiving and Christmases in front of the TV, too poor or poorly motivated to find a friend or family home to crash at. I remember listening to the Cowboy Junkies a lot on Scott's nice sound system, and that lyric "Something small and frail and plastic, baby, cause cheap is how I feel" captured me exactly. I was a hustling, busy, broken mess. Being poor was a full-time job.

The temp agency was situated in a nondescript white office somewhere downtown, and I'd catch the early bus down Aurora from Seventieth Street and hang out with the other poor fools until the office manager would come out and send one or two or three of us out to a call, whatever the need was. Once it was to a cardboard factory not far away. It was a couple of days gig, and all it entailed was cutting and stacking and loading cardboard for eight hours. The factory was a loud, big, darkened space, and there were paper particles hanging with a dusty haze in the air constantly. I came home coughing those couple days, and when one of the workers told me I was good enough to get hired permanently, I declined. The air was better at the temp office.

For another longer-term job, a couple of weeks I think it was, I took the early bus, hopped on an early ferry to Vashon Island for a short ride from the city, and spent the entire day filling foofy, artfully labeled little bags of gourmet pancake mix from an industrial, fifty-pound bag of Krusteaz pancake mix. It was a small, mail-order business run from a clean, well-lighted little trailer, and there were three or four of us in there filling one bag from another. We might have done chocolate-covered cherries and other Washingtony things as well. It was a weirdly unapologetic business model: hire temps, rip off one brand to sell another rip-off, and everyone got paid. It was a sweet and naive con, and we did it for our seven bucks an hour and were happy to do it. The ferry ride was unpaid, and the day was long with all of the travel, but it was untaxing, and the sea air was better than the cardboard particulates. I learned the valuable skill of heat-sealing plastic bags and the lesson of not buying cute tourist trinkets.

Back to the temp office for a few day jobs, and then I scored a gig at a fish stick factory down on the wharf. I would wake up at baker's hours, maybe four in the morning, catch the first bus down to near the Seattle P-I Building, and run over to the factory, built over the water next to a fisherman's terminal. I was working with mostly Filipino folks who distrusted my young, white boy self, and for good reason: the pace was grueling and fast, and it took me a while to get up to speed. Meanwhile, I was cramping their efficiency. The sheets of frozen fish slurry rolled down the conveyor, where a responsible worker ran the chopper, punching stick figures from the sheet and sending them rolling down to us. We would separate them so that the spray machine could get the entire piece wet and then the breadcrumb drizzler could completely coat it. Line after line of delicate work rolling down on us at breakneck speed. We were wearing plastic gloves, and the naked, wet, frozen sticks would attach to our fingers and impede our ability to distance the little slurry nuggets each from the other. If I got too many sticks on too many of my fingers, the workers near me would groan, and there would be a shout, and the conveyor would slow down. You got two minutes for a pee break, and if you took more, the next person got a minute and forty-five seconds. It was cutthroat. I was never able to watch that *I Love Lucy* scene where Lucy and Ethel are at the chocolate factory assembly line in the same way again. I still laugh at her and me, though. The work, at the time, was unfunny.

One day I took a job up north at the airplane factory in Everet, washing dishes at the corporate food service cafeteria next to the biggest indoor building space in the world. When our bus got to the gates, though, there were lines of workers with signs, and as we eased through them and the chain-link fencing, they were shouting and spitting and mocking us. My heart sank. I didn't know there was an airplane strike going on, and I'd been hired in as a scab to keep the bosses fed and their cutlery clean. A new low for me. But a boy needs to eat, and friends need their rent money, so I kept up at it, and the strike broke one way or another, and I stayed on washing dishes as a doubly subcontracted food service worker. Every day, I took the forty-minute bus ride up to the job, where I was ensconced within a huge metal web of tray racks and oblong conveyor belt about as big as a football field. I became a master of the Hobart industrial dishwasher.

The Hobart itself was the biggest dishwashing machine I ever met, maybe a twenty-foot-long sheet metal tunnel of high-pressure water jets and detergent strong enough to melt the skin from your bones. Dishes went in, cleared of major leftover debris, and came out in a cloud of steam, the plates and silver so hot they dried themselves instantly. I quickly, perforce, got hands of asbestos. The tray racks revolved around and were scraped, unloaded onto plastic sorting racks, and into the Hobie. It was work that required some speed, because if the revolving tray racks got too full, there wasn't space for the diners to put their trays onto the conveyor machine. Weighted down with hundreds of breakfast and lunch dishes, the whole assembly started to vibrate under the stress. As did I. With executives waiting, hands full, while trays bounced and crockery crashed and mess splattered out into the drop-off area, I would shut the system down and try to catch up. We were doing hundreds, maybe thousands of meals a day, and it was stressful. I stayed at the job, though, and it got into me somehow. I became a part of that proud and noble line of smart, educated, weirdo dishwashers. If you know, you know.

I became adept at sorting silverware in a blinding flash. I could service the minor workings of the Hobie and soon had the dish shack running like a well-oiled machine. I initially avoided the nearby pot shack, the turf of an ex-postal worker with PTSD who remained buried and struggling through a mountain of baked-on, scour-proof industrial-sized pots and pans all day every day. But his was a hard hell to ignore, so I intervened and discovered a few efficiencies where we could help, and soon, he was able to catch up enough to get a few breathers throughout the day. He came away from the edge of the abyss enough that he could smile and talk occasionally. He was grateful. After a month of exemplary work, the food service contractor bought out my contract with the temp agency, and I became the dishwasher lead, with four dishwashers under my supervision. I got a quilt-lined twill jacket with my name on it. I'd found a work home. I was a leader of men. If not in the armed services, at least the food service.

There were so many personalities in that place. The corporate folks were nameless and faceless, in the front of the house and unaware of the secret lives of their food service serfs, but behind the scenes, we lived vivid and memorable lives. There was the kid, Matt, who I found lying down on the floor of the dish shack while plates and trays careened around him, and at my shout, he almost literally did one of those kick-leaps from a prone to standing position. He had pretensions to be a ninja, and that was the closest I saw him to achieving it. His excuse was that he was stretching, but he was a poor liar, like most kids, and I told him to stretch when the dishes were caught up. Be a dish-ninja and then be one of your own choosing after that.

One of the cooks was a beautiful and flirtatious Black woman named Joy Promise, and we were intrigued by each other. She was thin as a rail and tall and fabulous and always had stories and words for me. I was awestruck and infatuated and all ears when she was talking. She had a knowledge of the world that I just didn't, would never, have access to. I was a good-looking, wordy, smart, white guy who talked with her, listened, and didn't hit on her. We were ciphers to each other. We would meet up as I ferried her cooking wares to the pot shack and checked invoices of the deliveries and put away stock on shelves and into the walk-in freezer, hence the quilted jacket, and she would talk food and boyfriends and raunchy sex that I only partly understood. She had range, in the kitchen and the bedroom, and I had zero interesting experiences in either realm. She told me that if she really liked a guy, she would put one of those little Andes mint chocolates on his pillow that said, "Thank you. Please come again," and hope to meet up with him for another time. She was clever, unsophisticated, hard-worn and soft-hearted. I was kind of in love with her. Joy sure lived up to her name. The promise was self-evident.

There was a point in that job where I hurt my back seriously, where something in my lower back unhinged and I could barely straighten up. I'd lift the trays and racks and limp through my days, and then, after the bus ride back to Seattle, walk the mile or so around Green Lake to our house at a decrepit, old-man pace, fearful of bikers and roller-bladers bumping me into spasms of pain. I visited a chiropractor for the first time, did my back exercises on the floor in my basement room, and lived that life of quiet desperation that my brother Jesse had warned me about in his note to me in my high school yearbook. I was so hard up for cash that I could make it through the week on five dollars of spending cash, getting meals at work and saving any extras for the weekend. I'd go out for a Saturday greasy-spoon breakfast on 45th Street and, once my back healed, walk the city for free miles. I wasn't much of a roommate. I wasn't much of a person. I wasn't living much of a life.

There were so many other jobs. A short-term shift as a line cook at a popular Green Lake breakfast joint, where I was always a little nervous that my friends would stop in so I could cook for them. Working as a cashier in a little garden store near the Honey Bear Bakery. The shop was an old car garage or filling station and had multiple metal and glass walls or doors that you could raise manually to the ceiling to improve air flow. There was a night when I was closing, and I balanced the till and set the alarms and headed home, only to realize, about twenty minutes' walk down the way, that I'd left the doors all up: the place was completely open to the night. I got back and everything was pristine, untouched. The air felt faintly judgy, but that might just have been my conscience. I walked home again wondering what the hell was wrong with me.

I started rowing a bit on weekends, just to remember something that I'd once been good at. The boats generally sucked, because crew requires a team of compensating and knowledgeable partners working together as one, and that's hard to get in a boat you just throw together with random individuals. You had to put in your time before you made a boat, joined a team with commensurate skills and goals, and so while it was fun to be rowing again, the experience didn't stroke my ego or pad my feelings of self-worth. But I met a girl, and that helped. She was rowing on an ergometer outside the boathouse, the sun shining on her short red hair and her strong, thin body, and my heart fluttered. She later told me she had the same experience, except while erging. She thought to herself, "He's cute, so he won't be interested in me," and that was pretty much my default thought process about romance as well, so I walked away fluttery, and she kept killing it on the erg, burning disenchantment for fuel.

We had a few mutual friends, so we got together a few times and moved rather quickly into the romance dance of visiting, talking, sitting on porches, and having meals together. We had the shared rowing experience between us, and that meant shared passion for working out, friend groups, nomenclature. When you've been through a lot of pain, it's natural to find others who know what that feels like, too. K and I had that, in sports and family and in our personal growth. We'd both learned about empathy and compassion from some of our own downswings, and it made for an early and strong bond for us.

O'Dell Farm, Omak, Okanogan Valley, Washington, Apples and Pears, 1993

In the Pears

Breaking with common farm wisdom
Jess drove tractor while his old man
daughter Sarah and I picked pears into plastic bins
a mottled and unlikely gang.

He shepherded us all the while moving the balky crew
of real pickers
late to move into the wet early morning orchard
ladders slick, fruit heavy, clothes sodden to hang low
and slow the pace
pushed the bin forward for us solicitously, patiently,
coaching and checking.

ARTIFACT: A MEMOIR

Down the rows of newly matured trees we walked
our picking bags crisscross applesauce, bandoleering our
shoulders
we grasped the two-pound, fist-full fruit, heavy in hand
and with quick upward twists, separated pear stem from
spur and branch.

Filled the bags snugged heavy to our chests.
Unlatched the knotted cords. Gently let the pears lower
onto the growing
mountain of green.

The old man had lost a step
his knee-slapping and barking laugh dulled
quicker to anger and confusion
he wandered down the row mulling silence and
unburdening trees
muscle-memory compensating for short-term loss

Sarah, all golden hair and eyebrows, taciturn and bright-
smiled
tenacious like all of her people
averted her eyes, like mine and we listened
as Padre finished the Alaska story again
companionable silence filled with wisdom of the aged.

Then she reached down, tore the pay stub from the bin,
and we were done
soon each on our own ways homeward.

I'd moved beyond rowing as a pursuit or even as a job, so while I rowed a bit and coached at the Mount Baker Club some, it didn't have a life-path pull for me anymore. I cobbled together some more short-term jobs and then grabbed an extended hand from the O'Dells up at their orchard in Omak, near the Canadian border, and went to pick baby's breath and apples for the late summer and fall. I'm not sure if I left my roommates in the lurch or not, but they knew me and didn't hold it against me, if so. I was not quite responsible, and that wasn't a secret. K was busy with lots of things, so it was easy enough for me to go away across the state and have her come visit on weekends now and then. She was a self-sufficient person, and there was no clinginess or demands on my time and emotional energy. We were devoted to each other and did our own things when apart, and we were congruent and like-minded when together. It felt comfortable and meaningful and sustainable, which wasn't something I'd experienced with a girlfriend before.

Living and working on the O'Dell place was a boon to me after living in the city. They set me up in one of the fancier picker's cabins, renovated with deluxe features like indoor plumbing and carpeting, and once I'd killed all of the spiders and removed many wasp's nests, it was a single guy's dream tiny home. And when K visited, it was a nice reminder that I wasn't single. I had meals provided by Madre, work from Padre, and I was actually getting paid this time, unlike my two previous farm experiences. This was an eighty-acre orchard of pears and apples, with some leases for ground growing baby's breath that we supplied to the floral market at a premium price, so if everyone worked, everyone got paid. That applied to the seasonal workers, who came up every year from Mexico to follow the crops across the western landscape. The O'Dells had a few crew leaders and many pickers who had worked at the place for many years, because they were fair employers and paid well. Jess knew some Spanish, and he and Padre didn't take advantage of their workers, regardless of their status or papers. If everyone worked, everyone got paid. It was a good place for a lot of people, including me.

The baby's breath, so-named because of the rather foul diaper-smell of the plant, was a niche crop for the O'Dells, and they'd picked up on the trade early and so had a set market for the product, which was not true for everyone in the trade. The breath was just a weed, classified as a noxious one at that, not so unlike tumbleweed with myriad small flowers, and there was a lot of competition for market share, just like in other weed markets. A fair amount of skullduggery and ne'er-do-wells in the business. The migrant crew workers, stay-overs from pruning season or early arrivers for apples and pears, did most of the picking and bundling and baling, and my job was to carry the bales off the field to the trucks, where we would unload and separate the bundles out to dry in the sun or hang-dry in the big apple warehouse from wires hung in the rafters. All of it was heavy, hot, itchy work, but it was better than washing dishes or working as a line cook. At the end of the day, we'd hang out on the O'Dell front porch and tell stories and drink a few beers before and after dinner. All manner of people would stop by and visit, looking for work or asking for favors or just being some kind of interesting and fatalistic passersby. A farm porch, on a rural agricultural highway-side draws a real crossroads of American life that most people never see. Town folks dropped off cats and dogs and roosters and sped away, thinking that we'd want any of them because we had room to roam and they didn't.

In a nod to the sketchy element of the breath business, we had to guard the drying bunches. They were pretty much cash money once they were ready. We rented the Okanagan County fairgrounds towards the end of the season, when there was no longer space anywhere else to dry the bundles. My job, as the guy with the least status and, really, the most expendable in all ways, was to be the night watchman and sleep with the baby's breath. Just my presence was all that was needed to keep the product safe, so I was pretty much an overeducated, under-skilled junkyard dog, without the growl or teeth. Or maybe a scarecrow, but marginally better dressed. No one ever came to rob us on my watch, so I guess I did my job. A few days of that, and then we boxed it all up and packed it into a long-haul fourteen-wheeler truck, and then we'd do it all over again. Nobody was sad to see the season end, but baby's breath put all three O'Dell boys through college, and me on the road to another short period of fiscal health, so no one complained too much, either. And then it was time to pick fruit.

I've always loved an orchard. The mix of human and nature, the symmetry and the orderly natural haze and lines of limbs and leaves and fruit. It is one of mankind's more notable achievements, I think, to enhance and build upon the biological proclivities of tree and fruit and make something more beautiful, productive, efficient, and worthy. You can still glimpse a bit of the Garden of Eden in a carefully and painstakingly maintained orchard. Of course, people never know when to stop, and orchardists are no different. I look at an espaliered apple tree and can't help but see a poor soul stretched upon a rack of torture. And many orchards today are grown in equally contrived fashions, limbs trained upon vertical trellises so that they can be machine-picked or more easily maintained for pruning, spraying, mowing. The artificiality and brutal efficiency kill any of the aesthetics that made people plant orchards in the first place. But the money is good, and again, the economies of scale demand it of many growers. As many fruit growers get bigger, more still are forced out. Bulldozers scrape the trees into huge slash piles for burning, and the next new fad variety is planted.

But like in my other farm experiences, Alfred O'Dell and his son Jess generally did things the old way and could get away with it because the land and equipment were paid for and they were frugal and conservative in their practice. Their place was small by current standards, and they had diversified varieties. Their Bosc pear orchard, twenty acres of forty-year-old graceful and gnarly, hugely canopied trees, was an anachronistic throwback to days when orchards were allowed to mature. The trees were productive and majestic and were an anchor for the economic and soul-aesthetic of what they were doing at the O'Dells. The pears were steady, long-range, sure, and a physical representation of the way tradition was followed here. People drove by, turned around, stopped at the porch, and talked about those trees. In the hot sun, it was always cool and green and shady there. They resisted pressure to replace them with a variety that would yield more dollars per acre. When they bulldozed a set of plantings, they chose younger, less loyal trees. Trees planted with a less far-seeing purpose. Al had planted that block of pears when he first transitioned from logging and timber-cruising to being a fruit grower, and that first choice had been right on. It was a monument to his life, during his life. And afterwards.

I never knew quite how much all of that beauty took to maintain though, until that summer and fall there in Omak. The famous fruit growing region of north central Washington was predicated on a dry climate, warm days and cool nights, and access to cheap and plentiful water from the Columbia River dam system. Just add water, and the desert will bear good crops. But that water took a lot of work. Changing the sprinklers was something I learned in college while staying at the place, when Thad or Jess or Lance would get up before the sun, put on running shoes, and move the lengths of irrigation pipe manually to water different parts of the alfalfa crop or the trees. They'd get back, wet with sweat and water, sandy mud on their shoes and calves, and report to the brothers their time. Records were hard to come by as all three brothers were stalwart cross-country runners.

The summer I worked there, we had an outbreak of fire blight, a disease that was highly infectious and could take out an entire orchard if left unchecked. After the already rigorous offseason pruning regime, there was a constant patrol with pruning saw and disinfectant spray to keep ahead of the killing disease. The trick was to prune enough away to get all the fire blight and stop the spread, but not so much as to take away the productiveness of the tree. It was the same kind of calculation a wartime doctor used in getting rid of gangrene. It was a constant and brutal process of triaging wounds.

Mowing in the rows was a constant, because of the regular watering of the trees, and spraying for pests was also on a regular, weekly schedule. Jess suited up in a complete Tyvek hazmat suit because, unlike his dad, he hadn't already had his maximum exposure to the carcinogens and let precautions, literally, go in the winds. Because he had a longer span of living in front of him and wanted to live it. All the work made for a never-ending set of tasks, until the last crop was picked and there was the abrupt coming of winter. And with that, pruning time again. Altogether it was much less of a burden than the work of dairying, but the same constraints of Mother Nature, the fluctuations of markets and prices, finding a pool of workers to bring in the fruit, the constant worry of whether you were doing all right or barely making it, all contrived to make a heavy burden. It was like the Garden after the fall: still a pretty great place, but with anxiety. The naked possibility of failure and foreclosure right in your face.

Jess, the oldest brother, chose to come back to keep the farm working and in the family, but it wasn't an easy decision, either in the making or living of it. He had a degree in English from Washington State University, and after he took over the daily working of the farm, we no longer had conversations about books so much. The work was all-consuming. He changed the farm, and the farm changed him. He became more serious and set in his ways than when I'd known him in college. But I was still welcome on that porch, even with my unchanging ideals and wayward views on religion and politics. The years together, successes and failures, hard work and play, set a foundation that lasted. After a hot day's work, we'd sit on the porch drinking cold drinks, and after a while, I'd grab the empties and place them on the ground in hopscotch fashion and leap and step and crush them like some great, shambling, Hi-C-punch-drunk kid. Years later, when Padre's old forestry buddy who shared time with us that summer was slowly devolving into dementia and became porch-bound himself, Al would visit, and the hopscotch would always come up. That's the kind of ephemeral, time-fuse immortality that I was yearning for. A legacy of unforgettability.

When the apple-picking season finally descended upon us, I joined the crew in a marginal, outside, friend of the farm kind of way. I got up with the Mexican crew and met for brief instructions and then set to work. Jess had given me the basics of wearing the bag, setting the ladder, grab and pinch and twist the fruit, but I was slow. They started me in the small new trees up on the hill by the pond, where I didn't have to use a ladder and the fruit was big and easy to grab from among the slender limbs. I got into the rhythm after a few days and picked five bins one day, which was about half to a third of what the real pickers were capable of. But no matter how carefully I picked, I still often removed the spur with the apple, or the stem, also removing the possibility of fruit from that spot next year, and marginally devaluing the apple. When I finally moved into the big trees and tried to set my ladder strategically, each time I found my ladder in an apple-free zone and would have to move it once again. Many times. The Mexican guys tried to show me. "Like this," Eduardo would say, and set once and picked half a bin. And they laughed a bit at my speed. "Fast fingers, Michael," Arturo would say, and reach out and pick two apples in each hand.

There was a good community feeling in the trees once I'd been picking a while. The Mexican guys flew through the rows, and I would mosey, worrying and overthinking and remorseful. But we'd get to the end of a block or a row at the end of the day, and we would all pick into a communal bin to finish the job. The guys would offer the ticket for the bin to me, but I smiled no and protested and waved it to them. Luis, Joachin, Miguel, those guys really knew how to work, and I thought they should get paid for it. My four or five or, occasionally, six bins a day, at eleven bucks a bin for the Red Delicious, fifteen for the Goldens, was small beer for them, but it was good money for me. Besides, they all had responsibilities to their families back home, and I was just a young, unaccompanied single guy with a girlfriend. We'd sometimes share a beer or a ride to town, and I felt a real appreciation in being accepted in a place that I didn't belong. The working man's world. I ended up picking sixty-five bins of apples, and Jess the paymaster counted out the tickets and paid me eight hundred dollars, plus a sixty-buck bonus that I felt was just him being nice. But I'd helped get the crop in, and that's no small thing. With the baby's breath money thrown in, I had about three thousand dollars to move on with. Financial breathing room for a semi-adult. It felt good to have money and options in my pocket again.

Little Rock, Arkansas, Church Ladies, 1994

The last time I visited Papa, it was a couple of weeks before Christmas,1994. He'd been writing me letters on his typewriter, the pages so covered with correction tape and crossed-out words that they were almost as illegible as his scrawling and crabbed handwriting, telling me how all of his children had deserted him but that he was determined to keep himself physically fit and busy writing and that maybe we'd one day recognize and repent of our disrespect and come visit him. Instead of heading directly to Peoria for Christmas with my girlfriend K to visit her family, I took a bus from Charlottesville to Little Rock and ended up at the doorstep of his latest apartment. He invited me in and said that lunch was almost ready. We sat and talked a bit of careful small talk, catching up in the nondescript, sparsely furnished living room until I noticed a burning smell and we hurried into the kitchen. I opened the oven, and a wave of acrid smoke billowed out.

Different Tupperware containers full of holiday food from the church ladies Papa always attracted the notice of were melting into the metal oven racks and catching fire on the heating elements below.

"Papa! You have to take the food out of the plastic if it's not a microwave!"

It was pretty clear Uncle Pat was not going to get his damage deposit back on this place, either, just like the countless others he had procured for his youngest brother in his brief breaks from his suffocating bipolar illness. We had a snack of some rolls and cold cuts and talked a while longer. I was short with Papa and angry at his foolishness, and it was a brief visit. He said that it was pretty obvious that I didn't love him and wondered why I'd bothered to come and see him at all. Thinking the same thing myself, I said that he'd wanted me to come, so I had. When I hugged him goodbye and kissed him on his stubbly, unshaven cheek, he said, "You probably won't see me again. My kids don't love me, my wife divorced me for one of those other men she was seeing. Even my brother doesn't care about me. This apartment is miles from the library, and I don't even have a library card. I'll probably kill myself."

I pooh-poohed his words; told him he was going to live forever and that I would love him the same length of time. The truth was, Papa was incredibly healthy and had lived so long with his illness that there didn't seem to be an ending point at all for any of us who knew and loved him. Who'd once loved him a lot and were finding it harder and harder to bring up those good memories of when he'd been more loveable. I was pretty sure he'd live forever.

When I was at K's parents' house a few days later, I was still stewing over the details of that visit with my dad. K and I had been together for two years and were talking marriage; we even went to a jewelry store looking at rings, so things were suddenly serious and getting complicated with details and binding the disparate parts of career paths, education and salary-earning potential, family-joining and family-breaking. I was stressed. The next day, I learned that Papa had killed himself with an overdose. K tried to help me make plans to go to the funeral and gave me the love and support that I'd always felt from her. On Christmas Eve, there was a formal family dinner, just the four of us. I'd never heard of such a thing. I came downstairs in my regular clothes and was told by my soon-to-be mother-in-law to go upstairs and get appropriately dressed. I did it under duress and endured the dinner, but I was mad. I'd had a lot of pride-swallowing all my life and didn't want to willingly sign up for more. Upstairs in our room afterwards, K and I had a quiet argument. I told her that the money her parents had was going to divide us, and that I needed to be able to be myself if I was going to be with her. And that wasn't going to happen. I decided that it would be for the best that we end our relationship, and then did what I always did best, and ran. No wedding, no funeral. I ran back to Mama's house in Greenville, South Carolina, and just checked out. Mama usually had a two-week visitation policy, but in this case, she just let me be, without time constraints or even much in the way of advice. She knew all of what I'd experienced and let me figure myself out. It was a great gift on the worst Christmas.

I had recently turned thirty, and I suddenly found that cliche of a biological clock a real thing. My lack of possessions and impact were painful to me. I wanted to be doing something more. I sent off an application for entry into the education department at Washington State University, my alma mater, and got a quick reply of a provisional yes but was informed that my grades wouldn't allow them to accept me into the department. "Come back," they told me. "Clean up your transcript, and we'll gladly take you." I left the demise of my long-term relationship and the suicide death of my father and departed for Pullman. Again.

The Palouse Region, Washington, Kamiak Butte, 1995

Each time I returned to Pullman, the place seemed different, although the changes were surface-level at best: this restaurant was now this other place; this dorm that once was special to me because a friend lived there was now mothballed as the student population dropped; this one greenspace beach where we had walked by the coconut-scented girls getting early summer tans was now paved over for parking. No, Pullman hadn't changed much, but I had. Five years of working in physically demanding jobs, gardening and dairy farming and line-cooking and dishwashing, salmon fishing—these jobs changed and hardened and informed me. Mostly, they told me that I wasn't built for nonstop physical labor, and I needed to find a different path.

I moved into the McEachern Graduate Center housing, McGeekern, I called it, and set down all of my worldly possessions, which included a heavy steel Raleigh ten-speed mountain bike, already years obsolete compared to the carbon-fiber lightweight bikes of my peers; an IBM Selectric typewriter that my mom had bought before computers came to rule the office, with exchangeable font and language wheels, fifty pounds if it was an ounce; some T-shirts; and a set of flannel cotton sheets. Not exactly David Carradine's *Kung Fu* walking in the world lightly, but not much encumbered. I had a room with a bed and a desk and a wall of windows that looked out onto shade. I felt like an adult. The woman who sat in the window of the lobby to give me my mail was pleasant and had a nice smile, so I asked her out. She said yes, and when we went downtown to have coffee, we just kind of stared at each other for as long as we could stand it and then, forlorn and depressed, we said bye. I wondered why I'd asked and why she'd accepted. Mail pickup became less of an anticipation. Less smiley. I was back to one of my good old cold spells again.

In the intervening years separating my first undergraduate degree in English and this second one in education, I had learned some things about work and learning. My introductory education classes and my old transcript Fs were embarrassingly easy to remedy and ace. This wasn't waking up at 4:30 on a cold winter morning to milk cows or carrying sixty-pound bales of baby's breath off a sandy plateau on a hundred-degree day. I coasted through my coursework, successfully this time. After being in jobs where I literally lived on the worksite, having a couple of classes a day was freeing. A cakewalk. I dutifully completed my English Fiction essays, wrote my daily logs for my education classes, retook History of WWII from a professor who spoke instead of droning this time around, and closed in on my history minor. One morning in one of our education classes, we learned that there had been a school shooting in Moses Lake, and the one teacher killed was the mother of one of our classmates. When my classmate offered up his take and sharing his knowledge of the event, he said that he wasn't surprised his mom was shot, that she was always too soft on kids. If I hadn't just a few days before confessed to another student in that class, in just the same off-the-cuff normalcy, that "every woman I'm interested in turns out to be a lesbian," a result of my latest attempt at asking another woman out and the aftermath of my almost-married relationship, I would have been shocked by his callousness. And of course I was. But I knew that mourning, trauma, and shock made us say dumb things. When you're in pain, you don't have a filter. It was one of the most powerful education lessons I learned in my year and a half getting that degree.

My new schedule opened up new opportunities and freedoms, so I returned to my running regimen and soon was flying down the roads of my old workout haunts. I ran without a shirt and got whistled at by a girl. I entered a campus fitness 5K race and found myself running stride for stride in the front with another runner. As I broke away at the end and sped through the tunnel and onto the turf of our football stadium and crossed the finish line first, I felt that old fierce joy that rowing had once given me. I won it in a time of 15:15, three five-minute miles, and got paid thirty dollars for the win. I joked that I was a professional now. But really, for me, who I was and who I'd been, getting whistled at by the girl was the better reward. And at that game, I was still a rank beginner and hopelessly outmatched.

During the semester, I had work study jobs frying three different sizes of burgers in the busiest dining hall on campus on Saturdays and working the pot shack early Sunday morning. I arrived to tottering stacks of burned-on gunky pots and pans, and three hours of scalding hot water and noxious chemicals later, the breakfast staff had a clean arsenal to cook from. My first summer back, I got a job with WSU Maintenance cleaning dormitory rooms, changing the batteries in thousands of smoke detectors and fixing the metal bedframes of thousands of screwless, bent, and stripped connections that had the mattresses listing and screeching. The crew of three of us would hit a room, straighten out any brokenness, and move on. If we were cruising, we could do a floor each day. There were lots of floors in lots of dormitories. If it was an endless and unsatisfying job, I'd had plenty of those. That was why I was here: to do the same old thing until I was qualified for something new. A teaching gig. Something that might actually pay me well enough to settle down and stay. Somewhere.

Those jobs, all my jobs after high school and a childhood without real work responsibilities, taught me important lessons in attitude and effort. One of the old boys in Maintenance, a pony-tailed, rough-cool, chain-smoker-skinny electrician, would often comment after a job he'd finished, "Good enough for the girls I go with." Oh, man, I loved that. Not just because it was literally true and he hung out with women who made questionable choices, like hanging out with him, but because the concept of good enough is a good and true place to hang your life-philosophy hat. For my second dad, Darius, good enough was a high achievement, an accomplishment to be proud of, and not something that was always a given. One time, he poured an old vintage wine, a special bottle for a special meal, and when I said it was "alright," he took the glass from me and drained it himself. And sometimes, good enough hits lower. Stocking shelves and fronting cans in a grocery store for the appearance of abundance, every shelf fully up front and standing in lockstep, is a job that doesn't carry a stain of sin for being pretty well done. That one coworker from my job in the vitamin health food store in Cambridge who always had to be "Great!" and told me he didn't want Satan to catch him in a down moment and catch him well and truly, well. I loved that weirdo, but how exhausting it must have been for him to always be up. I learned that just alright was pretty darn good.

My work also taught me to see behind facades and look and notice and acknowledge the people who do the hard and underappreciated labor of making our world work. After having worked in the anonymity of the pot shack, Sunday mornings before the sun came up, I remembered that there's a whole secret world out there of people in back rooms cleaning our dishes or sweeping floors and emptying trash and cleaning bathrooms like I'd done with the Emersons in high school. Painting parking lots in the early hours of the morning. Bakers working in big factories producing bread good enough for the masses, and bakers working in small, hot basement spaces making bread good enough for people to travel across town to buy. To stand in line for. All while never being good enough for their customers to take the time to meet and thank the person who made it. We lose something important when we say a prayer of thanks to our Maker for our daily bread, but don't do the kindness of a few simple words of praise for the bread maker.

I had a couple of education classes with great teachers named Eileen. One, in Ed Psych, focused her class on the crunching of numbers as a way of measuring student progress. I disagreed with her so strongly, but in an engaging and respectful challenge, that she told me one day after class, "Your distrust of standardized testing is going to dog you throughout your career in teaching unless you decide to embrace it." I said something to the effect that all of my strong beliefs dogged me, and that I was okay with the weight that I chose to drag around. The other Eileen, the more accomplished and experienced teacher of the two, taught an English reading class and introduced me to Sandra Cisneros and *The House on Mango Street* and other writers of color for young people. She also introduced me to another amazing woman. In her class, we had to earn tutoring credits by working with other students on literacy issues. She had me assigned to a remedial tutoring classroom that utilized the internet and all of the sources contained there. I begged off by telling her about my IBM Selectric, and she said that I definitely needed to be a part of this class.

When I showed up to the computer lab, there were a dozen students and one other teacher named Diane to help me run the tutorial session. The technology was new to all of us, the group rather hastily thrown together, so there was some confusion as to the class structure and leadership and purpose. We all kind of made it up as we went, and it quickly became a good cooperative learning model. I knew nothing about computers, but writing, though, that was deep in my comfort zone. So, the students, my peers, really, had their writing that they were trying to revise and improve upon for their English 101 classes, and I knew how to do that. They did research and wrote, and I looked over their shoulders and drafts and made helpful suggestions. The other young woman—tall, thin, pretty, businesslike—was obviously the one in charge of leading the classroom, and she did most of the direct instruction and goal setting for each session. We both did our job. It was good teacher prep and mentoring for me. I kept Eileen apprised of our progress and thanked her for the opportunity. I appreciated the challenge.

Diane later told me that when she'd been encouraged to join the class by a fellow writing center tutor because there was a cute organic farmer co-teacher, she told her friend, "I have a big new bed and a cute new puppy. I don't need a man." And I, upon seeing this tall, willowy, long-haired beauty, said to myself, "Oh, well. You can't hit on the teacher." It turned out we were both disabused of those views pretty quickly. One day after the class, she asked me if I wanted to come out to her place for a Sunday lunch. I told her I didn't have a car and couldn't make it out of town, and she said no problem, she could pick me up. I said yes. I went home and called all of my friends for their sage advice:

Was a Sunday lunch a date?

Yes, Michael.

Should I go out on a date with the teacher?

Are you sure she's the teacher? Is she cute? Nice? Do you like her?

The first an undecided no, followed by a string of yesses. I stewed all week in an agony of anticipation and fear, but when she showed up in her little blue Toyota Tercel—Beva, she called it—we immediately hit it off. She laughed at me when I asked her about the teacher thing, and she told me about the organic farmer comment. Although she'd been skeptical, she said, she figured he'd turned out to be right about me. I was cute. Swoon.

She and Beva drove me away from my sterile dormitory digs and north out of Pullman. We drove over the rolling Palouse landscape, past Kamiak Butte and almost to the town of Palouse. I kept looking over at her, dressed in her sturdy shoes and long denim skirt, her long auburn hair loose down her back, and freckled, upturned nose. It was like going on a date with Pippi Longstocking. I mean a super-cute, adult, smart, real Pippi. She was enchanting. When she finally turned off the highway, it was onto a gravel road heading up and over a hill and down into a charming farm hollow, an oasis with a big red barn, apple and fir trees, two large and upstanding if somewhat dilapidated farmhouses, and one little cabin. She drove up to the cabin and said, "This is it!"

The Bungalow, as it was known, consisted of one small main room of a kitchen and a table with chairs, an attached glass greenhouse off at a dogleg that brought a glow of exterior light inside, a curtained-off back room with a bed and a small loft above, and a separate curtained cubby with a composting toilet, all paneled in cherry-stained wood planks. Everything was warm and comfy in color, style, and substance, and Diane had a fluffy little border collie pup named Hannah. It was like walking into a Jan Brett children's picture book. There was a wonderful smell filling the interior, and I sat down and we talked while she put a few last touches on the meal she'd prepared. Out of the oven came a loaf of sourdough white bread, browned and crisp, while on the stovetop, a big, enameled pot of potato leek soup bubbled. As the bread came out, in went an apple tart with a lattice crust. I was pierced through the heart by so much beauty, by that poor kid hunger I always carried with me, by the magical appearance of a place and a person and a life that I'd dreamed about but had stopped hoping for. We shared our first meal, and I was pretty much ready to move in.

When we'd finished lunch and done the dishes, Diane suggested going for a walk up at Kamiak Butte, a state park we'd passed a couple miles away. It was early November and the days were short, so we were chasing the light of a beautiful sunset and setting out to claim a walk from the coming darkness. We weren't long into the hike when the trail forked, and she said, offhandedly, "Do you want to stay on the trail or head off across the field? I haven't been through here before." I readily agreed to go off-trail, and we trod over the roughly tilled wheatfields a while before making our way through the woods and back onto the more traveled path. When we made it back to Beva, we tarried, and kissed warm, sweet, soft, slow kisses. Driving back to the bungalow, that little spark of light in the big, dark Palouse night, it was decided that I'd stay the night.

We mooned around a bit, in that fresh joy of new romance, and then as we prepared for bed, I sat down and told her, "I've messed up this part a lot. I always move too fast and end up doing something wrong or rushing things, so they don't work. And I don't want to do that. I want us to work. Is it okay if we just sleep together?" She agreed, and so I waited across the room while she got out of her clothes and into her night things. I came back into the bedroom, the light so dim that it might as well have been candlelight, and there was a big bed with quilts and a duvet and the whole setting a fine little frontier love shack. I took off all of my things and climbed in next to her naked, and she gave a quick intake of breath and said, "Oh, my!" It was a sentiment we both shared. It was the best first date ever and, unbeknownst to me, the beginning of a whole new life.

Part V: Arrival

After that first date, so full of portents that escaped me in the moment, Diane and I were serious. Seriously in love, seriously devoted, seriously at that time when we were full of light and joy and purpose. I hadn't been clear about the deadly seriousness of her question about leaving the trail as we walked together, but she'd had enough of cookie-cutter, bean-counter, standardized guys, and if I had chosen the beaten path instead of going off-trail, it would have led me right back to my cheerless dormitory cubicle. I still had a semester and some change left in my teaching preparation, and she was uncomfortably aware of my unserious study habits. I spent a few all-nighters in the front room of the Bungalow writing essays after choosing to spend the prime daylight and evening hours enthralled by her. I'd sit at her tiny Apple IIe computer, the screen the size of a postcard, and rattle off a ten-page essay that would earn me a first-draft A the next day. Hannah, that lovely pup of hers, of ours, would accompany me through the wee hours and not judge as long as I patted her occasionally and took her out to pee under the stars every few hours.

Palouse, Washington, The Bungalow, 1996

Diane's graduate school master's work never made similar appearances at home: she took care of shit and got it done. I told her about my first undergraduate experience and how I'd struggled mightily to be a rower, and less so as a student. My pièce de résistance story was when I'd been disenrolled for the first time because of a particularly bad semester where I received a 1.55 GPA. She was awestruck. "How do you even get a GPA that low?" and I was like, "I KNOW! It takes effort." I told her that 155 was a holy number, the weight average for all eight rowers in a lightweight boat, and how I'd written "Lightweight in mind and body" under the grades. When I told her that it was a kind of magical occurrence, a proof of my commitment, and an outrageous display of allegiance to sport, she was unimpressed and not amused. "A more fitting commitment to the sport and your teammates might have been to row with them your senior year." There wasn't an answer to that. She steered me through my coursework, curse-work if you've ever taken education classes, and tried to gently encourage me to succeed. I wasn't very teachable in that context, but the whole reason I came back for my teaching certification was to be a new me, so I pushed back a little and also got my work done. She'd never had much experience failing herself, and she didn't want it for me. I didn't want it for us, so I tried a bit harder. We worked well together.

After a winter of working on school and loving this woman, her dog, our little shack in the folds of wheat fields, spring hit like a sledgehammer and everything reverberated into mass action. We planted a garden, got some chickens, and made the Bungalow a place for three, not two. Four if you count Qolus the cat, which I didn't. We were ambitious in our farmstead planning and lack of experience. We got ten Cornish Cross chickens and raised them to maturity in six short weeks. We knew they were a meat breed, and we were prepared to kill and eat them. What we weren't prepared for was their freakishly fast growth, the way their legs soon ceased to carry the incredible breastwork that they were genetically forced to grow. And that when we hesitated to kill them, they dropped over dead from heart attacks and asphyxiation on their own. We decided to pursue a more egg-production-oriented flock after that. My final semester was progressing similarly. Even though coming through coursework as an adult with motivation was easier on me than my first undergrad experience, I balked at a classroom management class that used an aged text called *You Can Handle Them All*. It had brief descriptions of students like "The Nose-

Picker" and "The Last-Worder," and directions on how to redirect or correct their behaviors. It was a mind-numbing and demoralizingly black-and-white lens for a class in an area of teaching I knew I was going to struggle with. I had always been a mix of apathetic and oppositional as a student myself, and leadership and imposing order was not an area in which I had a lot of experience or confidence.

Late on the last day of the semester, in the last class before I graduated to a semester of student teaching, a process contingent upon passing the management class, I finished a fifty-page classroom management plan and placed it in the carport of my least favorite teacher. Diane and I were both on tenterhooks as to whether he'd take it, and that created some stress. It was a kind of welcoming to the life of Riley moment for her: a life in which last second, hanging in the balance, unforced error events happen. But we needn't have worried, from my perspective at least, because he accepted the project and gave me the grade I needed. Usually that was the way it worked for me. Diane was learning to grip a bit less tightly, and I was learning to hold on a bit less loosely. We met in the middle and held each other firmly, with a connection that was part life preserver, part steadying hand to catch our balance, and part passionate embrace. All without leaving bruises. We were growing together.

Sometime that spring, Diane started making intimations of affirmations for our relationship. I was confused and taken aback. "What, like codifying our relationship? Like marriage?!

We've just met! Why would we want to change anything?" I was thinking of all of the things we were doing as gestures of our healthy togetherness and overtures of commitment. We were raising animals and a garden together. Sharing what little money we had and both working hard separately to provide for the other. Our love life was going swimmingly, always captured for me in the time I found myself with one foot on the couch and one in the dog dish, both of us laughing while lovemaking. There might have been a hamstring cramp thrown in as well. We were doing pretty damned good. Her response was something on the order of, "Well, why would we want to do anything else? Why not this time? Why not now?" I translated all of this into things, into words and aphorisms, that she didn't approve of. "Do anything" became "do anyone." I thought about "free milk from a cow" and, on the timeliness front, "biological clock ticking" and "shit or get off the pot." It was bleak and crude language to describe something that gave me the heebie-jeebies. It felt to me like marriage was a place where love went to die. I was upset and pressured and felt unnecessarily rushed, and if there is one thing people who love us know to be true, it's that you should never rush a Riley. In the end, though, I agreed. I wanted us to happen. I moseyed a bit more hurriedly.

On spring break, we drove down to California to bask in some iconic western beauty. I thought I'd pop the question. I made Michael Riley preparations, which consisted of two phone calls and one addition to our itinerary. We drove through middle-of-nowhere eastern Oregon and then through middle-of-nowhere northern California. Deep in the night on one mountain pass curve where Diane was foolishly allowing me to drive Beva, the blue Toyota, I attempted to turn off my brights and instead turned off the lights. The guy powering around the corner lost me as I assumed stealth mode, and I'm forever apologetic about the years of his life lost as he shouted, "Where'd he go! Where'd he go!" into his car interior. As we came into San Francisco, I had another malfunction as I pulled up to the toll gate for a busy bridge merge. Still in the days of coin-operated tollbooths, I dropped our only remaining coins short of the basket and watched them roll under the car. Horns blaring, traffic surging, yells and taunts imagined and real, I got on my knees and retrieved the coins. I paid the toll and had a panic attack trying to merge out of the gates and killed the engine while shifting the gears wrong. More shouting. I got it started and exited onto the shoulder, and we changed drivers. Like, pretty much permanently from that point onward. It was a painful exchange, but one that ultimately worked for me. I've always been more comfortable in the passenger seat than in the driver's. I wasn't driven to be the man.

We had a wonderful time visiting Big Sur, where we sat outside on a clifftop patio and enjoyed an expensive lunch that included a priceless view overlooking the ocean. We walked on beaches and among the redwoods, saw sights in the city, and did all of the done things. After that we drove out towards Gilroy, the Garlic Capital of the World, where even the McDonald's features garlic fries, and made our way into the countryside. I found myself in the driver's seat once again, this time metaphorically. We were headed to my old girlfriend's dad's ranch. Diane was skeptical. I was adamant. We bobbed and weaved into brown grassy hills and vineyards and dusty green coastal live oaks on a curvy, thin gray blacktop ribbon of road that finally turned to dirt. I spied the sign to the ranch, a faded, wooden, unprepossessing raised-letter affair that said *Vanumanutagi*, and breathed a sigh of relief. I had not steered us wrong. We wended up the now private road, deep into towering young redwoods and shade. Leo, Pam's dad, met us on the porch of the main house and showed us along the boardwalk to one of the newer suites he'd made available. He gave us the short-version tour of the gardens, livestock, swimming pool, all of the amenities. He gave me the keys and a couple of bottles of the house wine and took his leave. Leo was pure class. A great guy for a favor to a struggling young man that he had his eyes on and was expecting great things from.

Diane was in a mild state of shock. She knew me from my relative penniless state, the me that moved in with everything I owned in a box containing flannel sheets, a bunch of T-shirts and jeans, and a ten-speed bike, but here I was giving her a glimpse of luxury she hadn't seen before. I was full of surprises. Exceeding expectations. The main house was built in 1900 for Fanny Stevenson, the widow of Robert Louis Stevenson, and the Vanumanutagi moniker was Samoan for "Vale of the Singing Birds." It was living up to its name as we settled in, birdsong carrying through the peaceful shady yard and the surrounding hillsides. If Papa really was an honorary chief in Samoa, here I was being an honorary prince.

We had the place to ourselves. As Diane explored, I went to work in the kitchen, setting about making calzone dough from the recipe I got while I was the salad and calzone guy working in the kitchen at Swilly's in Pullman, the one fine dining place in our area. I put the dough together and left it aside while I began assembling and prepping the ingredients: spinach, Italian sausage, mushrooms, ricotta and mozzarella, tomato sauce, and herbs from the garden. Once I had everything ready to begin, I noticed the dough sitting in its dormant, dough-ball state. It was too late in the day to put together another meal, so I left the calzone idea behind and made a hearty pasta instead. We ate in a corner of the big dining room, a cozy nook with a table for two.

After the meal, I got down on my knee and presented her with an antique Austrian diamond ring that I'd procured in secrecy from my mom. I asked and she said yes. The proposal wouldn't win me any contests in *Wedding Magazine*, like Pam's friend who was helicoptered to a remote mesa-top where the waiter poured the wine, uncovered the entrees and hopped into the helicopter, leaving the couple to their own devices. But in terms of setting, planning, and budgetary constraints, it was a convincing display of love. It was a big day in my life, maybe the biggest. A turning point in finally starting to get things right.

The next morning, the dough had risen, and we made cinnamon rolls. I told her, "That's the life of Riley right there. It takes some time, and things don't always go according to plan, but in the end? Dolce, baby." Years later, when I'd tell the story to my eighth-grade students, one boy popped up with a crafty gleam and said, "The dough didn't rise, Mr. Riley?" It took a second for his implication to sink in, and I retorted with real heat, "Hey! That's my proposal story, you jerk. Don't you worry about the dough, mister. Ew!" But I eventually warmed to his addition to the story, because it really was a bit of an odd tale in the first place, asking a girl to marry me at my ex-girlfriend's country estate. I mean, who does that? Who gets away with that? The answer was and remains, me. The charmed person I'd grown into from that skinny young kid that my Uncle Pat had once told, "You were just so pitiful, Michael. We never thought you were going to make it." And that faint praise changed to his mantra of me later in his life, when he was fond of repeating that, "You met that Diane, and she just turned your life around." It turned out he was pretty damned right. The next night we were in Yosemite, and we were using the payphone to call our families and a few best friends and sharing the news that we were betrothed. It was a jubilation to us all.

The end of the spring semester and the start of summer allowed us time to start planning the wedding and playing with all the ideas and moving parts. I was to start my student teaching semester in Richland, Washington, at Hanford High at the end of August, so we set a date of August 10th and the place at Kamiak State Park, in the trees where we took that first-date walk and shared our first kiss. Since we were doing everything on a shoestring, perforce and according to our views on long-term success not beginning with long-term debt, we made it up as we went. Renting the space in the park might have been fifty bucks, and the view was spectacular, the setting among the green grass and towering pines bordering on ripe wheat fields Instagram-worthy even before the media existed. We had a Victorian garden party to test out the site of the after-wedding reception, on straw bales scattered around the farmyard in front of the Bungalow, and we made connections among friends for music and food and officiating the service. Diane borrowed her mom's wedding dress and went on a crash diet she only needed because her mom was tiny-waisted thirty years previously. Diane was skinny already, so we both worried: she if she would make it, me that she would lose too much weight. She was competitive, and there was no question that she was going to make it. I got fitted for a tux, and we were a matched pair—young, thin, and not hard on the eyes. And happy together.

With a week to go before the big day, old friends and family and the wedding party participants started showing up, pitching tents in our yard and pitching in with the yardwork, food, pickups and deliveries of the sundry things that make a wedding happen. Maybe the single most expensive part of the wedding was the cake, and we'd been lucky enough to secure the services of Edna Mae Schultheis of Colton, Washington, to make us one of her special creations. When it arrived, deconstructed, we needed three different refrigerators in three different houses to hold the many layers. Assembled and strewn with edible flowers, it looked straight out of *Sunset Magazine*. It was just us and our crew making it happen, and things were going swimmingly. Friends were set to work making mountains of pasta salad, enough, one said, that she might never need to eat it again for the rest of her life.

We went over plans with Kristine, our pastor at the Pullman Congregational Church, and she found the vows we'd written worthy. We were short on scripture in the service and long on secular humanism. We were marrying each other, after all, not God. The prayer, though, she told us, would need to be directed towards a deity. She remembered a couple who just wanted the words directed into the air and had a feeling that that's exactly where they went. "A prayer, like a letter, needs an addressee, or it won't find a home." We agreed with her on that and worked with her getting the people placement, words, rituals all set and practiced. I loved that the excitement exceeded the anxiety. That laughs and community superseded the inevitable stress-induced sharp words and the loneliness among crowds that I had grown up with. We were using all our life and love and support to make something beautiful together.

The day before the wedding arrived, and mostly things were in place. The keg of microbrew, cases of wine, meats and cheese that my restaurant-owner friend had provided at cost arrived. The farm was starting to look like the site of a Rainbow Gathering, tents sprung up like mushrooms and new people stopping in to say hi and announce their arrival. Most of the guests were staying fifteen miles away in Moscow, so the back-and-forth and comings and goings were legion. There were hikes at Kamiak Butte, organized runs, meals being prepared nonstop over gas cookstoves and in the three house kitchens on the farm. That evening, we went out and had the walk-through at the park and then came back to a feast. Grandmother Kelly discovered that Diane drank wine, a disappointment greater for her than learning that I didn't teach in a suit and tie. She wasn't the only one with concerns. My mom, who never drank alcohol because of the resulting loss of rigid self-control that it might precipitate, was imbibing on this occasion. She rounded on me and Diane in a side-swirl out of the main merriment and said, "This all seems so happy and beautiful. Let's see how we feel a year from now." Schatzi, who had already worked out that she was gaining a sister, not losing a brother, took her aside for some words. Other than a sharp, "Mama!" I'm not sure if I upbraided her. She was obviously in mourning for the end of her youngest boy's childhood, the loss of her *zucker-bulli*, her little sugar boy. We rolled on by her like the mighty Columbia, and the comment was just a small eddy in the powerful flow of good vibes.

I only remember being nervous at one point in the whole day of the wedding, and that was quickly resolved. I was upstairs in the big house, across the yard from the Bungalow and the place that would be our new home. Me and my guys were changing into our tuxes, and I came face to face with a cummerbund for the first time in my life. "What the FUCK is a cummerbund?!" I asked the room, as I struggled to attach the strange accoutrement to my middle. My best man, Dave Reeder, of course, came over and said, "Here you go, Michael," and closed the clasp behind me. I looked in the mirror, and found that I was a sharp-dressed, lovely man. I stood myself down. As stress and anxiety events for grooms go, it was way less dramatic than fainting in front of the whole party. And it was hot enough for that to happen. But such a display was unnecessary. I was ready.

We caravaned the three miles down the road to the state park and got all of the old people settled in under the trees and into folding chairs in the shade. It was a blazing hot day, but we'd just made it under the late-season park closure for fire hazard (it would take effect the following week), and we were in the green under-spaces, relatively cool, surrounded by fields of tawny ripe wheat. We could see the shimmer of heat waves over the grain, but we were shielded from it by ponderosa pines and manicured lawn.

Darius walked me down to where Kristine was waiting to begin the ceremony, and I might have cried. He had on an ugly paisley tie, wide and colorful, but he was a beautiful man. I loved him more than my own father. Probably more than my mother. It was a love we'd mutually worked out, given freely to each other, and one without requirements. Without the corruption of blood. He handed me off and stood back, and Diane walked down the path with her dad. In her white dress, crown of rose florets, her wide smile, she was dazzling. I was dazzled.

We said our vows, had readings from friends, both of our moms sang solos, and it went off without a hitch. We sealed the deal with a chaste and warm and romantic kiss worthy of the day. Years later, Kristine would say that we had kind of spoiled her for weddings. We were one of the first she officiated, and it all went so smoothly that it left her unprepared for the following years of glitches and mishaps that typically occur. After the vows, we climbed over the railing fence and posed for pictures of the wedding party, the bridesmaids and Diane holding me up, the groomsmen and me holding up the bride. We were comfortable in our close-fitting clothes, our skin, in the arrangements we'd made with each other. We were well met.

Michael is held by his bride and bridesmaids in the wheatfields of the Palouse (1996).

On the ride back to the farm in Beva, we popped the cork of a bottle of champagne, and I finally started sweating. It was ninety-five degrees out. I took off my jacket back at the place and we leapt into the festivities. It was time to party. Our friends Paul Smith and Mike Reilly were playing fiddle and guitar music, the keg was doing steady business under the trees, food was flying off the tables, and best of all, all of our friends and families were conversing and laughing and telling stories.

Everyone was having a good time. Diane and I cut the cake, and she fed me with a saucy smile and crinkly, laughing eyes. I did the same for her. We were tan and thin and dressed to the nines, and we would still be feeling fine even a year later. Even twenty-nine years later.

Michael Riley and Diane Kelly-Riley at their wedding reception, August 1996.

The party ran into the evening hours and showed no sign of slowing down. Diane and I did, exiting finally, exhausted and happy, and left the revelers to their celebration. Late in the night, long after we went to bed, some of our best buddies were in the hot tub, buoyantly drunk, and decided to run naked out into the moonlit hills of ripe wheat surrounding the farm. The next morning, decidedly sober and hobbling from the sharp chafing of the wheat awns, glumes, and spikes on their own softer tender parts, the self-styled Children of the Wheat suffered and commiserated and laughed with each other. It was the best wedding that any of us had ever attended.

The following day, we set off for our honeymoon in the Gulf Islands, the Canadian San Juans, with a few helpful and hardy souls doing us the service of clearing up, putting away, and returning all of the party gear. Beva was decked out with marriage graffiti, and cans clanked behind us as we rolled up the hill, ready for the open road. A solitary car descended towards us and rolled down their window as we both came to a stop. "Hello, Diane and Michael! Hey, um, where's the wedding?" I looked over my shoulder to the littered and trampled Shull Farm yard, and said, "Oh, MAN! You really missed a good one. There's not much left except some work to do. We're off. Sorry you couldn't be there." Time occasionally stands still, and you get to see an event with the omniscient view of a kid holding a snow globe. Our wedding still feels that way to me. But it doesn't stand so still that you can show up a day late. Sometimes, when you miss something, whether it be by minutes, hours, or a whole day, you miss it by lightyears. We said goodbye, and laughed, and didn't feel bad. The open road waits for no one.

We drove Beva over to Seattle, loaded her onto a car ferry bound for Victoria, BC, Canada, and let out some big, deep breaths. Holding a culminating life event, carrying it off and birthing a beautiful day in the life of us and our friends and family was no mean feat. We were exhausted. We stood out on the deck and railings and had some fellow traveler take a picture of us, exhilarated and groggy-eyed and happy. We had high tea at the Empress Hotel, as tourists on honeymoon would. Our first couple of nights, we stayed in the Oak Bay Guest House, an old-school English club-looking place with lots of floral decor and dark, heavy wood features: the masculine and feminine traditions rampant. It was beautiful, but it felt like a place for old people. When we ordered dinner, our waiter, a slow-moving ancient gentleman who could have been anywhere from sixty to a hundred years of age and who blended into the shadows and wood-paneling like a magician, heard our request for a Caesar salad with an audible sigh. He came back a few minutes later, silently pushing a service cart, and began a painstaking process of cutting the romaine leaves from their center ribs, mixing the egg and oil and cheese and anchovies in a whisking bowl, and assembling the whole dish in a tableside theatre tableau. It felt painful to watch. It was delicious to eat.

After two nights, we left the perpetual shade and Anglophile gloom of our lodgings and the pretty primness of Victoria and headed to Saltspring Island. The sea breezes and cool sunshiny days felt like a balm, fresh and clean. We were surprised by the dryness and lack of beaches. The Channel Islands, like their cousins the San Juans, lie in the rain-shadow of the westernmost coastal lands and are largely rocky outcrops in the ocean. We enjoyed a few casual days of lazing around, but it was difficult to access the natural beauty of the place. We wanted to be in it, and the island vibe seemed to be more about watching from a comfortable chair. We took the ferry over to Galiano Island to stay at a B & B that had looked interesting, in a rustic and casual way, from our searches while planning the trip. On our arrival, though, with a bit of a falling heart, we noticed that rustic was instead rather dumpy, the cabins roughly and inexpertly built in a way that we coined shape-shifter architecture. Buildings that had changed with available materials and in the years that had passed from concept to finished project. A key element of shape-shifter-built architecture is that it's never finished. The old guy showed us the rather grungy bathtubs set out on the rocks above the ocean, the feature that had looked so enticing from the online pictures, and mentioned that they were clothing optional. We glanced up at the big picture windows looming above from his own home, and winced. We wore our suits. The next day, we decided to cut the trip short and head back to the Palouse. We had a home, even if it was a rental, and it was cuter, homier, more picturesque than anything we'd seen so far. And it was ours together to share in the privacy of that little ten-acre wheatland bowl of a homestead. We missed it already. We went home

Little Rock, Arkansas, The Favorite, 1997

Of all my cousins, I'd always felt closest to Anne, Uncle Pat's youngest. When I would visit their house in the Heights, it was a nonstop education in Southern upper-class culture. I'd tag along to her neighbor-friend's and get mysterious insights into the lives of girls. They talked to each other, laughed a lot, lounged about, knew things. Since pretty much all I did was walk miles and read books, it all felt alien to me. We would play on the trampoline they had in their enclosed backyard, and Anne would show me acrobatic moves that I would try once and spectacularly fail at. I had near-death experiences and always left with pinch marks from the springs. Pat, Jr., on the other hand, was always slumped on the couch with food, watching TV and recovering from the miles he'd swam in the early morning and getting ready for the miles he'd swim in the afternoon. He had a drawer full of medals and was monosyllabic at his best. The other two sisters were older and had even less time for me, although Katharine could ante up for some rebellious fun on occasion. Anne and Katharine once got the idea of dressing me up as a girl and taking me over to the Little Rock Country Club across the street. I wore the dress and makeup well, and passed as a cute little girl, but the cousins loved telling me afterwards how everyone wondered what was wrong with my legs, whether I had some sort of disability, because we hadn't had time to practice walking in high heels. I was a toy, the sidekick, and it was a role I was familiar with. It got me good meals at the country club grill, so I was okay with slipping back into it.

When I was out of college, Anne had a serious bout of breast cancer that almost killed her. She recovered and took a job in Washington, DC, in the Clinton administration with the Council on Aging and built a good life for herself. I visited her and her husband and baby in Alexandria one fall day when I was living nearby in Charlottesville and had an afternoon carving pumpkins with them. She had these fancy pumpkin-carving tools that dumbfounded me. Did you need anything other than a sharp knife to carve two eyes, a nose, and a crinkly mouth? The answer was yes, and we filigreed and shaved and nuanced our fancy Halloween pumpkins into being. It was an idyllic setting, and I could see she and I growing up and into the selves we might have imagined as kids.

Just when I'd imagined her well and out of the woods again, the cancer surged back with a vengeance and killed her quickly. I was shocked and hammered by grief the way I never felt with either of my grandmothers' passings, not even with my dad's. I would find myself crying at regular intervals, and it confused me, because I'd never felt a death touch me before. With Papa, we kids had all felt an odd sense of relief when he finally died, after being sick most of our lives. For me, the relief was that I could still remember my love for him. In the last few years, he'd been getting vindictive and mean-spirited, and it was getting awful hard to like him, much less love him. With Anne, it was completely different. She was everyone's favorite. I went down to her funeral in Little Rock, and we gathered for a church service that I don't remember any part of, aside from when I went to the bathroom and peed for so long, with so much volume, a loud firehose of not-tears, that the guy next to me, in a church bathroom at a funeral, commented upon it and laughed. It felt odd to be laughing and talking over the urinal stall partitions, a breach of the social contract, but I was always one to show my emotional saturation in odd behavior. At the cemetery, at the interment, I watched as Uncle Pat was overcome with emotion, saw the earth swallow Anne's big personality and life into that small rectangle. Nothing about it felt alright.

At the dinner after the service, we all experienced a little miracle. We met in the kitchen of someone's house (was it Anne's?) and had all the good food that Anne loved to eat, all the good wine that she loved to drink, and stood and sat for hours telling stories of all the things we loved about her. It's not very often that we get those important days right, because how do you prepare for the unexpected devastation of a young death? It's hard enough to get a wedding right, and that's an event that people think through for their whole young lives. That night we said goodbye to Anne, heartbroken for us and for her young child and husband, and it was a good goodbye. A joyous remembering. A fitting sendoff for such a joyous, exuberant woman. We felt the blessing of that last gift from her to us.

309

Portrait of a Cousin (or the First Law of Thermodynamics)

I met an angel in the food court.
Not encumbered by perfection, but imbued by light:
just a bit worn by 6 a.m. workouts,
the cares of life and death,
and the penitentiary of childhood.

She shone

with a patina, a golden-shadowed circlet of sunshine.
She carried this corona aloft,
overcast and shadowed by love:
like ground diamond dust and
hard work and few failures,
past and present and future glittered from her.

Her wavy curled wings she tied back to reveal a portrait,
much like the one I kept, remembered and known but
locked,
in the hope chest of necessary treasures.
In with the heartbreaks and dreams that seldom came to
light.

A portrait of her mother.

With her grace and light she lifted me and memories
The backlit past and present buoyed
in knowledge that life replicates itself anew,
and that while one cousin is forever lost,
another remains.

Little Rock, Arkansas, Death of the Patriarch, 2016

Uncle Pat's funeral was altogether different. The patriarch had spent the last decade and a half of his life planning his funeral, and he had it fine-tuned and managed down to the last detail. Walking down the center aisle of the Pulaski Heights Baptist Church, heading to the front family section, we were met with Pat's voice singing his favorite hymns. He had a decent crooning voice and regularly sent us CD compilations of him singing popular standards from a different era or a Christmas album, and hearing him again was odd. I hadn't anticipated him being quite so present. The cousins and select friends lauded him and said a few words of surprising humor and grace, and the pastor tried to keep the event going forward. At one point, the crowd restive and the ceremony going over time, the pastor said, "I'm going to pass over a few of these items you have in the program, and I'm sure Pat wouldn't mind." I leaned over to my sister and said that Uncle Pat was totally going to lobby for a spot in hell for that guy. Pat could sing the songs, write the obituary, choose the speakers, and choreograph the funeral to within an inch of its life, but he was dead, and the orchestration was left to the man, the living man, whom he'd paid well for his services. Dying means all the best-laid plans, all the control, all of the managing of yourself and others was done. I'm sure he never planned for that.

The burial, the flag-draped coffin for his service in WWII, the bugler playing taps, the words and forms being met, were less important than me seeing Papa's grave for the first time. Pat was placed in the family plot, near Anne and I think his parents, too, but me and my siblings went for a short walk down the cemetery road and found a more modest site of sparse grass and red earth where Papa lay. Schatzi pointed out where she wanted to be buried, at the right side of the father, and Jesse chose the other side. It was incredible to me that they were so loyal and loving and orderly and normal in their decision to be there. Next to Papa. I had such a visceral reaction against that for myself and was surprised that I already knew by then that I'd be buried anywhere but Arkansas.

Afterwards, we met at the athletic club that Pat had founded, one of his many business pursuits and perhaps the one that worked best in the end. Like his father, he always had a lot of sticks in the fire, from a book depository when that was a business opportunity, to an empire of nursing home facilities, to the health and fitness clubs that were his pride and joy. I wandered around feeling at odds with the scene, because I don't do somber so well. When I saw a rugged old square-jawed guy, I recognized Hunter Douglas, my older cousin from our childhood experiment in parenting, and we had a good conversation about our families and our shared interest in history. I met second cousins I hadn't met before and remembered that this was the real meaning of the day, the takeaway from the death of the patriarch: that there were smart, beautiful, strong, weird, partially broken new Rileys to take the family story forward, and that we were not done yet. Sure, they were Shoulders and Knights, and somehow, Papa's children were the ones bringing the Riley name forward, but they were all Rileys, and the kids were all alright.

When the day was done and we were doing that most Southern of things, sitting around a kitchen table laden with food and drink and carefully sharing politic funeral talk, I was relaxing into everything except the drink situation. There was white wine and beer, maybe a box of red, but it seemed to me that the evening deserved a stronger libation. When the last of the old guard passes, it is incumbent upon the next generation to send off the past with appropriate pomp and circumstance, and a hard seltzer would not do the job. I went into the bar and found only more of the same and some old, derelict-looking bottles that didn't fit the occasion. I remembered that Pat had a storage cupboard under the stairs for boxes of wine opposite the laundry room, so I went there and found cases of Kendall Jackson Chardonnay, but nothing else. I scrambled into the darkened space and spied another door on the back wall. I opened it and peered in to find, like some Indiana Jones treasure in a lost tomb, a small wooden casket. I pulled it out and found that I had unearthed a McCallan twenty-five-year-old Scotch. And it wasn't lost on me that it was in a casket. I brought it out to the table, and we cheered and toasted and, long after I went to bed, killed that bottle off with extreme prejudice. I was proud to have contributed, proud of Uncle Pat for having the bottle. But I was reminded to make sure that when I died, I hadn't surrounded myself with pedestrian fare and found that I'd saved the best for too late.

A few years after Uncle Pat's funeral, and when we thought that the last thing that could bring us all together again had passed, the cousins entered into an email thread and started planning a family reunion. We hadn't had such a thing since my early teens, when the Douglases and Rileys would have a great feast at a park in North Little Rock. It was always a feast of Southern cooking and a chance to meet parts of the family that we didn't know. None of my first cousins or uncles and aunts ever attended, so it was sort of the offshoot-Riley family reunion. This time, though, we kept it close: the Pat and Ed Rileys, Sarah's Cross family kids, and that was it. No one knew where Eddie Hicks was, and no one thought to invite our cousin Pam, now living out in Virginia. It was the Little Rock Rileys plus one from Idaho.

We all brought stacks of pictures and family documents and talked over questions and stories and people that had always intrigued us. It was another kind of family magic. I had told my students before leaving that my one job was not to get into a fistfight with my oldest brother, John, because old men fighting was just common. In the months leading up to the reunion, off to the side of our long email thread, John had been sending me reply-only messages about how stupid my contributions were and how no one wanted to read them. It was a shock to me to see him still bullying after all the years. From the time I came back home from college for a Christmas visit and, fresh off daily rowing practices and a lot of time in the weight room, firmly and decisively beat him in arm wrestling, I'd been willing to let bygones be gone. But he wasn't willing to let that ancient habit die, so I gave him space and we avoided eye contact and we glided past each other like air-hockey pucks. No blows were traded. I was relieved.

My sister took ill just before the weekend reunion was to take place, but we went ahead without her. I was sad that she had missed such a fruitful and pleasant family event, which wasn't something we often shared, and so, after the history and storytelling and punches not thrown, I got in my rental car and headed off to the Baptist Hospital in Conway, AR to see her. I was shocked when I made it to her room and saw the condition she was in. There were tubes running from her nose, tubes running everywhere, and Schatzi out of her head and looking ragged and wan. She couldn't quite make complete sentences and was groggy and couldn't remember a thing. With the juxtaposition of a morning remembering the last of our parents and the generations before them, I wasn't ready to ante up my sister from our generation just yet. She was near death, and all I could do was run a few errands for her, stopping by her house up on rural Wye Mountain and dropping off Frosted Flakes and frozen pizzas so her boys would have enough to eat if she was gone for a while.

By the time I visited the next day, she was on the mend, and she was starting to come back from the effects of the viral infection that had so quickly felled her. She was lucid and making sense again. It was curious to me and gave me so many obvious questions that I couldn't answer, but of the fifteen siblings and cousins at our reunion, I was the only one that visited her. I know that all families are their own cauldrons of long-standing enmities and misplaced loves and loyalties, and I wasn't surprised so much as disappointed that no one came to check on her. It was clear evidence to me that the Rileys were a special sort of messed up.

I found time to meet and spend real time with two of my older cousins, Junius and Pat, whom I'd never really talked with in any meaningful way, and it was the thing that cemented some of the reunion's good work and made the trip worthwhile for me. Pat, Jr. and I met at the Big Dam Bridge over the Arkansas River, and we talked over some of the joys and tribulations of our lives, some of the hidden dynamics of his father and mine, his siblings and mine, and it was such a gift to tell each other important truths after a lifetime, really, of never having spoken to each other about anything of importance. After eight miles of walking, we'd established a bond. With my cousin June, I traveled up to his wife's ancestral land up on Petit Jean Mountain, a tabletop land formation her great-grandfather had surveyed and liked enough to parcel out to himself, and was thunderstruck by the natural beauty of their old hunting cabin and new cathedral-like country home, both perched upon the edge of limestone cliffs that dropped down hundreds of feet to the Arkansas River below. It was fall and the ticks were gone, the oak leaves were mostly down, and I could see just about forever. I think it might have been the first time I could ever pinpoint a specific example of pride in my home state. I knew I loved Arkansas, I knew it was important to me, but I'd never really seen it being the kind of beautiful that I could appreciate. It was a coming to terms with the geography of family. Maybe that is how the mantle of generations is exchanged, with the old leaving and entrusting us with finding the best we can out of what they've left us.

Coda: Greenville, South Carolina, A Body of Work, 2025

Yesterday I woke up to the phone call that told me my mom had died. I laughed-cried over the phone, "Well, I guess I won't need to visit her today." When the court-appointed guardian asked if I did want to see her, I told her truthfully that I didn't have an answer to that right then. I decided against chasing the ambulance already in progress to load her up and cart her away, seeing myself on that beast of a Southern highway with its high-speed, no-turn-signal merges, thunderous downpours, and breakdown lanes littered with crashes. I decided I was not dying to see her. When I did finally see her later in the day, lying in state at the West Greenville funeral home, I got the shock of my life. There she was, resting peacefully, with her hair done, makeup applied, and a cute outfit, ready for a day on the town. A far cry from the open-mouth, gasping, death-mask pale and drawn face, all energy and effort to keep her failing machine of a body driving on that I'd seen a few hours earlier.

I'd flown into Greenville late Thursday night, and first saw her Friday morning, when she was groaning and agitated and disturbing to see. A different Mama even than the vacant and mumbling, smiling vestiges of Helene I'd seen on video calls the months prior. I met with one of her hospice nurses, a nice young man who was keen to tell me about her conjunctivitis and upper respiratory ailments and answer any questions I had as to her condition. I was never the facts guy, and since she was dying, I wasn't overly interested in her health. I showed him some pictures of a young girl, woman, a lady in her prime, so he could see a little more of who she was. How she was. One picture, the one of her in the jeans and cowboy hat, a mustache drawn realistically on her upper lip, had him and the guardian gobsmacked. What was that about? Why was she dressed like that? And the mustache? That was just my mom gender-bending in 1959. Being fabulous and artsy and, well, being Helene. "Well, I never. Huh." And that's the message that I wanted conveyed to them. That no, you didn't ever see a woman like my mom before. She's special, like Chrissie Hynde in that Pretenders song. That Mama is gone now, but this woman here, when she's gone? Well, we're losing something important and irreplaceable. She was something apart, different, other. Special.

I got together a video call with Mama's family in Vienna, and we talked a bit beforehand, while Mama got the finishing touches of her bed made and clothes arranged. Seeing her was going to be a shock for her younger brother and sister-in-law and niece. Mama had always been a lot more than beautiful, but that was the ground-floor expectation. She was lovely and fierce. Not so anymore. I brought them in on my phone screen, and they managed their shock gracefully, as the Viennese are capable of, and it was a wonder to hear eighty-three-year-old brother Josef's voice, childlike and eager, asking Helli how she was, reminding her of who he was. The kid brother hopefully asking big sister to play. We all chimed in and gave our love and talked some, but those one-way conversations, especially with the six-hour time difference lag and the small phone screen, were difficult to keep up. The momentum was hard to generate. A lot like Mama's body. The breaths came, but they were painfully labored. The lungs and heart and mind lagged, her time-difference years in the making. The conversation of the parts degrading. Waiting for the call to drop. We got done and said our goodbyes, and I went to my Airbnb and crashed into sleep. When I woke from my nap, I knew I wasn't going back for an afternoon session. Physically and mentally, sure, I was sharp and on-point enough. But emotionally, I lay gasping painfully, wondering if I could grab a deep enough breath to return. Not that day.

By Saturday, I had recovered my equilibrium enough to visit Mama twice. I sat by her beside and sang some of my favorite songs in a range that I could sing, from Josh Ritter's "Idaho" to Iris DeMent's version of "Leaning on the Everlasting Arms" and a couple from Alison Krauss, "A Living Prayer" and "Down to the River to Pray." I figured she didn't want to hear me butcher beautiful songs, so I tried my best to stay low and on key. I read her a few sections from this memoir, some of the lighter notes, and held her hand and kissed her. When I left for the day, I felt good about the visit, even though she was struggling so hard to keep alive that it was painful to listen and watch and not be able to help. I was awoken early the next morning with a call that told me she was gone.

The rest of the day after she died, and the rest of the week after that, was full of small, demeaning details, all the death industry remoras clamoring for their share of Mama's body of work. There was a sixteen-hundred-dollar obituary, the blow softened by "it has already been set aside for that purpose," so we might as well use it up; many emails surrounding the corpus and her desire to be cremated, which necessitated, under South Carolina law, all four offspring signing on to that, in email and in printed copy, times four; the extra storage fees when not all of us could navigate the cremation paperwork process. Refrigeration is not free, after all; if her ashes are to be commingled with Darius's, as both of their wills stipulate, there needs to be a family member of his to sign a paper to disinter his ashes. So many indignities. The probate for Mama's accounts and property will take three lawyers in three different jurisdictions, so the process might reasonably be wrapped up in eighteen months. Oh, and don't forget, your mom just died, so take a break from all these emails, urgent requests, and planning details to recognize that you might be feeling something. It's probably grief. We can help you with that. The estate will pay for it. Ugh.

There was a long legal process that took considerable time and money for Schatzi, Jesse, and I to get Mama the care she needed, once it became apparent that she was lapsing into dementia and paranoia and would need to be moved, against her daunting will, into a care facility. At one point, I had to face off against Mama in a courtroom, as she testified to the woman judge and was told repeatedly to hold her remarks short. It took a strong woman to cut Mama off. When it came time for her to agree to a guardian or not, she looked at me from across the room, her in the witness box in her black jacket with epaulets and me in a suit coat in my seat next to my lawyer, another strong woman, and asked me, "Should I do this, Michael?" I breathed a relieved, "Yes, Mama, you should," and she agreed. Two years of maxed-out credit cards and family leave and court appearances that ended up providing a court-appointed conservator and a guardian, as well as a facility for her to live her last years out safely.

Playing out this last part, finishing the arrangements of a life she had fought so hard to gain control of, and taking care of her money that she so painstakingly accumulated so that she could exercise control of herself in the world, is something we do because we loved her. It rewards us monetarily and with humiliation and conflict. We're keeping the graveside interment simple and without too much God stuff, the way she would have wanted. A few of us are singing. I don't think anyone will tell us to shut up like we did to her when we were growing up in Denton and Houston, and she was always singing. I like to think she's singing still.

When Mama Actually Passed

I was preparing to see my mom on Mother's Day,
symbolic and typical but still a visit, can't deny it.
Her Guardian called me, a woman appointed
to see to affairs that the legendary Frau Doctor Professor
Helene Riley could no longer manage herself,
she said, Come now.

So I did, just like she had over and over for her mother,
a woman constantly on the verge of dying for decades.
But Mama didn't disappoint. After five years of memory
loss
that meant she lost everything, mostly autonomy, I
found her
eyes closed, mouth gaping open, labored breathing,
waxen and waning.

It was hard to know what was left of her except for will,
the body enduring, driving and pumping, lungs and
heart.
I sang her some hymns, because I liked to sing
and Soprano was her acknowledged religion, while she
could
still acknowledge. After she could no longer sing.
That one always makes me cry, I told her.

I read to her words I'd written about her. Not anything
that might trouble her, trapped inside what was left of
her
after eighty-five years of hard laboring thought-work.

I gave her back the stories she'd given me,
the ones we'd always laughed about. And unfunny ones,
too. I laughed for us both.

After I'd held her hand a while, kissed her cheek, and
then again,
I told her that she could stop now, if she wanted. If she
was able.
That she'd been a good mother and I loved her. I told
her
in two languages. I used our common vernacular. And I
left her.
When I got a call early the next morning that you'd
actually died,
I cried for us both.

Acknowledgements

This book exists because of all the kind words from friends, colleagues, family, and teachers who encouraged me in my writing all throughout my life. Through my journal volumes across the years, letters of correspondence, poems entered in the county fair, opinion letters to the editor, and essays published in the local newspaper, so many people gave me the affirmation that allowed this to finally reach the light of day, instead of just living in my head.

Principal among those deserving thanks are Norbert Elliot and Frances Ward, who on one of their afternoon power-walks with their indefatigable dog, that off-site meeting space where their real publishing decisions are made, agreed that me and my story were worth taking a chance on. And to the entire Purple Breeze Press staff. Thanks Meg Vezzu for the myriad spacing, capitalization, and comma interventions you took to make this better.

And thanks to all of my family. Schatzi, who was my first reader and number one fan of my writing. To my sons, Will and Steffen, who encouraged me and assured that I would have at least two important readers to take this story and continue running with it. And to Diane, who always says and does the things that help make me and my writing better. I'm so lucky to have you in my life.

About the Author

Michael Riley is a retired middle school English and history teacher who now spends his time walking the back logging roads and forest service hiking trails near his home in Potlach, Idaho, and traveling the world looking for new paths to wander. When he's not out and about, he's at home with his two dogs, Orla and Finn, and his very old cat, Scout. Reading is his favorite sport.